Just The facts101

Textbook Key Facts

Bangladesh Customs, Trade Regulations and Procedures Handbook

Table of Contents

Just The Facts101

Exam Prep for

Bangladesh Customs, Trade Regulations and Procedures Handbook

Just The Facts101 Exam Prep is your link from
the textbook and lecture to your exams.

**Just The Facts101 Exam Preps are unauthorized and comprehensive reviews
of your textbooks.**

All material provided by CTI Publications (c) 2019

Textbook publishers and textbook authors do not participate in or contribute to these reviews.

Just The Facts101 Exam Prep

eAIN 444439

Foundations of Business

A business, also known as an enterprise, agency or a firm, is an entity
involved in the provision of goods and/or services to consumers. Businesses are
prevalent in capitalist economies, where most of them are privately owned and
provide goods and services to customers in exchange for other goods, services,
or money.

:: Business law ::

A _____ is an arrangement where parties, known as partners, agree to cooperate to advance their mutual interests. The partners in a _____ may be individuals, businesses, interest-based organizations, schools, governments or combinations. Organizations may partner to increase the likelihood of each achieving their mission and to amplify their reach. A _____ may result in issuing and holding equity or may be only governed by a contract.

Exam Probability: **High**

1. *Answer choices:*

(see index for correct answer)

- a. Free agent
- b. Unfair preference
- c. Perfection
- d. Partnership

Guidance: level 1

:: Stock market ::

_____ is a form of stock which may have any combination of features not possessed by common stock including properties of both an equity and a debt instrument, and is generally considered a hybrid instrument. _____ s are senior to common stock, but subordinate to bonds in terms of claim and may have priority over common stock in the payment of dividends and upon liquidation. Terms of the _____ are described in the issuing company's articles of association or articles of incorporation.

2. *Answer choices:*

(see index for correct answer)

- a. Preferred stock
- b. Smaller reporting company
- c. Mark Twain effect
- d. Securities offering

Guidance: level 1

:: ::

Business is the activity of making one's living or making money by producing or buying and selling products . Simply put, it is "any activity or enterprise entered into for profit. It does not mean it is a company, a corporation, partnership, or have any such formal organization, but it can range from a street peddler to General Motors."

3. *Answer choices:*

(see index for correct answer)

- a. Sarbanes-Oxley act of 2002
- b. Firm

- c. similarity-attraction theory
- d. hierarchical

Guidance: level 1

:: Regression analysis ::

A _____ often refers to a set of documented requirements to be satisfied by a material, design, product, or service. A _____ is often a type of technical standard.

Exam Probability: **High**

4. *Answer choices:*

(see index for correct answer)

- a. moderator variable
- b. Specification
- c. Generalized least squares
- d. Truncated regression model

Guidance: level 1

:: E-commerce ::

_____ is the activity of buying or selling of products on online services or over the Internet. Electronic commerce draws on technologies such as mobile commerce, electronic funds transfer, supply chain management, Internet marketing, online transaction processing, electronic data interchange , inventory management systems, and automated data collection systems.

Exam Probability: **Medium**

5. *Answer choices:*

(see index for correct answer)

- a. EatOye
- b. Impulse economy
- c. MonkeySports
- d. E-commerce

Guidance: level 1

:: Financial regulatory authorities of the United States ::

The _____ is the revenue service of the United States federal government. The government agency is a bureau of the Department of the Treasury, and is under the immediate direction of the Commissioner of Internal Revenue, who is appointed to a five-year term by the President of the United States. The IRS is responsible for collecting taxes and administering the Internal Revenue Code, the main body of federal statutory tax law of the United States. The duties of the IRS include providing tax assistance to taxpayers and pursuing and resolving instances of erroneous or fraudulent tax filings. The IRS has also overseen various benefits programs, and enforces portions of the Affordable Care Act.

Exam Probability: **High**

6. *Answer choices:*

(see index for correct answer)

- a. U.S. Securities and Exchange Commission
- b. National Credit Union Administration
- c. Office of Thrift Supervision
- d. Farm Credit Administration

Guidance: level 1

:: Employment ::

_____ is a relationship between two parties, usually based on a contract where work is paid for, where one party, which may be a corporation, for profit, not-for-profit organization, co-operative or other entity is the employer and the other is the employee. Employees work in return for payment, which may be in the form of an hourly wage, by piecework or an annual salary, depending on the type of work an employee does or which sector she or he is working in. Employees in some fields or sectors may receive gratuities, bonus payment or stock options. In some types of _____ , employees may receive benefits in addition to payment. Benefits can include health insurance, housing, disability insurance or use of a gym. _____ is typically governed by _____ laws, regulations or legal contracts.

Exam Probability: **Low**

7. *Answer choices:*

(see index for correct answer)

- a. ThinkTalk
- b. Clodomir Santos de Morais
- c. Goldbricking
- d. In-basket test

Guidance: level 1

:: Marketing ::

_____ comes from the Latin neg and otsia referring to businessmen who, unlike the patricians, had no leisure time in their industriousness; it held the meaning of business until the 17th century when it took on the diplomatic connotation as a dialogue between two or more people or parties intended to reach a beneficial outcome over one or more issues where a conflict exists with respect to at least one of these issues. Thus, _____ is a process of combining divergent positions into a joint agreement under a decision rule of unanimity.

Exam Probability: **Low**

8. *Answer choices:*

(see index for correct answer)

- a. Negotiation
- b. Lead generation
- c. Customer franchise
- d. Customer insight

Guidance: level 1

:: Training ::

_____ is teaching, or developing in oneself or others, any skills and knowledge that relate to specific useful competencies. _____ has specific goals of improving one's capability, capacity, productivity and performance. It forms the core of apprenticeships and provides the backbone of content at institutes of technology . In addition to the basic _____ required for a trade, occupation or profession, observers of the labor-market recognize as of 2008 the need to continue _____ beyond initial qualifications: to maintain, upgrade and update skills throughout working life. People within many professions and occupations may refer to this sort of _____ as professional development.

Exam Probability: **High**

9. *Answer choices:*

(see index for correct answer)

- a. Training camp
- b. Training
- c. Jeff Phillips
- d. Fartlek

Guidance: level 1

:: Industrial Revolution ::

The _____ , now also known as the First _____ , was the transition to new manufacturing processes in Europe and the US, in the period from about 1760 to sometime between 1820 and 1840. This transition included going from hand production methods to machines, new chemical manufacturing and iron production processes, the increasing use of steam power and water power, the development of machine tools and the rise of the mechanized factory system. The _____ also led to an unprecedented rise in the rate of population growth.

Exam Probability: **Medium**

10. *Answer choices:*

(see index for correct answer)

- a. Pocasset Manufacturing Company
- b. Masson Mill
- c. Industrial Revolution
- d. Derwent Valley Mills

Guidance: level 1

:: ::

_____ is the collection of techniques, skills, methods, and processes used in the production of goods or services or in the accomplishment of objectives, such as scientific investigation. _____ can be the knowledge of techniques, processes, and the like, or it can be embedded in machines to allow for operation without detailed knowledge of their workings. Systems applying _____ by taking an input, changing it according to the system's use, and then producing an outcome are referred to as _____ systems or technological systems.

Exam Probability: **Medium**

11. *Answer choices:*

(see index for correct answer)

- a. Technology
- b. surface-level diversity
- c. imperative
- d. corporate values

Guidance: level 1

:: Investment ::

In finance, the benefit from an _____ is called a return. The return may consist of a gain realised from the sale of property or an _____ , unrealised capital appreciation , or _____ income such as dividends, interest, rental income etc., or a combination of capital gain and income. The return may also include currency gains or losses due to changes in foreign currency exchange rates.

12. *Answer choices:*

(see index for correct answer)

- a. Financial sponsor
- b. Emerging market
- c. Capital market line
- d. Laddering

Guidance: level 1

:: Evaluation ::

_____ is the practice of being honest and showing a consistent and uncompromising adherence to strong moral and ethical principles and values.In ethics, _____ is regarded as the honesty and truthfulness or accuracy of one's actions. _____ can stand in opposition to hypocrisy, in that judging with the standards of _____ involves regarding internal consistency as a virtue, and suggests that parties holding within themselves apparently conflicting values should account for the discrepancy or alter their beliefs. The word _____ evolved from the Latin adjective integer, meaning whole or complete. In this context, _____ is the inner sense of "wholeness" deriving from qualities such as honesty and consistency of character. As such, one may judge that others "have _____" to the extent that they act according to the values, beliefs and principles they claim to hold.

13. *Answer choices:*

(see index for correct answer)

- a. Integrity
- b. International Association for the Evaluation of Educational Achievement
- c. American Evaluation Association
- d. Technology assessment

Guidance: level 1

:: Evaluation ::

A _____ is an evaluation of a publication, service, or company such as a movie , video game , musical composition , book ; a piece of hardware like a car, home appliance, or computer; or an event or performance, such as a live music concert, play, musical theater show, dance show, or art exhibition. In addition to a critical evaluation, the _____ 's author may assign the work a rating to indicate its relative merit. More loosely, an author may _____ current events, trends, or items in the news. A compilation of _____ s may itself be called a _____ . The New York _____ of Books, for instance, is a collection of essays on literature, culture, and current affairs. National _____ , founded by William F. Buckley, Jr., is an influential conservative magazine, and Monthly _____ is a long-running socialist periodical.

Exam Probability: **Low**

14. *Answer choices:*

(see index for correct answer)

- a. Common Criteria Testing Laboratory
- b. Teaching and Learning International Survey
- c. Encomium
- d. Review

Guidance: level 1

:: Bribery ::

_____ is the act of giving or receiving something of value in exchange for some kind of influence or action in return, that the recipient would otherwise not offer. _____ is defined by Black's Law Dictionary as the offering, giving, receiving, or soliciting of any item of value to influence the actions of an official or other person in charge of a public or legal duty. Essentially, _____ is offering to do something for someone for the expressed purpose of receiving something in exchange. Gifts of money or other items of value which are otherwise available to everyone on an equivalent basis, and not for dishonest purposes, is not _____ . Offering a discount or a refund to all purchasers is a legal rebate and is not _____ . For example, it is legal for an employee of a Public Utilities Commission involved in electric rate regulation to accept a rebate on electric service that reduces their cost for electricity, when the rebate is available to other residential electric customers. Giving the rebate to influence them to look favorably on the electric utility's rate increase applications, however, would be considered _____ .

Exam Probability: **High**

15. *Answer choices:*

(see index for correct answer)

- a. Holyland Case
- b. Cunningham scandal
- c. Bribery
- d. GSIS-Meralco bribery case

Guidance: level 1

:: Marketing ::

A _____ is a group of customers within a business's serviceable available market at which a business aims its marketing efforts and resources. A _____ is a subset of the total market for a product or service. The _____ typically consists of consumers who exhibit similar characteristics and are considered most likely to buy a business's market offerings or are likely to be the most profitable segments for the business to service.

Exam Probability: **Low**

16. *Answer choices:*

(see index for correct answer)

- a. Market environment
- b. Masstige
- c. Private label
- d. Target market

Guidance: level 1

:: Cash flow ::

_____ s are narrowly interconnected with the concepts of value, interest rate and liquidity. A _____ that shall happen on a future day tN can be transformed into a _____ of the same value in t0.

Exam Probability: **High**

17. *Answer choices:*

(see index for correct answer)

- a. Operating cash flow
- b. Cash flow
- c. Cash flow forecasting
- d. Invoice discounting

Guidance: level 1

:: Stock market ::

A _____ , securities exchange or bourse, is a facility where stock brokers and traders can buy and sell securities, such as shares of stock and bonds and other financial instruments. _____ s may also provide for facilities the issue and redemption of such securities and instruments and capital events including the payment of income and dividends. Securities traded on a _____ include stock issued by listed companies, unit trusts, derivatives, pooled investment products and bonds. _____ s often function as "continuous auction" markets with buyers and sellers consummating transactions via open outcry at a central location such as the floor of the exchange or by using an electronic trading platform.

Exam Probability: **Low**

18. *Answer choices:*

(see index for correct answer)

- a. Nifty Fifty
- b. Stock exchange
- c. Long squeeze
- d. Slippage

Guidance: level 1

:: Management ::

In business, a _____ is the attribute that allows an organization to outperform its competitors. A _____ may include access to natural resources, such as high-grade ores or a low-cost power source, highly skilled labor, geographic location, high entry barriers, and access to new technology.

Exam Probability: **Medium**

19. *Answer choices:*

(see index for correct answer)

- a. Executive development
- b. Adhocracy
- c. Operations management
- d. Project management simulation

Guidance: level 1

:: National accounts ::

_____ is a monetary measure of the market value of all the final goods and services produced in a period of time, often annually. GDP per capita does not, however, reflect differences in the cost of living and the inflation rates of the countries; therefore using a basis of GDP per capita at purchasing power parity is arguably more useful when comparing differences in living standards between nations.

Exam Probability: **Medium**

20. *Answer choices:*

(see index for correct answer)

- a. Fixed capital
- b. National Income

- c. Gross domestic product

Guidance: level 1

:: Foreign direct investment ::

A _____ is an investment in the form of a controlling ownership in a business in one country by an entity based in another country. It is thus distinguished from a foreign portfolio investment by a notion of direct control.

Exam Probability: **Medium**

21. *Answer choices:*

(see index for correct answer)

- a. Foreign direct investments in Kosovo
- b. Immigrant investor programs
- c. FDi magazine
- d. Foreign direct investment

Guidance: level 1

:: ::

_____ refers to a business or organization attempting to acquire goods or services to accomplish its goals. Although there are several organizations that attempt to set standards in the _____ process, processes can vary greatly between organizations. Typically the word " _____ " is not used interchangeably with the word "procurement", since procurement typically includes expediting, supplier quality, and transportation and logistics in addition to _____ .

Exam Probability: **High**

22. *Answer choices:*

(see index for correct answer)

- a. Purchasing
- b. levels of analysis
- c. empathy
- d. interpersonal communication

Guidance: level 1

:: Financial accounting ::

_____ is a financial metric which represents operating liquidity available to a business, organisation or other entity, including governmental entities. Along with fixed assets such as plant and equipment, _____ is considered a part of operating capital. Gross _____ is equal to current assets. _____ is calculated as current assets minus current liabilities. If current assets are less than current liabilities, an entity has a _____ deficiency, also called a _____ deficit.

23. *Answer choices:*

(see index for correct answer)

- a. Working capital
- b. Associate company
- c. Deferred financing cost
- d. Mark-to-market accounting

Guidance: level 1

:: Goods ::

In most contexts, the concept of _____ denotes the conduct that should be preferred when posed with a choice between possible actions. _____ is generally considered to be the opposite of evil, and is of interest in the study of morality, ethics, religion and philosophy. The specific meaning and etymology of the term and its associated translations among ancient and contemporary languages show substantial variation in its inflection and meaning depending on circumstances of place, history, religious, or philosophical context.

24. *Answer choices:*

(see index for correct answer)

- a. Goods and services
- b. Superior good
- c. excludable
- d. Good

Guidance: level 1

:: Globalization-related theories ::

_____ is an economic system based on the private ownership of the means of production and their operation for profit. Characteristics central to _____ include private property, capital accumulation, wage labor, voluntary exchange, a price system, and competitive markets. In a capitalist market economy, decision-making and investment are determined by every owner of wealth, property or production ability in financial and capital markets, whereas prices and the distribution of goods and services are mainly determined by competition in goods and services markets.

Exam Probability: **Low**

25. *Answer choices:*

(see index for correct answer)

- a. postmodernism
- b. Economic Development
- c. Capitalism

Guidance: level 1

:: ::

An _____ is an area of the production, distribution, or trade, and consumption of goods and services by different agents. Understood in its broadest sense, `The _____ is defined as a social domain that emphasize the practices, discourses, and material expressions associated with the production, use, and management of resources'. Economic agents can be individuals, businesses, organizations, or governments. Economic transactions occur when two parties agree to the value or price of the transacted good or service, commonly expressed in a certain currency. However, monetary transactions only account for a small part of the economic domain.

Exam Probability: **High**

26. *Answer choices:*

(see index for correct answer)

- a. process perspective
- b. functional perspective
- c. surface-level diversity
- d. levels of analysis

Guidance: level 1

:: Business models ::

_____ es are privately owned corporations, partnerships, or sole proprietorships that have fewer employees and/or less annual revenue than a regular-sized business or corporation. Businesses are defined as "small" in terms of being able to apply for government support and qualify for preferential tax policy varies depending on the country and industry. _____ es range from fifteen employees under the Australian Fair Work Act 2009, fifty employees according to the definition used by the European Union, and fewer than five hundred employees to qualify for many U.S. _____ Administration programs. While _____ es can also be classified according to other methods, such as annual revenues, shipments, sales, assets, or by annual gross or net revenue or net profits, the number of employees is one of the most widely used measures.

Exam Probability: **Low**

27. *Answer choices:*

(see index for correct answer)

- a. Home business
- b. Micro-enterprise
- c. Gratis
- d. Market game

Guidance: level 1

:: Business ::

_____ is a trade policy that does not restrict imports or exports; it can also be understood as the free market idea applied to international trade. In government, _____ is predominantly advocated by political parties that hold liberal economic positions while economically left-wing and nationalist political parties generally support protectionism, the opposite of _____ .

Exam Probability: **Medium**

28. *Answer choices:*

(see index for correct answer)

- a. Business directory
- b. Les Vergers du Mekong
- c. Uncorporation
- d. Free trade

Guidance: level 1

:: Consumer theory ::

_____ is the quantity of a good that consumers are willing and able to purchase at various prices during a given period of time.

Exam Probability: **High**

29. *Answer choices:*

(see index for correct answer)

- a. Demand
- b. Lexicographic preferences
- c. Supply and demand
- d. Permanent income hypothesis

Guidance: level 1

:: Service industries ::

_____ are the economic services provided by the finance industry, which encompasses a broad range of businesses that manage money, including credit unions, banks, credit-card companies, insurance companies, accountancy companies, consumer-finance companies, stock brokerages, investment funds, individual managers and some government-sponsored enterprises. _____ companies are present in all economically developed geographic locations and tend to cluster in local, national, regional and international financial centers such as London, New York City, and Tokyo.

Exam Probability: **Low**

30. *Answer choices:*

(see index for correct answer)

- a. Financial services
- b. Graham Company
- c. Allotment
- d. Financial services in China

:: ::

Some scenarios associate "this kind of planning" with learning "life skills". Schedules are necessary, or at least useful, in situations where individuals need to know what time they must be at a specific location to receive a specific service, and where people need to accomplish a set of goals within a set time period.

Exam Probability: **Low**

31. *Answer choices:*

(see index for correct answer)

- a. co-culture
- b. cultural
- c. process perspective
- d. Scheduling

:: Credit cards ::

A _____ is a payment card issued to users to enable the cardholder to pay a merchant for goods and services based on the cardholder's promise to the card issuer to pay them for the amounts plus the other agreed charges. The card issuer creates a revolving account and grants a line of credit to the cardholder, from which the cardholder can borrow money for payment to a merchant or as a cash advance.

Exam Probability: **Low**

32. *Answer choices:*

(see index for correct answer)

- a. Barclaycard
- b. Netbanx
- c. Credit card
- d. Diners Club International

Guidance: level 1

:: Management ::

A _____ is when two or more people come together to discuss one or more topics, often in a formal or business setting, but _____ s also occur in a variety of other environments. Many various types of _____ s exist.

Exam Probability: **Medium**

33. *Answer choices:*

(see index for correct answer)

- a. Financial planning
- b. Fall guy
- c. Certified management consultant
- d. Just in time

Guidance: level 1

:: Export and import control ::

" _____ " means the Government Service which is responsible for the administration of _____ law and the collection of duties and taxes and which also has the responsibility for the application of other laws and regulations relating to the importation, exportation, movement or storage of goods.

Exam Probability: **Medium**

34. *Answer choices:*

(see index for correct answer)

- a. GOST R Conformity Declaration
- b. Bureau of Industry and Security
- c. Neutron scanner
- d. United States Munitions List

:: Derivatives (finance) ::

_____ is any bodily activity that enhances or maintains physical fitness and overall health and wellness. It is performed for various reasons, to aid growth and improve strength, preventing aging, developing muscles and the cardiovascular system, honing athletic skills, weight loss or maintenance, improving health and also for enjoyment. Many individuals choose to _____ outdoors where they can congregate in groups, socialize, and enhance well-being.

Exam Probability: **Low**

35. *Answer choices:*

(see index for correct answer)

- a. Forward-forward agreement
- b. Foreign exchange option
- c. Exercise
- d. Swap ratio

:: Insolvency ::

_____ is a legal process through which people or other entities who cannot repay debts to creditors may seek relief from some or all of their debts. In most jurisdictions, _____ is imposed by a court order, often initiated by the debtor.

Exam Probability: **High**

36. *Answer choices:*

(see index for correct answer)

- a. Bankruptcy
- b. Personal Insolvency Arrangement
- c. Preferential creditor
- d. Insolvency law of Russia

Guidance: level 1

:: Loans ::

In finance, a _____ is the lending of money by one or more individuals, organizations, or other entities to other individuals, organizations etc. The recipient incurs a debt, and is usually liable to pay interest on that debt until it is repaid, and also to repay the principal amount borrowed.

Exam Probability: **Medium**

37. *Answer choices:*

(see index for correct answer)

- a. amortizing bond
- b. FHA insured loan
- c. Loan servicing
- d. Construction loan

Guidance: level 1

:: Free trade agreements ::

A _____ is a wide-ranging taxes, tariff and trade treaty that often includes investment guarantees. It exists when two or more countries agree on terms that helps them trade with each other. The most common _____ s are of the preferential and free trade types are concluded in order to reduce tariffs, quotas and other trade restrictions on items traded between the signatories.

Exam Probability: **Medium**

38. *Answer choices:*
(see index for correct answer)

- a. New West Partnership
- b. Trade agreement
- c. South Asia Free Trade Agreement
- d. African Free Trade Zone

:: Analysis ::

_____ is the process of breaking a complex topic or substance into smaller parts in order to gain a better understanding of it. The technique has been applied in the study of mathematics and logic since before Aristotle , though _____ as a formal concept is a relatively recent development.

Exam Probability: **High**

39. *Answer choices:*

(see index for correct answer)

- a. Paradox of analysis
- b. Gompertz constant
- c. Situational analysis
- d. Deviation analysis

:: Mathematical finance ::

In economics and finance, _____ , also known as present discounted value, is the value of an expected income stream determined as of the date of valuation. The _____ is always less than or equal to the future value because money has interest-earning potential, a characteristic referred to as the time value of money, except during times of negative interest rates, when the _____ will be more than the future value. Time value can be described with the simplified phrase, "A dollar today is worth more than a dollar tomorrow". Here, `worth more` means that its value is greater. A dollar today is worth more than a dollar tomorrow because the dollar can be invested and earn a day's worth of interest, making the total accumulate to a value more than a dollar by tomorrow. Interest can be compared to rent. Just as rent is paid to a landlord by a tenant without the ownership of the asset being transferred, interest is paid to a lender by a borrower who gains access to the money for a time before paying it back. By letting the borrower have access to the money, the lender has sacrificed the exchange value of this money, and is compensated for it in the form of interest. The initial amount of the borrowed funds is less than the total amount of money paid to the lender.

Exam Probability: **Medium**

40. *Answer choices:*

(see index for correct answer)

- a. Risk-neutral measure
- b. Markov switching multifractal
- c. Self-financing portfolio
- d. Present value

Guidance: level 1

:: Materials ::

A _____ , also known as a feedstock, unprocessed material, or primary commodity, is a basic material that is used to produce goods, finished products, energy, or intermediate materials which are feedstock for future finished products. As feedstock, the term connotes these materials are bottleneck assets and are highly important with regard to producing other products. An example of this is crude oil, which is a _____ and a feedstock used in the production of industrial chemicals, fuels, plastics, and pharmaceutical goods; lumber is a _____ used to produce a variety of products including all types of furniture. The term " _____ " denotes materials in minimally processed or unprocessed in states; e.g., raw latex, crude oil, cotton, coal, raw biomass, iron ore, air, logs, or water i.e. "...any product of agriculture, forestry, fishing and any other mineral that is in its natural form or which has undergone the transformation required to prepare it for internationally marketing in substantial volumes."

Exam Probability: **Medium**

41. *Answer choices:*

(see index for correct answer)

- a. Muka
- b. Lute
- c. Microporous material
- d. Raw material

Guidance: level 1

:: Macroeconomics ::

_____ is the increase in the inflation-adjusted market value of the goods and services produced by an economy over time. It is conventionally measured as the percent rate of increase in real gross domestic product, or real GDP.

Exam Probability: **Low**

42. *Answer choices:*

(see index for correct answer)

- a. Gonzalo Garland
- b. Original sin
- c. Economic growth
- d. MEMEnomics

Guidance: level 1

:: International trade ::

The law or principle of _____ holds that under free trade, an agent will produce more of and consume less of a good for which they have a _____ . _____ is the economic reality describing the work gains from trade for individuals, firms, or nations, which arise from differences in their factor endowments or technological progress. In an economic model, agents have a _____ over others in producing a particular good if they can produce that good at a lower relative opportunity cost or autarky price, i.e. at a lower relative marginal cost prior to trade. One shouldn't compare the monetary costs of production or even the resource costs of production. Instead, one must compare the opportunity costs of producing goods across countries.

43. *Answer choices:*

(see index for correct answer)

- a. Trade mission
- b. Spice trade
- c. Comparative advantage
- d. Trade mandate

Guidance: level 1

:: Competition regulators ::

The _____ is an independent agency of the United States government, established in 1914 by the _____ Act. Its principal mission is the promotion of consumer protection and the elimination and prevention of anticompetitive business practices, such as coercive monopoly. It is headquartered in the _____ Building in Washington, D.C.

Exam Probability: **Low**

44. *Answer choices:*

(see index for correct answer)

- a. Industrial Commission
- b. Jersey Competition Regulatory Authority

- c. Superintendency of Industry and Commerce
- d. Federal Trade Commission

Guidance: level 1

:: Alchemical processes ::

In chemistry, a _____ is a special type of homogeneous mixture composed of two or more substances. In such a mixture, a solute is a substance dissolved in another substance, known as a solvent. The mixing process of a _____ happens at a scale where the effects of chemical polarity are involved, resulting in interactions that are specific to solvation. The _____ assumes the phase of the solvent when the solvent is the larger fraction of the mixture, as is commonly the case. The concentration of a solute in a _____ is the mass of that solute expressed as a percentage of the mass of the whole _____ . The term aqueous _____ is when one of the solvents is water.

Exam Probability: **Medium**

45. *Answer choices:*

(see index for correct answer)

- a. Fixation
- b. Solution
- c. Fermentation
- d. Unity of opposites

Guidance: level 1

:: Costs ::

In microeconomic theory, the _____ , or alternative cost, of making a particular choice is the value of the most valuable choice out of those that were not taken. In other words, opportunity that will require sacrifices.

Exam Probability: **High**

46. *Answer choices:*

(see index for correct answer)

- a. Opportunity cost
- b. Sliding scale
- c. Opportunity cost of capital
- d. Sliding scale fees

Guidance: level 1

:: Shareholders ::

A _____ is a payment made by a corporation to its shareholders, usually as a distribution of profits. When a corporation earns a profit or surplus, the corporation is able to re-invest the profit in the business and pay a proportion of the profit as a _____ to shareholders. Distribution to shareholders may be in cash or, if the corporation has a _____ reinvestment plan, the amount can be paid by the issue of further shares or share repurchase. When _____ s are paid, shareholders typically must pay income taxes, and the corporation does not receive a corporate income tax deduction for the _____ payments.

Exam Probability: **Medium**

47. *Answer choices:*

(see index for correct answer)

- a. Shareholder yield
- b. Shareholders in the United Kingdom
- c. Institutional Shareholder Services
- d. Dividend

Guidance: level 1

:: Project management ::

_____ is the right to exercise power, which can be formalized by a state and exercised by way of judges, appointed executives of government, or the ecclesiastical or priestly appointed representatives of a God or other deities.

48. *Answer choices:*

(see index for correct answer)

- a. Association for Project Management
- b. Arrow diagramming method
- c. Theory X and Theory Y
- d. Authority

Guidance: level 1

:: ::

An _____ is the production of goods or related services within an economy. The major source of revenue of a group or company is the indicator of its relevant _____ . When a large group has multiple sources of revenue generation, it is considered to be working in different industries.
Manufacturing _____ became a key sector of production and labour in European and North American countries during the Industrial Revolution, upsetting previous mercantile and feudal economies. This came through many successive rapid advances in technology, such as the production of steel and coal.

49. *Answer choices:*

(see index for correct answer)

- a. corporate values
- b. Industry
- c. hierarchical
- d. information systems assessment

Guidance: level 1

:: Asset ::

In financial accounting, an _____ is any resource owned by the business. Anything tangible or intangible that can be owned or controlled to produce value and that is held by a company to produce positive economic value is an _____ . Simply stated, _____ s represent value of ownership that can be converted into cash . The balance sheet of a firm records the monetary value of the _____ s owned by that firm. It covers money and other valuables belonging to an individual or to a business.

Exam Probability: **High**

50. *Answer choices:*
(see index for correct answer)

- a. Asset
- b. Fixed asset

Guidance: level 1

:: Stochastic processes ::

_____ is a system of rules that are created and enforced through social or governmental institutions to regulate behavior. It has been defined both as "the Science of Justice" and "the Art of Justice". _____ is a system that regulates and ensures that individuals or a community adhere to the will of the state. State-enforced _____ s can be made by a collective legislature or by a single legislator, resulting in statutes, by the executive through decrees and regulations, or established by judges through precedent, normally in common _____ jurisdictions. Private individuals can create legally binding contracts, including arbitration agreements that may elect to accept alternative arbitration to the normal court process. The formation of _____ s themselves may be influenced by a constitution, written or tacit, and the rights encoded therein. The _____ shapes politics, economics, history and society in various ways and serves as a mediator of relations between people.

Exam Probability: **Medium**

51. *Answer choices:*

(see index for correct answer)

- a. Law
- b. Polynomial chaos
- c. Stochastic thinking
- d. Dissociated press

Guidance: level 1

:: Statistical terminology ::

_____ is the magnitude or dimensions of a thing. _____ can be measured as length, width, height, diameter, perimeter, area, volume, or mass.

52. *Answer choices:*

(see index for correct answer)

- a. Probable error
- b. Size
- c. Completeness
- d. Endogeneity

Guidance: level 1

:: Treaties ::

An _____ is a relationship among people, groups, or states that have joined together for mutual benefit or to achieve some common purpose, whether or not explicit agreement has been worked out among them. Members of an _____ are called allies. _____ s form in many settings, including political _____ s, military _____ s, and business _____ s. When the term is used in the context of war or armed struggle, such associations may also be called allied powers, especially when discussing World War I or World War II.

53. *Answer choices:*

(see index for correct answer)

- a. Reservation
- b. Treaty
- c. Alliance
- d. Quasi alliance

Guidance: level 1

:: Organizational behavior ::

_____ is the state or fact of exclusive rights and control over property, which may be an object, land/real estate or intellectual property. _____ involves multiple rights, collectively referred to as title, which may be separated and held by different parties.

Exam Probability: **Low**

54. *Answer choices:*

(see index for correct answer)

- a. Ownership
- b. Organizational Expedience
- c. Organizational citizenship behavior
- d. Managerial grid model

:: ::

Competition arises whenever at least two parties strive for a goal which cannot be shared: where one's gain is the other's loss .

Exam Probability: **High**

55. *Answer choices:*

(see index for correct answer)

- a. surface-level diversity
- b. Competitor
- c. process perspective
- d. information systems assessment

:: Management ::

A _____ is a formal written document containing business goals, the methods on how these goals can be attained, and the time frame within which these goals need to be achieved. It also describes the nature of the business, background information on the organization, the organization's financial projections, and the strategies it intends to implement to achieve the stated targets. In its entirety, this document serves as a road map that provides direction to the business.

Exam Probability: **Low**

56. *Answer choices:*

(see index for correct answer)

- a. Business plan
- b. Stovepipe
- c. Investment control
- d. PhD in management

Guidance: level 1

:: Consumer theory ::

A _____ is a technical term in psychology, economics and philosophy usually used in relation to choosing between alternatives. For example, someone prefers A over B if they would rather choose A than B.

Exam Probability: **Low**

57. *Answer choices:*

(see index for correct answer)

- a. Marginal rate of substitution
- b. Marshallian demand function
- c. Preference
- d. Convex preferences

Guidance: level 1

:: Marketing ::

_____ is based on a marketing concept which can be adopted by an organization as a strategy for business expansion. Where implemented, a franchisor licenses its know-how, procedures, intellectual property, use of its business model, brand, and rights to sell its branded products and services to a franchisee. In return the franchisee pays certain fees and agrees to comply with certain obligations, typically set out in a Franchise Agreement.

Exam Probability: **Low**

58. *Answer choices:*

(see index for correct answer)

- a. Penetration pricing
- b. Fifth screen
- c. Beat-sheet
- d. Franchising

:: Generally Accepted Accounting Principles ::

In accounting, _____ is the income that a business have from its normal business activities, usually from the sale of goods and services to customers. _____ is also referred to as sales or turnover. Some companies receive _____ from interest, royalties, or other fees. _____ may refer to business income in general, or it may refer to the amount, in a monetary unit, earned during a period of time, as in "Last year, Company X had _____ of $42 million". Profits or net income generally imply total _____ minus total expenses in a given period. In accounting, in the balance statement it is a subsection of the Equity section and _____ increases equity, it is often referred to as the "top line" due to its position on the income statement at the very top. This is to be contrasted with the "bottom line" which denotes net income .

Exam Probability: **Medium**

59. *Answer choices:*
(see index for correct answer)

- a. Revenue
- b. Access to finance
- c. Deferred income
- d. Gross profit

Management

Management is the administration of an organization, whether it is a business, a not-for-profit organization, or government body. Management includes the activities of setting the strategy of an organization and coordinating the efforts of its employees (or of volunteers) to accomplish its objectives through the application of available resources, such as financial, natural, technological, and human resources.

:: Human resource management ::

A _____ is a group of people with different functional expertise working toward a common goal. It may include people from finance, marketing, operations, and human resources departments. Typically, it includes employees from all levels of an organization. Members may also come from outside an organization .

1. *Answer choices:*

- a. Cross-functional team
- b. Pay in lieu of notice
- c. Cultural capital
- d. Talascend

Guidance: level 1

:: Management ::

A _____ is a method or technique that has been generally accepted as superior to any alternatives because it produces results that are superior to those achieved by other means or because it has become a standard way of doing things, e.g., a standard way of complying with legal or ethical requirements.

Exam Probability: **High**

2. *Answer choices:*

- a. Design management
- b. Data Item Descriptions
- c. Best practice

- d. PDCA

Guidance: level 1

:: Management ::

In organizational studies, _____ is the efficient and effective development of an organization's resources when they are needed. Such resources may include financial resources, inventory, human skills, production resources, or information technology and natural resources.

Exam Probability: **High**

3. *Answer choices:*

(see index for correct answer)

- a. Manager Tools Podcast
- b. Shrinkage
- c. Customer Benefit Package
- d. Resource management

Guidance: level 1

:: Behaviorism ::

In behavioral psychology, _____ is a consequence applied that will strengthen an organism's future behavior whenever that behavior is preceded by a specific antecedent stimulus. This strengthening effect may be measured as a higher frequency of behavior , longer duration , greater magnitude , or shorter latency . There are two types of _____ , known as positive _____ and negative _____ ; positive is where by a reward is offered on expression of the wanted behaviour and negative is taking away an undesirable element in the persons environment whenever the desired behaviour is achieved.

Exam Probability: **High**

4. *Answer choices:*

(see index for correct answer)

- a. Matching Law
- b. Systematic desensitization
- c. chaining
- d. Reinforcement

Guidance: level 1

:: Commercial item transport and distribution ::

In commerce, supply-chain management , the management of the flow of goods and services, involves the movement and storage of raw materials, of work-in-process inventory, and of finished goods from point of origin to point of consumption. Interconnected or interlinked networks, channels and node businesses combine in the provision of products and services required by end customers in a supply chain. Supply-chain management has been defined as the "design, planning, execution, control, and monitoring of supply-chain activities with the objective of creating net value, building a competitive infrastructure, leveraging worldwide logistics, synchronizing supply with demand and measuring performance globally."SCM practice draws heavily from the areas of industrial engineering, systems engineering, operations management, logistics, procurement, information technology, and marketing and strives for an integrated approach. Marketing channels play an important role in supply-chain management. Current research in supply-chain management is concerned with topics related to sustainability and risk management, among others. Some suggest that the "people dimension" of SCM, ethical issues, internal integration, transparency/visibility, and human capital/talent management are topics that have, so far, been underrepresented on the research agenda.

Exam Probability: **Low**

5. *Answer choices:*

(see index for correct answer)

- a. Inland navigation
- b. Wholesale fashion distribution
- c. Semi-trailer truck
- d. Supply chain management

Guidance: level 1

:: Management ::

In the field of management, _____ involves the formulation and implementation of the major goals and initiatives taken by an organization's top management on behalf of owners, based on consideration of resources and an assessment of the internal and external environments in which the organization operates.

Exam Probability: **Medium**

6. *Answer choices:*

(see index for correct answer)

- a. Records manager
- b. middle manager
- c. Strategic management
- d. Management cockpit

Guidance: level 1

:: Organizational theory ::

Decentralisation is the process by which the activities of an organization, particularly those regarding planning and decision making, are distributed or delegated away from a central, authoritative location or group. Concepts of _____ have been applied to group dynamics and management science in private businesses and organizations, political science, law and public administration, economics, money and technology.

7. *Answer choices:*

(see index for correct answer)

- a. Decentralization
- b. Contingency theory
- c. Organizational field
- d. Organization theory

Guidance: level 1

:: Systems thinking ::

Systems theory is the interdisciplinary study of systems. A system is a cohesive conglomeration of interrelated and interdependent parts that is either natural or man-made. Every system is delineated by its spatial and temporal boundaries, surrounded and influenced by its environment, described by its structure and purpose or nature and expressed in its functioning. In terms of its effects, a system can be more than the sum of its parts if it expresses synergy or emergent behavior. Changing one part of the system usually affects other parts and the whole system, with predictable patterns of behavior. For systems that are self-learning and self-adapting, the positive growth and adaptation depend upon how well the system is adjusted with its environment. Some systems function mainly to support other systems by aiding in the maintenance of the other system to prevent failure. The goal of systems theory is systematically discovering a system's dynamics, constraints, conditions and elucidating principles that can be discerned and applied to systems at every level of nesting, and in every field for achieving optimized equifinality.

8. *Answer choices:*

(see index for correct answer)

- a. Interdependence
- b. Real-time Delphi
- c. Club of Rome
- d. Involution

Guidance: level 1

:: ::

A _____ is the ability to carry out a task with determined results often within a given amount of time, energy, or both. _____ s can often be divided into domain-general and domain-specific _____ s. For example, in the domain of work, some general _____ s would include time management, teamwork and leadership, self-motivation and others, whereas domain-specific _____ s would be used only for a certain job. _____ usually requires certain environmental stimuli and situations to assess the level of _____ being shown and used.

9. *Answer choices:*

(see index for correct answer)

- a. corporate values
- b. Character
- c. Skill
- d. hierarchical

Guidance: level 1

:: Personality tests ::

The Myers–Briggs Type Indicator is an introspective self-report questionnaire with the purpose of indicating differing psychological preferences in how people perceive the world around them and make decisions. . Though the test superficially resembles some psychological theories it is commonly classified as pseudoscience, especially as pertains to its supposed predictive abilities.

Exam Probability: **Medium**

10. *Answer choices:*

(see index for correct answer)

- a. Keirsey Temperament Sorter
- b. Myers-Briggs Type Indicator
- c. personality quiz
- d. Myers-Briggs type

Guidance: level 1

:: ::

_____ is the moral stance, political philosophy, ideology, or social outlook that emphasizes the moral worth of the individual. Individualists promote the exercise of one's goals and desires and so value independence and self-reliance and advocate that interests of the individual should achieve precedence over the state or a social group, while opposing external interference upon one's own interests by society or institutions such as the government. _____ is often defined in contrast to totalitarianism, collectivism, and more corporate social forms.

Exam Probability: Low

11. *Answer choices:*

(see index for correct answer)

- a. Individualism
- b. functional perspective
- c. corporate values
- d. co-culture

Guidance: level 1

:: Television commercials ::

_____ is a phenomenon whereby something new and somehow valuable is formed. The created item may be intangible or a physical object .

12. *Answer choices:*

(see index for correct answer)

- a. Gay Mountain
- b. Eyebrows
- c. St George
- d. Creativity

Guidance: level 1

:: Product management ::

_____ s, also known as Shewhart charts or process-behavior charts, are a statistical process control tool used to determine if a manufacturing or business process is in a state of control.

Exam Probability: **High**

13. *Answer choices:*

(see index for correct answer)

- a. Brand equity
- b. Product manager
- c. Control chart
- d. Dwinell-Wright Company

:: Monopoly (economics) ::

A _____ is a form of intellectual property that gives its owner the legal right to exclude others from making, using, selling, and importing an invention for a limited period of years, in exchange for publishing an enabling public disclosure of the invention. In most countries _____ rights fall under civil law and the _____ holder needs to sue someone infringing the _____ in order to enforce his or her rights. In some industries _____ s are an essential form of competitive advantage; in others they are irrelevant.

Exam Probability: **High**

14. *Answer choices:*

(see index for correct answer)

- a. Intellectual property
- b. Patent
- c. Ramsey problem
- d. Cost per procedure

:: ::

In mathematics, a _____ is a relationship between two numbers indicating how many times the first number contains the second. For example, if a bowl of fruit contains eight oranges and six lemons, then the _____ of oranges to lemons is eight to six . Similarly, the _____ of lemons to oranges is 6:8 and the _____ of oranges to the total amount of fruit is 8:14 .

Exam Probability: **Medium**

15. *Answer choices:*

(see index for correct answer)

- a. Ratio
- b. similarity-attraction theory
- c. Character
- d. surface-level diversity

Guidance: level 1

:: Organizational structure ::

An _____ defines how activities such as task allocation, coordination, and supervision are directed toward the achievement of organizational aims.

Exam Probability: **Medium**

16. *Answer choices:*

- a. The Starfish and the Spider
- b. Unorganisation
- c. Organizational structure
- d. Automated Bureaucracy

Guidance: level 1

:: Business ::

The seller, or the provider of the goods or services, completes a sale in response to an acquisition, appropriation, requisition or a direct interaction with the buyer at the point of sale. There is a passing of title of the item, and the settlement of a price, in which agreement is reached on a price for which transfer of ownership of the item will occur. The seller, not the purchaser typically executes the sale and it may be completed prior to the obligation of payment. In the case of indirect interaction, a person who sells goods or service on behalf of the owner is known as a _____ man or _____ woman or _____ person, but this often refers to someone selling goods in a store/shop, in which case other terms are also common, including _____ clerk, shop assistant, and retail clerk.

Exam Probability: **Medium**

17. *Answer choices:*

- a. Crowdsourcing

- b. Organizational life cycle
- c. Sales
- d. Westnile Distilling Company Limited

Guidance: level 1

:: ::

A _____ is a type of job aid used to reduce failure by compensating for potential limits of human memory and attention. It helps to ensure consistency and completeness in carrying out a task. A basic example is the "to do list". A more advanced _____ would be a schedule, which lays out tasks to be done according to time of day or other factors. A primary task in _____ is documentation of the task and auditing against the documentation.

Exam Probability: **High**

18. *Answer choices:*

(see index for correct answer)

- a. hierarchical
- b. cultural
- c. empathy
- d. Checklist

Guidance: level 1

:: Regression analysis ::

A _____ often refers to a set of documented requirements to be satisfied by a material, design, product, or service. A _____ is often a type of technical standard.

Exam Probability: **Medium**

19. *Answer choices:*

(see index for correct answer)

- a. Censored regression model
- b. Multinomial logistic regression
- c. Proper linear model
- d. Specification

Guidance: level 1

:: Lean manufacturing ::

A continual improvement process, also often called a _____ process , is an ongoing effort to improve products, services, or processes. These efforts can seek "incremental" improvement over time or "breakthrough" improvement all at once. Delivery processes are constantly evaluated and improved in the light of their efficiency, effectiveness and flexibility.

Exam Probability: **High**

20. *Answer choices:*

(see index for correct answer)

- a. No value added
- b. Value stream mapping
- c. Kanban board
- d. Agent-assisted automation

Guidance: level 1

:: Organizational behavior ::

In organizational behavior and industrial and organizational psychology, _____ is an individual's psychological attachment to the organization. The basis behind many of these studies was to find ways to improve how workers feel about their jobs so that these workers would become more committed to their organizations. _____ predicts work variables such as turnover, organizational citizenship behavior, and job performance. Some of the factors such as role stress, empowerment, job insecurity and employability, and distribution of leadership have been shown to be connected to a worker's sense of _____ .

Exam Probability: **Low**

21. *Answer choices:*

(see index for correct answer)

- a. Positive organizational behavior
- b. Organizational retaliatory behavior

- c. Organizational commitment
- d. Satisficing

Guidance: level 1

:: ::

_____ is an evaluative or corrective exercise that can occur in any area of human life. _____ can therefore take many different forms . How people go about criticizing, can vary a great deal. In specific areas of human endeavour, the form of _____ can be highly specialized and technical; it often requires professional knowledge to appreciate the _____ . For subject-specific information, see the Varieties of _____ page.

Exam Probability: **Low**

22. *Answer choices:*

(see index for correct answer)

- a. interpersonal communication
- b. hierarchical perspective
- c. Criticism
- d. information systems assessment

Guidance: level 1

:: Data analysis ::

In statistics, the _____ is a measure that is used to quantify the amount of variation or dispersion of a set of data values. A low _____ indicates that the data points tend to be close to the mean of the set, while a high _____ indicates that the data points are spread out over a wider range of values.

Exam Probability: **Medium**

23. *Answer choices:*

(see index for correct answer)

- a. Outlier
- b. Data transformation
- c. Boolean analysis
- d. Neighbourhood components analysis

Guidance: level 1

:: Decision theory ::

A _____ is a decision support tool that uses a tree-like model of decisions and their possible consequences, including chance event outcomes, resource costs, and utility. It is one way to display an algorithm that only contains conditional control statements.

Exam Probability: **Medium**

24. *Answer choices:*

(see index for correct answer)

- a. Expected value of sample information
- b. Omission bias
- c. Decision tree
- d. Causal decision theory

Guidance: level 1

:: Legal terms ::

_____ is a type of meaning in which a phrase, statement or resolution is not explicitly defined, making several interpretations plausible. A common aspect of _____ is uncertainty. It is thus an attribute of any idea or statement whose intended meaning cannot be definitively resolved according to a rule or process with a finite number of steps.

Exam Probability: **Low**

25. *Answer choices:*

(see index for correct answer)

- a. Abstract of judgment
- b. Fuero
- c. Plenary power
- d. Ambiguity

:: Information science ::

_____ is the resolution of uncertainty; it is that which answers the question of "what an entity is" and thus defines both its essence and nature of its characteristics. _____ relates to both data and knowledge, as data is meaningful _____ representing values attributed to parameters, and knowledge signifies understanding of a concept. _____ is uncoupled from an observer, which is an entity that can access _____ and thus discern what it specifies; _____ exists beyond an event horizon for example. In the case of knowledge, the _____ itself requires a cognitive observer to be obtained.

Exam Probability: **Medium**

26. *Answer choices:*

(see index for correct answer)

- a. Information ethics
- b. Metamedia
- c. Science communication
- d. Library and Information Science Abstracts

:: Production economics ::

In microeconomics, _____ are the cost advantages that enterprises obtain due to their scale of operation , with cost per unit of output decreasing with increasing scale.

Exam Probability: **High**

27. *Answer choices:*

(see index for correct answer)

- a. Division of work
- b. Economies of scale
- c. Product pipeline
- d. HMI quality

Guidance: level 1

:: Human resource management ::

_____ is a core function of human resource management and it is related to the specification of contents, methods and relationship of jobs in order to satisfy technological and organizational requirements as well as the social and personal requirements of the job holder or the employee. Its principles are geared towards how the nature of a person's job affects their attitudes and behavior at work, particularly relating to characteristics such as skill variety and autonomy. The aim of a _____ is to improve job satisfaction, to improve through-put, to improve quality and to reduce employee problems .

28. *Answer choices:*

(see index for correct answer)

- a. Talascend
- b. On-ramping
- c. Job design
- d. E-HRM

Guidance: level 1

:: Strategic management ::

_____ is a strategic planning technique used to help a person or organization identify strengths, weaknesses, opportunities, and threats related to business competition or project planning. It is intended to specify the objectives of the business venture or project and identify the internal and external factors that are favorable and unfavorable to achieving those objectives. Users of a _____ often ask and answer questions to generate meaningful information for each category to make the tool useful and identify their competitive advantage. SWOT has been described as the tried-and-true tool of strategic analysis.

Exam Probability: **High**

29. *Answer choices:*

(see index for correct answer)

- a. Segment architecture
- b. SWOT analysis
- c. Operational responsiveness
- d. Strategic service management

Guidance: level 1

:: Human resource management ::

_____ encompasses values and behaviors that contribute to the unique social and psychological environment of a business. The _____ influences the way people interact, the context within which knowledge is created, the resistance they will have towards certain changes, and ultimately the way they share knowledge. _____ represents the collective values, beliefs and principles of organizational members and is a product of factors such as history, product, market, technology, strategy, type of employees, management style, and national culture; culture includes the organization's vision, values, norms, systems, symbols, language, assumptions, environment, location, beliefs and habits.

Exam Probability: **Low**

30. *Answer choices:*

(see index for correct answer)

- a. Inclusive business
- b. Attendance management
- c. Functional job analysis
- d. Organizational culture

:: Training ::

_____ is teaching, or developing in oneself or others, any skills and knowledge that relate to specific useful competencies. _____ has specific goals of improving one's capability, capacity, productivity and performance. It forms the core of apprenticeships and provides the backbone of content at institutes of technology . In addition to the basic _____ required for a trade, occupation or profession, observers of the labor-market recognize as of 2008 the need to continue _____ beyond initial qualifications: to maintain, upgrade and update skills throughout working life. People within many professions and occupations may refer to this sort of _____ as professional development.

Exam Probability: **Low**

31. *Answer choices:*

(see index for correct answer)

- a. Training
- b. International Society for Performance Improvement
- c. Endurance training
- d. Jeff Phillips

:: Business terms ::

A _____ is a short statement of why an organization exists, what its overall goal is, identifying the goal of its operations: what kind of product or service it provides, its primary customers or market, and its geographical region of operation. It may include a short statement of such fundamental matters as the organization's values or philosophies, a business's main competitive advantages, or a desired future state—the "vision".

Exam Probability: **High**

32. *Answer choices:*

(see index for correct answer)

- a. operating cost
- b. granular
- c. back office
- d. Strategic partner

Guidance: level 1

:: Marketing ::

_____ or stock control can be broadly defined as "the activity of checking a shop's stock." However, a more focused definition takes into account the more science-based, methodical practice of not only verifying a business' inventory but also focusing on the many related facets of inventory management "within an organisation to meet the demand placed upon that business economically." Other facets of _____ include supply chain management, production control, financial flexibility, and customer satisfaction. At the root of _____ , however, is the _____ problem, which involves determining when to order, how much to order, and the logistics of those decisions.

Exam Probability: **Medium**

33. *Answer choices:*

(see index for correct answer)

- a. Inventory control
- b. Price premium
- c. Interactive collateral management
- d. Brand

Guidance: level 1

:: Human resource management ::

_____ expands the capacity of individuals to perform in leadership roles within organizations. Leadership roles are those that facilitate execution of a company's strategy through building alignment, winning mindshare and growing the capabilities of others. Leadership roles may be formal, with the corresponding authority to make decisions and take responsibility, or they may be informal roles with little official authority .

Exam Probability: **Low**

34. *Answer choices:*

(see index for correct answer)

- a. Functional job analysis
- b. Organizational culture
- c. Public service motivation
- d. Leadership development

Guidance: level 1

:: ::

_____ is the process of two or more people or organizations working together to complete a task or achieve a goal. _____ is similar to cooperation. Most _____ requires leadership, although the form of leadership can be social within a decentralized and egalitarian group. Teams that work collaboratively often access greater resources, recognition and rewards when facing competition for finite resources.

35. *Answer choices:*

(see index for correct answer)

- a. functional perspective
- b. Collaboration
- c. deep-level diversity
- d. cultural

Guidance: level 1

:: ::

_____ is the assignment of any responsibility or authority to another person to carry out specific activities. It is one of the core concepts of management leadership. However, the person who delegated the work remains accountable for the outcome of the delegated work. _____ empowers a subordinate to make decisions, i.e. it is a shifting of decision-making authority from one organizational level to a lower one. _____ , if properly done, is not fabrication. The opposite of effective _____ is micromanagement, where a manager provides too much input, direction, and review of delegated work. In general, _____ is good and can save money and time, help in building skills, and motivate people. On the other hand, poor _____ might cause frustration and confusion to all the involved parties. Some agents, however, do not favour a _____ and consider the power of making a decision rather burdensome.

36. *Answer choices:*

(see index for correct answer)

- a. Delegation
- b. levels of analysis
- c. co-culture
- d. interpersonal communication

Guidance: level 1

:: Elementary mathematics ::

_____ is a numerical measurement of how far apart objects are. In physics or everyday usage, _____ may refer to a physical length or an estimation based on other criteria . In most cases, " _____ from A to B" is interchangeable with " _____ from B to A". In mathematics, a _____ function or metric is a generalization of the concept of physical _____ . A metric is a function that behaves according to a specific set of rules, and is a way of describing what it means for elements of some space to be "close to" or "far away from" each other.

Exam Probability: **Medium**

37. *Answer choices:*

(see index for correct answer)

- a. Natural number
- b. Function

- c. Distance
- d. Point plotting

Guidance: level 1

:: ::

_____ , in its broadest context, includes both the attainment of that which is just and the philosophical discussion of that which is just. The concept of _____ is based on numerous fields, and many differing viewpoints and perspectives including the concepts of moral correctness based on ethics, rationality, law, religion, equity and fairness. Often, the general discussion of _____ is divided into the realm of social _____ as found in philosophy, theology and religion, and, procedural _____ as found in the study and application of the law.

Exam Probability: **Medium**

38. *Answer choices:*
(see index for correct answer)

- a. empathy
- b. levels of analysis
- c. Justice
- d. process perspective

Guidance: level 1

:: Project management ::

A _____ is a source or supply from which a benefit is produced and it has some utility. _____ s can broadly be classified upon their availability—they are classified into renewable and non-renewable _____ s.Examples of non renewable _____ s are coal ,crude oil natural gas nuclear energy etc. Examples of renewable _____ s are air,water,wind,solar energy etc. They can also be classified as actual and potential on the basis of level of development and use, on the basis of origin they can be classified as biotic and abiotic, and on the basis of their distribution, as ubiquitous and localized . An item becomes a _____ with time and developing technology. Typically, _____ s are materials, energy, services, staff, knowledge, or other assets that are transformed to produce benefit and in the process may be consumed or made unavailable. Benefits of _____ utilization may include increased wealth, proper functioning of a system, or enhanced well-being. From a human perspective a natural _____ is anything obtained from the environment to satisfy human needs and wants. From a broader biological or ecological perspective a _____ satisfies the needs of a living organism .

Exam Probability: **High**

39. *Answer choices:*

(see index for correct answer)

- a. Social project management
- b. Milestone
- c. Iteration
- d. overdue

Guidance: level 1

:: Organizational behavior ::

_____ is the term now used more commonly in business management, particularly human resource management. _____ refers to the number of subordinates a supervisor has.

Exam Probability: **High**

40. *Answer choices:*

(see index for correct answer)

- a. Counterproductive norms
- b. History of contingency theories of leadership
- c. Span of control
- d. Organizational Expedience

Guidance: level 1

:: ::

_____ is the reason for people`s actions, willingness and goals. _____ is derived from the word motive in the English language which is defined as a need that requires satisfaction. These needs could also be wants or desires that are acquired through influence of culture, society, lifestyle, etc. or generally innate. _____ is one`s direction to behaviour, or what causes a person to want to repeat a behaviour, a set of force that acts behind the motives. An individual`s _____ may be inspired by others or events or it may come from within the individual . _____ has been considered as one of the most important reasons that inspires a person to move forward in life. _____ results from the interaction of both conscious and unconscious factors. Mastering _____ to allow sustained and deliberate practice is central to high levels of achievement e.g. in the worlds of elite sport, medicine or music.

Exam Probability: **Medium**

41. *Answer choices:*

(see index for correct answer)

- a. similarity-attraction theory
- b. Motivation
- c. hierarchical perspective
- d. deep-level diversity

Guidance: level 1

:: ::

_____ is the stock of habits, knowledge, social and personality attributes embodied in the ability to perform labor so as to produce economic value.

Exam Probability: **Low**

42. *Answer choices:*

(see index for correct answer)

- a. personal values
- b. empathy
- c. Sarbanes-Oxley act of 2002
- d. process perspective

Guidance: level 1

:: Labour relations ::

_____ is a field of study that can have different meanings depending on the context in which it is used. In an international context, it is a subfield of labor history that studies the human relations with regard to work – in its broadest sense – and how this connects to questions of social inequality. It explicitly encompasses unregulated, historical, and non-Western forms of labor. Here, _____ define "for or with whom one works and under what rules. These rules determine the type of work, type and amount of remuneration, working hours, degrees of physical and psychological strain, as well as the degree of freedom and autonomy associated with the work."

43. *Answer choices:*

(see index for correct answer)

- a. Scranton Declaration
- b. Featherbedding
- c. Impasse
- d. Big labor

Guidance: level 1

:: Production and manufacturing ::

Automatic _____ in continuous production processes is a combination of control engineering and chemical engineering disciplines that uses industrial control systems to achieve a production level of consistency, economy and safety which could not be achieved purely by human manual control. It is implemented widely in industries such as oil refining, pulp and paper manufacturing, chemical processing and power generating plants.

Exam Probability: **High**

44. *Answer choices:*

(see index for correct answer)

- a. CTQ tree
- b. Simatic S5 PLC

- c. Advanced product quality planning
- d. Process control

Guidance: level 1

:: ::

In communications and information processing, _____ is a system of rules to convert information—such as a letter, word, sound, image, or gesture—into another form or representation, sometimes shortened or secret, for communication through a communication channel or storage in a storage medium. An early example is the invention of language, which enabled a person, through speech, to communicate what they saw, heard, felt, or thought to others. But speech limits the range of communication to the distance a voice can carry, and limits the audience to those present when the speech is uttered. The invention of writing, which converted spoken language into visual symbols, extended the range of communication across space and time.

Exam Probability: **Low**

45. *Answer choices:*
(see index for correct answer)

- a. hierarchical perspective
- b. levels of analysis
- c. corporate values
- d. Code

Guidance: level 1

:: Security compliance ::

A _____ is a communicated intent to inflict harm or loss on another person. A _____ is considered an act of coercion. _____ s are widely observed in animal behavior, particularly in a ritualized form, chiefly in order to avoid the unnecessary physical violence that can lead to physical damage or the death of both conflicting parties.

Exam Probability: **Medium**

46. *Answer choices:*

(see index for correct answer)

- a. Vulnerability
- b. Threat
- c. Month of bugs
- d. Security Content Automation Protocol

Guidance: level 1

:: ::

_____ involves the development of an action plan designed to motivate and guide a person or group toward a goal. _____ can be guided by goal-setting criteria such as SMART criteria. _____ is a major component of personal-development and management literature.

47. *Answer choices:*

(see index for correct answer)

- a. Goal setting
- b. interpersonal communication
- c. hierarchical
- d. Character

Guidance: level 1

:: Power (social and political) ::

In a notable study of power conducted by social psychologists John R. P. French and Bertram Raven in 1959, power is divided into five separate and distinct forms. In 1965 Raven revised this model to include a sixth form by separating the informational power base as distinct from the _____ base.

Exam Probability: **Low**

48. *Answer choices:*

(see index for correct answer)

- a. Expert power
- b. need for power
- c. Referent power

:: Business models ::

A _____ is "an autonomous association of persons united voluntarily to meet their common economic, social, and cultural needs and aspirations through a jointly-owned and democratically-controlled enterprise". _____ s may include.

Exam Probability: **High**

49. *Answer choices:*

(see index for correct answer)

- a. Cooperative
- b. Business model pattern
- c. Copy to China
- d. Collective business system

Guidance: level 1

:: Business models ::

A _____ , _____ company or daughter company is a company that is owned or controlled by another company, which is called the parent company, parent, or holding company. The _____ can be a company, corporation, or limited liability company. In some cases it is a government or state-owned enterprise. In some cases, particularly in the music and book publishing industries, subsidiaries are referred to as imprints.

Exam Probability: **Low**

50. *Answer choices:*

(see index for correct answer)

- a. Consumer cooperative
- b. Subsidiary
- c. Freemium
- d. Business-agile enterprise

Guidance: level 1

:: ::

An _____ in international trade is a good or service produced in one country that is bought by someone in another country. The seller of such goods and services is an _____ er; the foreign buyer is an importer.

Exam Probability: **Medium**

51. *Answer choices:*

(see index for correct answer)

- a. co-culture
- b. Export
- c. cultural
- d. process perspective

Guidance: level 1

:: ::

In organizational behavior and industrial/organizational psychology, proactivity or _____ behavior by individuals refers to anticipatory, change-oriented and self-initiated behavior in situations. _____ behavior involves acting in advance of a future situation, rather than just reacting. It means taking control and making things happen rather than just adjusting to a situation or waiting for something to happen. _____ employees generally do not need to be asked to act, nor do they require detailed instructions.

Exam Probability: **High**

52. *Answer choices:*

(see index for correct answer)

- a. Sarbanes-Oxley act of 2002
- b. Proactive
- c. Character

- d. co-culture

Guidance: level 1

:: Office administration ::

An _____ is generally a room or other area where an organization's employees perform administrative work in order to support and realize objects and goals of the organization. The word " _____ " may also denote a position within an organization with specific duties attached to it ; the latter is in fact an earlier usage, _____ as place originally referring to the location of one's duty. When used as an adjective, the term " _____ " may refer to business-related tasks. In law, a company or organization has _____ s in any place where it has an official presence, even if that presence consists of a storage silo rather than an establishment with desk-and-chair. An _____ is also an architectural and design phenomenon: ranging from a small _____ such as a bench in the corner of a small business of extremely small size , through entire floors of buildings, up to and including massive buildings dedicated entirely to one company. In modern terms an _____ is usually the location where white-collar workers carry out their functions. As per James Stephenson, " _____ is that part of business enterprise which is devoted to the direction and co-ordination of its various activities."

Exam Probability: **Low**

53. *Answer choices:*

(see index for correct answer)

- a. Fish! Philosophy
- b. Office

- c. Office administration
- d. Inter departmental communication

Guidance: level 1

:: Human resource management ::

_____ involves improving the effectiveness of organizations and the individuals and teams within them. Training may be viewed as related to immediate changes in organizational effectiveness via organized instruction, while development is related to the progress of longer-term organizational and employee goals. While _____ technically have differing definitions, the two are oftentimes used interchangeably and/or together. _____ has historically been a topic within applied psychology but has within the last two decades become closely associated with human resources management, talent management, human resources development, instructional design, human factors, and knowledge management.

Exam Probability: **Low**

54. *Answer choices:*

(see index for correct answer)

- a. On-ramping
- b. Workforce planning
- c. Income bracket
- d. Potential analysis

Guidance: level 1

:: Management ::

_____ is a process by which entities review the quality of all factors involved in production. ISO 9000 defines _____ as "A part of quality management focused on fulfilling quality requirements".

Exam Probability: **Low**

55. *Answer choices:*

(see index for correct answer)

- a. Duality
- b. Quality control
- c. Backsourcing
- d. Capability management

Guidance: level 1

:: ::

According to Torrington, a _____ is usually developed by conducting a job analysis, which includes examining the tasks and sequences of tasks necessary to perform the job. The analysis considers the areas of knowledge and skills needed for the job. A job usually includes several roles. According to Hall, the _____ might be broadened to form a person specification or may be known as "terms of reference". The person/job specification can be presented as a stand-alone document, but in practice it is usually included within the _____ . A _____ is often used by employers in the recruitment process.

Exam Probability: **Medium**

56. *Answer choices:*

(see index for correct answer)

- a. Job description
- b. information systems assessment
- c. levels of analysis
- d. Character

Guidance: level 1

:: Operations research ::

_____ is a method to achieve the best outcome in a mathematical model whose requirements are represented by linear relationships. _____ is a special case of mathematical programming .

57. *Answer choices:*

(see index for correct answer)

- a. Linear programming
- b. European Working Group on Multiple Criteria Decision Aiding
- c. Semidefinite programming
- d. Fractional programming

Guidance: level 1

:: Human resource management ::

_____ are the people who make up the workforce of an organization, business sector, or economy. "Human capital" is sometimes used synonymously with "_____", although human capital typically refers to a narrower effect . Likewise, other terms sometimes used include manpower, talent, labor, personnel, or simply people.

Exam Probability: **Low**

58. *Answer choices:*

(see index for correct answer)

- a. Human resources
- b. Focal Point Review

- c. Resource-based view
- d. Contractor management

Guidance: level 1

:: ::

_____ Corporation was an American energy, commodities, and services company based in Houston, Texas. It was founded in 1985 as a merger between Houston Natural Gas and InterNorth, both relatively small regional companies. Before its bankruptcy on December 3, 2001, _____ employed approximately 29,000 staff and was a major electricity, natural gas, communications and pulp and paper company, with claimed revenues of nearly $101 billion during 2000. Fortune named _____ "America's Most Innovative Company" for six consecutive years.

Exam Probability: **Medium**

59. *Answer choices:*
(see index for correct answer)

- a. Enron
- b. hierarchical perspective
- c. open system
- d. co-culture

Guidance: level 1

Business law

    Corporate law (also known as business law) is the body of law governing the rights, relations, and conduct of persons, companies, organizations and businesses. It refers to the legal practice relating to, or the theory of corporations. Corporate law often describes the law relating to matters which derive directly from the life-cycle of a corporation. It thus encompasses the formation, funding, governance, and death of a corporation.

:: ::

_____ is the assignment of any responsibility or authority to another person to carry out specific activities. It is one of the core concepts of management leadership. However, the person who delegated the work remains accountable for the outcome of the delegated work. _____ empowers a subordinate to make decisions, i.e. it is a shifting of decision-making authority from one organizational level to a lower one. _____ , if properly done, is not fabrication. The opposite of effective _____ is micromanagement, where a manager provides too much input, direction, and review of delegated work. In general, _____ is good and can save money and time, help in building skills, and motivate people. On the other hand, poor _____ might cause frustration and confusion to all the involved parties. Some agents, however, do not favour a _____ and consider the power of making a decision rather burdensome.

Exam Probability: **Low**

1. *Answer choices:*

(see index for correct answer)

- a. Delegation
- b. empathy
- c. co-culture
- d. Character

Guidance: level 1

:: ::

_____ , in United States trademark law, is a statutory cause of action that permits a party to petition the Trademark Trial and Appeal Board of the Patent and Trademark Office to cancel a trademark registration that "may disparage or falsely suggest a connection with persons, living or dead, institutions, beliefs, or national symbols, or bring them into contempt or disrepute." Unlike claims regarding the validity of the mark, a _____ claim can be brought "at any time," subject to equitable defenses such as laches.

Exam Probability: **High**

2. *Answer choices:*

(see index for correct answer)

- a. hierarchical perspective
- b. interpersonal communication
- c. surface-level diversity
- d. functional perspective

Guidance: level 1

:: Real estate valuation ::

_____ or OMV is the price at which an asset would trade in a competitive auction setting. _____ is often used interchangeably with open _____ , fair value or fair _____ , although these terms have distinct definitions in different standards, and may or may not differ in some circumstances.

3. *Answer choices:*

(see index for correct answer)

- a. Highest and best use
- b. E.surv
- c. Market value
- d. Uniform Standards of Professional Appraisal Practice

Guidance: level 1

:: ::

In legal terminology, a _____ is any formal legal document that sets out the facts and legal reasons that the filing party or parties believes are sufficient to support a claim against the party or parties against whom the claim is brought that entitles the plaintiff to a remedy . For example, the Federal Rules of Civil Procedure that govern civil litigation in United States courts provide that a civil action is commenced with the filing or service of a pleading called a _____ . Civil court rules in states that have incorporated the Federal Rules of Civil Procedure use the same term for the same pleading.

Exam Probability: **Low**

4. *Answer choices:*

(see index for correct answer)

- a. empathy
- b. information systems assessment
- c. Character
- d. Complaint

Guidance: level 1

:: ::

_____ is a judicial device in common law legal systems whereby a court may prevent, or "estop" a person from making assertions or from going back on his or her word; the person being sanctioned is "estopped". _____ may prevent someone from bringing a particular claim. Legal doctrines of _____ are based in both common law and equity.

Exam Probability: **Medium**

5. *Answer choices:*

(see index for correct answer)

- a. cultural
- b. similarity-attraction theory
- c. Character
- d. imperative

Guidance: level 1

:: Insolvency ::

_____ is the state of being unable to pay the money owed, by a person or company, on time; those in a state of _____ are said to be insolvent. There are two forms: cash-flow _____ and balance-sheet _____ .

Exam Probability: **Low**

6. *Answer choices:*

(see index for correct answer)

- • a. Bankruptcy
- • b. Financial distress
- • c. Debt consolidation
- • d. Insolvency

Guidance: level 1

:: ::

An _____ is a criminal accusation that a person has committed a crime. In jurisdictions that use the concept of felonies, the most serious criminal offence is a felony; jurisdictions that do not use the felonies concept often use that of an indictable offence, an offence that requires an _____ .

Exam Probability: **Low**

7. *Answer choices:*

(see index for correct answer)

- a. information systems assessment
- b. Indictment
- c. hierarchical perspective
- d. surface-level diversity

Guidance: level 1

:: ::

In international relations, _____ is – from the perspective of governments – a voluntary transfer of resources from one country to another.

Exam Probability: **Low**

8. *Answer choices:*

(see index for correct answer)

- a. corporate values
- b. open system
- c. functional perspective
- d. Aid

Guidance: level 1

:: ::

In financial markets, a share is a unit used as mutual funds, limited partnerships, and real estate investment trusts. The owner of _____ in the corporation/company is a shareholder of the corporation. A share is an indivisible unit of capital, expressing the ownership relationship between the company and the shareholder. The denominated value of a share is its face value, and the total of the face value of issued _____ represent the capital of a company, which may not reflect the market value of those _____ .

Exam Probability: **Low**

9. *Answer choices:*

(see index for correct answer)

- a. Shares
- b. hierarchical
- c. Sarbanes-Oxley act of 2002
- d. process perspective

Guidance: level 1

:: Insolvency ::

_____ is a legal process through which people or other entities who cannot repay debts to creditors may seek relief from some or all of their debts. In most jurisdictions, _____ is imposed by a court order, often initiated by the debtor.

Exam Probability: **Medium**

10. *Answer choices:*

(see index for correct answer)

- a. George Samuel Ford
- b. Personal Insolvency Arrangement
- c. Debt consolidation
- d. United Kingdom insolvency law

Guidance: level 1

:: ::

A _____ is a person or firm who arranges transactions between a buyer and a seller for a commission when the deal is executed. A _____ who also acts as a seller or as a buyer becomes a principal party to the deal. Neither role should be confused with that of an agent—one who acts on behalf of a principal party in a deal.

Exam Probability: **High**

11. *Answer choices:*

(see index for correct answer)

- a. hierarchical perspective
- b. similarity-attraction theory
- c. Broker
- d. Sarbanes-Oxley act of 2002

Guidance: level 1

:: ::

A _____ is a sworn body of people convened to render an impartial verdict officially submitted to them by a court, or to set a penalty or judgment. Modern juries tend to be found in courts to ascertain the guilt or lack thereof in a crime. In Anglophone jurisdictions, the verdict may be guilty or not guilty . The old institution of grand juries still exists in some places, particularly the United States, to investigate whether enough evidence of a crime exists to bring someone to trial.

Exam Probability: **Low**

12. *Answer choices:*

(see index for correct answer)

- a. co-culture
- b. hierarchical
- c. open system

- d. Jury

:: ::

The Sherman Antitrust Act of 1890 was a United States antitrust law that regulates competition among enterprises, which was passed by Congress under the presidency of Benjamin Harrison.

Exam Probability: **High**

13. *Answer choices:*

(see index for correct answer)

- a. corporate values
- b. levels of analysis
- c. Sherman Act
- d. process perspective

:: Working time ::

Labour law is the area of law most commonly relating to the relationship between trade unions, employers and the government.

Exam Probability: **Low**

14. *Answer choices:*

(see index for correct answer)

- a. Break
- b. Graveyard shift
- c. Sunday Trading Act 1994
- d. Employment law

Guidance: level 1

:: Abuse of the legal system ::

_____ occurs when a person is restricted in their personal movement within any area without justification or consent. Actual physical restraint is not necessary for _____ to occur. A _____ claim may be made based upon private acts, or upon wrongful governmental detention. For detention by the police, proof of _____ provides a basis to obtain a writ of habeas corpus.

Exam Probability: **High**

15. *Answer choices:*

(see index for correct answer)

- a. Forum shopping
- b. False arrest
- c. False imprisonment

Guidance: level 1

:: Legal doctrines and principles ::

In law, a _____ is an event sufficiently related to an injury that the courts deem the event to be the cause of that injury. There are two types of causation in the law: cause-in-fact, and proximate cause. Cause-in-fact is determined by the "but for" test: But for the action, the result would not have happened. The action is a necessary condition, but may not be a sufficient condition, for the resulting injury. A few circumstances exist where the but for test is ineffective . Since but-for causation is very easy to show , a second test is used to determine if an action is close enough to a harm in a "chain of events" to be legally valid. This test is called _____ . _____ is a key principle of Insurance and is concerned with how the loss or damage actually occurred. There are several competing theories of _____ . For an act to be deemed to cause a harm, both tests must be met; _____ is a legal limitation on cause-in-fact.

Exam Probability: **High**

16. *Answer choices:*
(see index for correct answer)

- a. Act of state

- b. Assumption of risk
- c. Proximate cause
- d. Caveat emptor

Guidance: level 1

:: ::

Punishment is the imposition of an undesirable or unpleasant outcome upon a group or individual, meted out by an authority—in contexts ranging from child discipline to criminal law—as a response and deterrent to a particular action or behaviour that is deemed undesirable or unacceptable. The reasoning may be to condition a child to avoid self-endangerment, to impose social conformity , to defend norms, to protect against future harms , and to maintain the law—and respect for rule of law—under which the social group is governed. Punishment may be self-inflicted as with self-flagellation and mortification of the flesh in the religious setting, but is most often a form of social coercion.

Exam Probability: **Medium**

17. *Answer choices:*
(see index for correct answer)

- a. hierarchical perspective
- b. Punitive
- c. functional perspective
- d. personal values

Guidance: level 1

_____ is the collection of techniques, skills, methods, and processes used in the production of goods or services or in the accomplishment of objectives, such as scientific investigation. _____ can be the knowledge of techniques, processes, and the like, or it can be embedded in machines to allow for operation without detailed knowledge of their workings. Systems applying _____ by taking an input, changing it according to the system's use, and then producing an outcome are referred to as _____ systems or technological systems.

Exam Probability: **High**

18. *Answer choices:*

(see index for correct answer)

- a. levels of analysis
- b. similarity-attraction theory
- c. hierarchical
- d. Sarbanes-Oxley act of 2002

Guidance: level 1

:: Mortgage ::

_____ is a legal process in which a lender attempts to recover the balance of a loan from a borrower who has stopped making payments to the lender by forcing the sale of the asset used as the collateral for the loan.

Exam Probability: **High**

19. *Answer choices:*

(see index for correct answer)

- a. Foreclosure
- b. Mortgage equity withdrawal
- c. Mortgage analytics
- d. April Charney

Guidance: level 1

:: Business law ::

A _____ is a business entity created by two or more parties, generally characterized by shared ownership, shared returns and risks, and shared governance. Companies typically pursue _____ s for one of four reasons: to access a new market, particularly emerging markets; to gain scale efficiencies by combining assets and operations; to share risk for major investments or projects; or to access skills and capabilities.

Exam Probability: **Low**

20. *Answer choices:*

(see index for correct answer)

- a. Security interest
- b. Negotiable instrument
- c. Joint venture
- d. Unfair business practices

Guidance: level 1

:: ::

In logic and philosophy, an _____ is a series of statements , called the premises or premisses , intended to determine the degree of truth of another statement, the conclusion. The logical form of an _____ in a natural language can be represented in a symbolic formal language, and independently of natural language formally defined " _____ s" can be made in math and computer science.

Exam Probability: **Low**

21. *Answer choices:*

(see index for correct answer)

- a. cultural
- b. levels of analysis
- c. Argument
- d. imperative

:: ::

An _____ is a formal or official change made to a law, contract, constitution, or other legal document. It is based on the verb to amend, which means to change for better. _____ s can add, remove, or update parts of these agreements. They are often used when it is better to change the document than to write a new one.

Exam Probability: **Low**

22. *Answer choices:*

(see index for correct answer)

- a. corporate values
- b. co-culture
- c. Amendment
- d. empathy

:: ::

A _____ is a person who holds a legal or ethical relationship of trust with one or more other parties . Typically, a _____ prudently takes care of money or other assets for another person. One party, for example, a corporate trust company or the trust department of a bank, acts in a _____ capacity to another party, who, for example, has entrusted funds to the _____ for safekeeping or investment. Likewise, financial advisers, financial planners, and; asset managers, including managers of pension plans, endowments, and other tax-exempt assets, are considered fiduciaries under applicable statutes and laws. In a _____ relationship, one person, in a position of vulnerability, justifiably vests confidence, good faith, reliance, and trust in another whose aid, advice, or protection is sought in some matter. In such a relation good conscience requires the _____ to act at all times for the sole benefit and interest of the one who trusts.

Exam Probability: **High**

23. *Answer choices:*

(see index for correct answer)

- a. Fiduciary
- b. hierarchical
- c. personal values
- d. open system

Guidance: level 1

:: ::

A federation is a political entity characterized by a union of partially self-governing provinces, states, or other regions under a central _____ . In a federation, the self-governing status of the component states, as well as the division of power between them and the central government, is typically constitutionally entrenched and may not be altered by a unilateral decision of either party, the states or the federal political body. Alternatively, federation is a form of government in which sovereign power is formally divided between a central authority and a number of constituent regions so that each region retains some degree of control over its internal affairs. It is often argued that federal states where the central government has the constitutional authority to suspend a constituent state's government by invoking gross mismanagement or civil unrest, or to adopt national legislation that overrides or infringe on the constituent states' powers by invoking the central government's constitutional authority to ensure "peace and good government" or to implement obligations contracted under an international treaty, are not truly federal states.

Exam Probability: **High**

24. *Answer choices:*

(see index for correct answer)

- a. Sarbanes-Oxley act of 2002
- b. cultural
- c. functional perspective
- d. imperative

Guidance: level 1

:: ::

The _____ of 1973, , is a federal law, codified as 29 U.S.C. § 701 et seq. The principal sponsor of the bill was Rep. John Brademas [IN-3]. The _____ of 1973 replaces the Vocational _____ of 1973, to extend and revise the authorization of grants to States for vocational rehabilitation services, with special emphasis on services to those with the most severe disabilities, to expand special Federal responsibilities and research and training programs with respect to individuals with disabilities, to establish special responsibilities in the Secretary of Health, Education, and Welfare for coordination of all programs with respect to individuals with disabilities within the Department of Health, Education, and Welfare, and for other purposes.

Exam Probability: **High**

25. *Answer choices:*

(see index for correct answer)

- a. Sarbanes-Oxley act of 2002
- b. Character
- c. imperative
- d. levels of analysis

Guidance: level 1

:: ::

Employment is a relationship between two parties, usually based on a contract where work is paid for, where one party, which may be a corporation, for profit, not-for-profit organization, co-operative or other entity is the employer and the other is the employee. Employees work in return for payment, which may be in the form of an hourly wage, by piecework or an annual salary, depending on the type of work an employee does or which sector she or he is working in. Employees in some fields or sectors may receive gratuities, bonus payment or stock options. In some types of employment, employees may receive benefits in addition to payment. Benefits can include health insurance, housing, disability insurance or use of a gym. Employment is typically governed by employment laws, regulations or legal contracts.

Exam Probability: **Medium**

26. *Answer choices:*

(see index for correct answer)

- a. Character
- b. hierarchical
- c. levels of analysis
- d. personal values

Guidance: level 1

:: Contract law ::

_____ of Contract is a legal term. In contract law, it is the implied ability of an individual to make a legally binding contract on behalf of an organization, by way of uniform or interaction with the public on behalf of that organization. When a person is wearing a uniform or nametag bearing the logo or trademark of a business or organization; or if that person is functioning in an obviously authorized capacity on behalf of a business or organization, that person carries an _____ of Contract. _____ is authority that is not express or written into the contract, but which the agent is assumed to have in order to transact the business of insurance for the principal. _____ is incidental to express authority since not every single detail of an agent's authority can be spelled out in the written contract.

Exam Probability: **High**

27. *Answer choices:*

(see index for correct answer)

- a. Implied authority
- b. Heads of Agreement
- c. Redhibition
- d. Pactum de quota litis

Guidance: level 1

:: Real property law ::

A _____ is the grant of authority or rights, stating that the granter formally recognizes the prerogative of the recipient to exercise the rights specified. It is implicit that the granter retains superiority, and that the recipient admits a limited status within the relationship, and it is within that sense that _____ s were historically granted, and that sense is retained in modern usage of the term.

Exam Probability: **Medium**

28. *Answer choices:*

(see index for correct answer)

- a. Primogeniture
- b. United States Court of Private Land Claims
- c. Charter
- d. Fee farm grant

Guidance: level 1

:: ::

The _____ Act of 1890 was a United States antitrust law that regulates competition among enterprises, which was passed by Congress under the presidency of Benjamin Harrison.

Exam Probability: **Low**

29. *Answer choices:*

(see index for correct answer)

- a. empathy
- b. open system
- c. cultural
- d. Sherman Antitrust

Guidance: level 1

:: Business law ::

A _____ is a form of security interest granted over an item of property to secure the payment of a debt or performance of some other obligation. The owner of the property, who grants the _____ , is referred to as the _____ ee and the person who has the benefit of the _____ is referred to as the _____ or or _____ holder.

Exam Probability: **Medium**

30. *Answer choices:*

(see index for correct answer)

- a. Lessor
- b. OHADA
- c. Jurisdictional strike
- d. De facto corporation and corporation by estoppel

:: Actuarial science ::

_____ is the possibility of losing something of value. Values can be gained or lost when taking _____ resulting from a given action or inaction, foreseen or unforeseen. _____ can also be defined as the intentional interaction with uncertainty. Uncertainty is a potential, unpredictable, and uncontrollable outcome; _____ is a consequence of action taken in spite of uncertainty.

Exam Probability: **Low**

31. *Answer choices:*

(see index for correct answer)

- a. Years of potential life lost
- b. Risk
- c. Catastrophe modeling
- d. Compound interest

:: Criminal procedure ::

_____ is the adjudication process of the criminal law. While _____ differs dramatically by jurisdiction, the process generally begins with a formal criminal charge with the person on trial either being free on bail or incarcerated, and results in the conviction or acquittal of the defendant. _____ can be either in form of inquisitorial or adversarial _____ .

Exam Probability: **Medium**

32. *Answer choices:*

(see index for correct answer)

- a. directed verdict
- b. Criminal procedure

Guidance: level 1

:: Sureties ::

In finance, a _____ , _____ bond or guaranty involves a promise by one party to assume responsibility for the debt obligation of a borrower if that borrower defaults. The person or company providing the promise is also known as a " _____ " or as a "guarantor".

Exam Probability: **Medium**

33. *Answer choices:*

(see index for correct answer)

- a. Payment bond
- b. Miller Act
- c. Surety
- d. Aval

Guidance: level 1

:: ::

An _____ is the production of goods or related services within an economy. The major source of revenue of a group or company is the indicator of its relevant _____ . When a large group has multiple sources of revenue generation, it is considered to be working in different industries. Manufacturing _____ became a key sector of production and labour in European and North American countries during the Industrial Revolution, upsetting previous mercantile and feudal economies. This came through many successive rapid advances in technology, such as the production of steel and coal.

Exam Probability: **High**

34. *Answer choices:*

(see index for correct answer)

- a. cultural
- b. corporate values
- c. Industry
- d. surface-level diversity

:: Corporate finance ::

_____ is a contract law concept about the purchase of the release from a debt obligation. It is one of the methods by which parties to a contract may terminate their agreement. The release is completed by the transfer of valuable consideration that must not be the actual performance of the obligation itself. The accord is the agreement to discharge the obligation and the satisfaction is the legal "consideration" which binds the parties to the agreement. A valid accord does not discharge the prior contract; instead it suspends the right to enforce it in accordance with the terms of the accord contract, in which satisfaction, or performance of the contract will discharge both contracts . If the creditor breaches the accord, then the debtor will be able to bring up the existence of the accord in order to enjoin any action against him.

Exam Probability: **Medium**

35. *Answer choices:*

(see index for correct answer)

- a. Accord and satisfaction
- b. Avellum Partners
- c. NOPLAT
- d. Liquidity forecast

:: Trade secrets ::

The _____ of 1996 was a 6 title Act of Congress dealing with a wide range of issues, including not only industrial espionage , but the insanity defense, matters regarding the Boys & Girls Clubs of America, requirements for presentence investigation reports, and the United States Sentencing Commission reports regarding encryption or scrambling technology, and other technical and minor amendments.

Exam Probability: **Medium**

36. *Answer choices:*

(see index for correct answer)

- a. Christou v. Beatport, LLC
- b. Trade secret
- c. Apple v. Does
- d. Economic Espionage Act

Guidance: level 1

:: Decision theory ::

Within economics the concept of _____ is used to model worth or value, but its usage has evolved significantly over time. The term was introduced initially as a measure of pleasure or satisfaction within the theory of utilitarianism by moral philosophers such as Jeremy Bentham and John Stuart Mill. But the term has been adapted and reapplied within neoclassical economics, which dominates modern economic theory, as a _____ function that represents a consumer's preference ordering over a choice set. As such, it is devoid of its original interpretation as a measurement of the pleasure or satisfaction obtained by the consumer from that choice.

Exam Probability: **High**

37. *Answer choices:*

(see index for correct answer)

- a. Aggregated indices randomization method
- b. Utility
- c. TOPSIS
- d. Binary decision

Guidance: level 1

:: Judgment (law) ::

In law, a _____ is a judgment entered by a court for one party and against another party summarily, i.e., without a full trial. Such a judgment may be issued on the merits of an entire case, or on discrete issues in that case.

38. *Answer choices:*

(see index for correct answer)

- a. Summary judgment
- b. judgment as a matter of law

Guidance: level 1

:: Debt ::

A _____ is a party that has a claim on the services of a second party. It is a person or institution to whom money is owed. The first party, in general, has provided some property or service to the second party under the assumption that the second party will return an equivalent property and service. The second party is frequently called a debtor or borrower. The first party is called the _____ , which is the lender of property, service, or money.

Exam Probability: **High**

39. *Answer choices:*

(see index for correct answer)

- a. Phantom debt
- b. Debt club
- c. Creditor

- d. Charge-off

Guidance: level 1

:: Employment discrimination ::

_____ is a form of discrimination based on race, gender, religion, national origin, physical or mental disability, age, sexual orientation, and gender identity by employers. Earnings differentials or occupational differentiation—where differences in pay come from differences in qualifications or responsibilities—should not be confused with _____ . Discrimination can be intended and involve disparate treatment of a group or be unintended, yet create disparate impact for a group.

Exam Probability: **High**

40. *Answer choices:*

(see index for correct answer)

- a. Employment discrimination
- b. Marriage bars
- c. Glass ceiling
- d. Glass cliff

Guidance: level 1

:: Marketing ::

_____ comes from the Latin neg and otsia referring to businessmen who, unlike the patricians, had no leisure time in their industriousness; it held the meaning of business until the 17th century when it took on the diplomatic connotation as a dialogue between two or more people or parties intended to reach a beneficial outcome over one or more issues where a conflict exists with respect to at least one of these issues. Thus, _____ is a process of combining divergent positions into a joint agreement under a decision rule of unanimity.

Exam Probability: **High**

41. *Answer choices:*

(see index for correct answer)

- a. Adobe Experience Manager
- b. HyTrust
- c. Fixed value-added resource
- d. Marketing operations

Guidance: level 1

:: Psychometrics ::

_____ is a dynamic, structured, interactive process where a neutral third party assists disputing parties in resolving conflict through the use of specialized communication and negotiation techniques. All participants in _____ are encouraged to actively participate in the process. _____ is a "party-centered" process in that it is focused primarily upon the needs, rights, and interests of the parties. The mediator uses a wide variety of techniques to guide the process in a constructive direction and to help the parties find their optimal solution. A mediator is facilitative in that she/he manages the interaction between parties and facilitates open communication. _____ is also evaluative in that the mediator analyzes issues and relevant norms , while refraining from providing prescriptive advice to the parties .

Exam Probability: **High**

42. *Answer choices:*
(see index for correct answer)

- a. Psychological statistics
- b. paired comparisons
- c. Mediation
- d. Test

Guidance: level 1

:: Commercial item transport and distribution ::

_____ s may be negotiable or non-negotiable. Negotiable _____ s allow transfer of ownership of that commodity without having to deliver the physical commodity. See Delivery order.

43. *Answer choices:*

(see index for correct answer)

- a. Fulfillment house
- b. Currency adjustment factor
- c. Global TransPark
- d. Wholesale

Guidance: level 1

:: Notes (finance) ::

A _____ , sometimes referred to as a note payable, is a legal instrument , in which one party promises in writing to pay a determinate sum of money to the other , either at a fixed or determinable future time or on demand of the payee, under specific terms.

Exam Probability: **High**

44. *Answer choices:*

(see index for correct answer)

- a. Large-sized note
- b. Compound Interest Treasury Note
- c. Promissory note

- d. note payable

Guidance: level 1

:: Personal property law ::

Bailment describes a legal relationship in common law where physical possession of personal property, or a chattel, is transferred from one person to another person who subsequently has possession of the property. It arises when a person gives property to someone else for safekeeping, and is a cause of action independent of contract or tort.

Exam Probability: **Medium**

45. *Answer choices:*
(see index for correct answer)

- a. Bailee
- b. bailor

Guidance: level 1

:: ::

_____ is the production of products for use or sale using labour and machines, tools, chemical and biological processing, or formulation. The term may refer to a range of human activity, from handicraft to high tech, but is most commonly applied to industrial design, in which raw materials are transformed into finished goods on a large scale. Such finished goods may be sold to other manufacturers for the production of other, more complex products, such as aircraft, household appliances, furniture, sports equipment or automobiles, or sold to wholesalers, who in turn sell them to retailers, who then sell them to end users and consumers.

Exam Probability: **Low**

46. *Answer choices:*

(see index for correct answer)

- a. process perspective
- b. deep-level diversity
- c. Character
- d. Manufacturing

Guidance: level 1

:: Industrial agreements ::

_____ is a process of negotiation between employers and a group of employees aimed at agreements to regulate working salaries, working conditions, benefits, and other aspects of workers' compensation and rights for workers. The interests of the employees are commonly presented by representatives of a trade union to which the employees belong. The collective agreements reached by these negotiations usually set out wage scales, working hours, training, health and safety, overtime, grievance mechanisms, and rights to participate in workplace or company affairs.

Exam Probability: **Medium**

47. *Answer choices:*

(see index for correct answer)

- a. Federal Labor Relations Act
- b. McCrone Agreement
- c. Collective bargaining
- d. Collaborative bargaining

Guidance: level 1

:: Legal terms ::

An _____ is a legal and equitable remedy in the form of a special court order that compels a party to do or refrain from specific acts. "When a court employs the extraordinary remedy of _____ , it directs the conduct of a party, and does so with the backing of its full coercive powers." A party that fails to comply with an _____ faces criminal or civil penalties, including possible monetary sanctions and even imprisonment. They can also be charged with contempt of court. Counter _____ s are _____ s that stop or reverse the enforcement of another _____ .

Exam Probability: **Medium**

48. *Answer choices:*

(see index for correct answer)

- a. Dissenting opinion
- b. Liberal legalism
- c. Informed assent
- d. Injunction

Guidance: level 1

:: ::

_____ is widespread, interconnected digital technology. The term entered the popular culture from science fiction and the arts but is now used by technology strategists, security professionals, government, military and industry leaders and entrepreneurs to describe the domain of the global technology environment. Others consider _____ to be just a notional environment in which communication over computer networks occurs. The word became popular in the 1990s when the uses of the Internet, networking, and digital communication were all growing dramatically and the term "_____ " was able to represent the many new ideas and phenomena that were emerging. It has been called the largest unregulated and uncontrolled domain in the history of mankind, and is also unique because it is a domain created by people vice the traditional physical domains.

Exam Probability: **Medium**

49. *Answer choices:*

(see index for correct answer)

- a. co-culture
- b. functional perspective
- c. Character
- d. Cyberspace

Guidance: level 1

:: ::

In law, a _____ is the formal finding of fact made by a jury on matters or questions submitted to the jury by a judge. In a bench trial, the judge's decision near the end of the trial is simply referred to as a finding. In England and Wales, a coroner's findings are called _____ s .

Exam Probability: **Low**

50. *Answer choices:*
(see index for correct answer)

- a. interpersonal communication
- b. levels of analysis
- c. functional perspective
- d. surface-level diversity

Guidance: level 1

:: Data management ::

_____ is a form of intellectual property that grants the creator of an original creative work an exclusive legal right to determine whether and under what conditions this original work may be copied and used by others, usually for a limited term of years. The exclusive rights are not absolute but limited by limitations and exceptions to _____ law, including fair use. A major limitation on _____ on ideas is that _____ protects only the original expression of ideas, and not the underlying ideas themselves.

Exam Probability: **Low**

51. *Answer choices:*

(see index for correct answer)

- a. Copyright
- b. H-Store
- c. Computer-aided software engineering
- d. Operational data store

Guidance: level 1

:: Business law ::

An _____ is a clause in a contract that requires the parties to resolve their disputes through an arbitration process. Although such a clause may or may not specify that arbitration occur within a specific jurisdiction, it always binds the parties to a type of resolution outside the courts, and is therefore considered a kind of forum selection clause.

Exam Probability: **Medium**

52. *Answer choices:*

(see index for correct answer)

- a. Business license
- b. Administration
- c. Country of origin
- d. Novation

:: ::

According to the philosopher Piyush Mathur , "Tangibility is the property that a phenomenon exhibits if it has and/or transports mass and/or energy and/or momentum".

Exam Probability: **Medium**

53. *Answer choices:*

(see index for correct answer)

- a. cultural
- b. information systems assessment
- c. Character
- d. personal values

:: ::

Competition law is a law that promotes or seeks to maintain market competition by regulating anti-competitive conduct by companies. Competition law is implemented through public and private enforcement. Competition law is known as " _____ law" in the United States for historical reasons, and as "anti-monopoly law" in China and Russia. In previous years it has been known as trade practices law in the United Kingdom and Australia. In the European Union, it is referred to as both _____ and competition law.

Exam Probability: **Low**

54. *Answer choices:*

(see index for correct answer)

- a. imperative
- b. Antitrust
- c. Sarbanes-Oxley act of 2002
- d. Character

Guidance: level 1

:: Business law ::

The term is used to designate a range of diverse, if often kindred, concepts. These have historically been addressed in a number of discrete disciplines, notably mathematics, physics, chemistry, ethics, aesthetics, ontology, and theology.

Exam Probability: **Low**

55. *Answer choices:*

(see index for correct answer)

- a. Statutory liability
- b. Uniform Commercial Code
- c. Product defect
- d. Consularization

Guidance: level 1

:: Legal doctrines and principles ::

In the United States, the _____ is a legal rule, based on constitutional law, that prevents evidence collected or analyzed in violation of the defendant's constitutional rights from being used in a court of law. This may be considered an example of a prophylactic rule formulated by the judiciary in order to protect a constitutional right. The _____ may also, in some circumstances at least, be considered to follow directly from the constitutional language, such as the Fifth Amendment's command that no person "shall be compelled in any criminal case to be a witness against himself" and that no person "shall be deprived of life, liberty or property without due process of law".

Exam Probability: **Medium**

56. *Answer choices:*

(see index for correct answer)

- a. Attractive nuisance

- b. Act of state
- c. Exclusionary rule
- d. Assumption of risk

Guidance: level 1

:: Contract law ::

In the United States, the _____ rule refers to the legal right for a buyer of goods to insist upon " _____ " by the seller. In a contract for the sale of goods, if the goods fail to conform exactly to the description in the contract the buyer may nonetheless accept the goods, or reject the goods, or reject the nonconforming part of the tender and accept the conforming part. The buyer does not have an unfettered ability to reject tender.

Exam Probability: **Medium**

57. *Answer choices:*
(see index for correct answer)

- a. Perfect tender
- b. Memorandum of understanding
- c. Executory contract
- d. Good faith

Guidance: level 1

:: ::

Business is the activity of making one's living or making money by producing or buying and selling products . Simply put, it is "any activity or enterprise entered into for profit. It does not mean it is a company, a corporation, partnership, or have any such formal organization, but it can range from a street peddler to General Motors."

Exam Probability: **Low**

58. *Answer choices:*

(see index for correct answer)

- a. co-culture
- b. process perspective
- c. corporate values
- d. cultural

Guidance: level 1

:: Legal doctrines and principles ::

The _____ rule is a rule in the Anglo-American common law that governs what kinds of evidence parties to a contract dispute can introduce when trying to determine the specific terms of a contract. The rule also prevents parties who have reduced their agreement to a final written document from later introducing other evidence, such as the content of oral discussions from earlier in the negotiation process, as evidence of a different intent as to the terms of the contract. The rule provides that "extrinsic evidence is inadmissible to vary a written contract". The term "parol" derives from the Anglo-Norman French parol or parole, meaning "word of mouth" or "verbal", and in medieval times referred to oral pleadings in a court case.

Exam Probability: **High**

59. *Answer choices:*

(see index for correct answer)

- a. Caveat emptor
- b. Parol evidence
- c. Res ipsa loquitur
- d. Mutual assent

Guidance: level 1

Finance

Finance is a field that is concerned with the allocation (investment) of assets and liabilities over space and time, often under conditions of risk or uncertainty. Finance can also be defined as the science of money management. Participants in the market aim to price assets based on their risk level, fundamental value, and their expected rate of return. Finance can be split into three sub-categories: public finance, corporate finance and personal finance.

:: Stock market ::

A share price is the price of a single share of a number of saleable stocks of a company, derivative or other financial asset.In layman`s terms, the _____ is the highest amount someone is willing to pay for the stock, or the lowest amount that it can be bought for.

1. *Answer choices:*

(see index for correct answer)

- a. Indirect finance
- b. Central securities depository
- c. Intermarket sweep order
- d. Flash trading

Guidance: level 1

:: Accounting journals and ledgers ::

The subledger, or _____ , provides details behind entries in the general ledger used in accounting. The subledger shows detail for part of the accounting records such as property and equipment, prepaid expenses, etc. The detail would include such items as date the item was purchased or expense incurred, a description of the item, the original balance, and the net book value. The total of the subledger would match the line item amount on the general ledger. This corresponding line item in the general ledger is referred to as the controlling account. The _____ balance is compared with its controlling account balance as part of the process of preparing a trial balance.

Exam Probability: **High**

2. *Answer choices:*

(see index for correct answer)

- a. Sales journal
- b. Subsidiary ledger
- c. Cash receipts journal
- d. Check register

:: Financial ratios ::

A _____ or accounting ratio is a relative magnitude of two selected numerical values taken from an enterprise's financial statements. Often used in accounting, there are many standard ratios used to try to evaluate the overall financial condition of a corporation or other organization. _____ s may be used by managers within a firm, by current and potential shareholders of a firm, and by a firm's creditors. Financial analysts use _____ s to compare the strengths and weaknesses in various companies. If shares in a company are traded in a financial market, the market price of the shares is used in certain _____ s.

Exam Probability: **High**

3. *Answer choices:*

(see index for correct answer)

- a. Market-to-book
- b. Financial ratio
- c. Texas ratio
- d. Reserve requirement

:: Financial markets ::

A _____ is a financial market in which long-term debt or equity-backed securities are bought and sold. _____ s channel the wealth of savers to those who can put it to long-term productive use, such as companies or governments making long-term investments. Financial regulators like the Bank of England and the U.S. Securities and Exchange Commission oversee _____ s to protect investors against fraud, among other duties.

Exam Probability: **Medium**

4. *Answer choices:*

(see index for correct answer)

- a. Market clearing
- b. Capital market
- c. Time-weighted average price
- d. Public offering

:: Financial accounting ::

_____ is a financial metric which represents operating liquidity available to a business, organisation or other entity, including governmental entities. Along with fixed assets such as plant and equipment, _____ is considered a part of operating capital. Gross _____ is equal to current assets. _____ is calculated as current assets minus current liabilities. If current assets are less than current liabilities, an entity has a _____ deficiency, also called a _____ deficit.

Exam Probability: **High**

5. *Answer choices:*

(see index for correct answer)

- a. Floating capital
- b. Working capital
- c. Finance charge
- d. Asset recovery

Guidance: level 1

:: ::

A _____ is the process of presenting a topic to an audience. It is typically a demonstration, introduction, lecture, or speech meant to inform, persuade, inspire, motivate, or to build good will or to present a new idea or product. The term can also be used for a formal or ritualized introduction or offering, as with the _____ of a debutante. _____ s in certain formats are also known as keynote address.

6. *Answer choices:*

(see index for correct answer)

- a. hierarchical perspective
- b. levels of analysis
- c. similarity-attraction theory
- d. Presentation

Guidance: level 1

:: Generally Accepted Accounting Principles ::

A _____ , in accrual accounting, is any account where the asset or liability is not realized until a future date , e.g. annuities, charges, taxes, income, etc. The deferred item may be carried, dependent on type of _____ , as either an asset or liability. See also accrual.

Exam Probability: **Medium**

7. *Answer choices:*

(see index for correct answer)

- a. Contributed capital
- b. Write-off
- c. Net realizable value

- d. Income statement

Guidance: level 1

:: Generally Accepted Accounting Principles ::

_____ is the accounting classification of an account. It is part of double-entry book-keeping technique.

Exam Probability: **Medium**

8. *Answer choices:*
(see index for correct answer)

- a. Cost pool
- b. Normal balance
- c. Indian Accounting Standards
- d. AICPA Statements of Position

Guidance: level 1

:: Consumer theory ::

A _____ is a technical term in psychology, economics and philosophy usually used in relation to choosing between alternatives. For example, someone prefers A over B if they would rather choose A than B.

Exam Probability: **Low**

9. *Answer choices:*

(see index for correct answer)

- a. Income elasticity of demand
- b. Consumption
- c. Bliss point
- d. Joint demand

Guidance: level 1

:: Data management ::

_____ is a form of intellectual property that grants the creator of an original creative work an exclusive legal right to determine whether and under what conditions this original work may be copied and used by others, usually for a limited term of years. The exclusive rights are not absolute but limited by limitations and exceptions to _____ law, including fair use. A major limitation on _____ on ideas is that _____ protects only the original expression of ideas, and not the underlying ideas themselves.

Exam Probability: **High**

10. *Answer choices:*

(see index for correct answer)

- a. British Oceanographic Data Centre
- b. Address space
- c. Sales intelligence
- d. Online complex processing

Guidance: level 1

:: Shareholders ::

A _____ is a payment made by a corporation to its shareholders, usually as a distribution of profits. When a corporation earns a profit or surplus, the corporation is able to re-invest the profit in the business and pay a proportion of the profit as a _____ to shareholders. Distribution to shareholders may be in cash or, if the corporation has a _____ reinvestment plan, the amount can be paid by the issue of further shares or share repurchase. When _____ s are paid, shareholders typically must pay income taxes, and the corporation does not receive a corporate income tax deduction for the _____ payments.

Exam Probability: **High**

11. *Answer choices:*

(see index for correct answer)

- a. Dividend
- b. Say on pay

- c. Proxy statement
- d. Shareholders in the United Kingdom

Guidance: level 1

:: ::

_____ is a costing method that identifies activities in an organization and assigns the cost of each activity to all products and services according to the actual consumption by each. This model assigns more indirect costs into direct costs compared to conventional costing.

Exam Probability: **High**

12. *Answer choices:*
(see index for correct answer)

- a. corporate values
- b. Activity-based costing
- c. empathy
- d. cultural

Guidance: level 1

:: Personal finance ::

_____ is income not spent, or deferred consumption. Methods of _____ include putting money aside in, for example, a deposit account, a pension account, an investment fund, or as cash. _____ also involves reducing expenditures, such as recurring costs. In terms of personal finance, _____ generally specifies low-risk preservation of money, as in a deposit account, versus investment, wherein risk is a lot higher; in economics more broadly, it refers to any income not used for immediate consumption.

Exam Probability: **High**

13. *Answer choices:*

(see index for correct answer)

- a. Short refinance
- b. LEC billing
- c. Saving
- d. Prestige Bulletin

Guidance: level 1

:: ::

In business, economics or investment, market _____ is a market's feature whereby an individual or firm can quickly purchase or sell an asset without causing a drastic change in the asset's price. _____ is about how big the trade-off is between the speed of the sale and the price it can be sold for. In a liquid market, the trade-off is mild: selling quickly will not reduce the price much. In a relatively illiquid market, selling it quickly will require cutting its price by some amount.

14. *Answer choices:*

(see index for correct answer)

- a. open system
- b. deep-level diversity
- c. Liquidity
- d. hierarchical

Guidance: level 1

:: Inventory ::

_____ is the amount of inventory a company has in stock at the end of its fiscal year. It is closely related with _____ cost, which is the amount of money spent to get these goods in stock. It should be calculated at the lower of cost or market.

Exam Probability: **Medium**

15. *Answer choices:*

(see index for correct answer)

- a. Inventory control problem
- b. Item-level tagging
- c. Ending inventory

- d. Safety stock

Guidance: level 1

:: ::

The U.S. _____ is an independent agency of the United States federal government. The SEC holds primary responsibility for enforcing the federal securities laws, proposing securities rules, and regulating the securities industry, the nation's stock and options exchanges, and other activities and organizations, including the electronic securities markets in the United States.

Exam Probability: **Medium**

16. *Answer choices:*

(see index for correct answer)

- a. cultural
- b. Character
- c. deep-level diversity
- d. functional perspective

Guidance: level 1

:: Fraud ::

In law, _____ is intentional deception to secure unfair or unlawful gain, or to deprive a victim of a legal right. _____ can violate civil law , a criminal law , or it may cause no loss of money, property or legal right but still be an element of another civil or criminal wrong. The purpose of _____ may be monetary gain or other benefits, for example by obtaining a passport, travel document, or driver's license, or mortgage _____ , where the perpetrator may attempt to qualify for a mortgage by way of false statements.

Exam Probability: **Medium**

17. *Answer choices:*

(see index for correct answer)

- a. Fraud
- b. SHERIFF
- c. Essay mill
- d. Credit card kiting

Guidance: level 1

:: Financial markets ::

As money became a commodity, the _____ became a component of the financial market for assets involved in short-term borrowing, lending, buying and selling with original maturities of one year or less. Trading in _____ s is done over the counter and is wholesale.

Exam Probability: **Medium**

18. *Answer choices:*

(see index for correct answer)

- a. Money market
- b. Faroese Securities Market
- c. Portfolios with Purpose
- d. Fourth market

Guidance: level 1

:: ::

_____ is a concept of English common law and is a necessity for simple contracts but not for special contracts . The concept has been adopted by other common law jurisdictions, including the US.

Exam Probability: **Low**

19. *Answer choices:*

(see index for correct answer)

- a. personal values
- b. corporate values
- c. deep-level diversity
- d. Consideration

:: Financial ratios ::

_____ is a financial ratio that indicates the percentage of a company's assets that are provided via debt. It is the ratio of total debt and total assets .

Exam Probability: **High**

20. *Answer choices:*

(see index for correct answer)

- a. Envy ratio
- b. Net capital outflow
- c. Return on capital employed
- d. Debt ratio

Guidance: level 1

:: Investment ::

In finance, the benefit from an _____ is called a return. The return may consist of a gain realised from the sale of property or an _____, unrealised capital appreciation, or _____ income such as dividends, interest, rental income etc., or a combination of capital gain and income. The return may also include currency gains or losses due to changes in foreign currency exchange rates.

Exam Probability: **Low**

21. *Answer choices:*

(see index for correct answer)

- a. Equity repositioning
- b. Option naming convention
- c. Bullish
- d. Investment

Guidance: level 1

:: Bonds (finance) ::

A _____ is a fund established by an economic entity by setting aside revenue over a period of time to fund a future capital expense, or repayment of a long-term debt.

Exam Probability: **Medium**

22. *Answer choices:*

(see index for correct answer)

- a. Savings bonds
- b. Sinking fund
- c. Inflation-indexed bond
- d. Inverse floating rate note

Guidance: level 1

:: Accounting terminology ::

_____ of something is, in finance, the adding together of interest or different investments over a period of time. It holds specific meanings in accounting, where it can refer to accounts on a balance sheet that represent liabilities and non-cash-based assets used in _____ -based accounting. These types of accounts include, among others, accounts payable, accounts receivable, goodwill, deferred tax liability and future interest expense.

Exam Probability: **Medium**

23. *Answer choices:*

(see index for correct answer)

- a. Capital appreciation
- b. Accounting equation
- c. Accounts payable
- d. Statement of financial position

:: Asset ::

In financial accounting, an _____ is any resource owned by the business. Anything tangible or intangible that can be owned or controlled to produce value and that is held by a company to produce positive economic value is an _____ . Simply stated, _____ s represent value of ownership that can be converted into cash . The balance sheet of a firm records the monetary value of the _____ s owned by that firm. It covers money and other valuables belonging to an individual or to a business.

Exam Probability: **Low**

24. *Answer choices:*

(see index for correct answer)

- a. Current asset
- b. Fixed asset

Guidance: level 1

:: Business ethics ::

In accounting and in most Schools of economic thought, _____ is a rational and unbiased estimate of the potential market price of a good, service, or asset. It takes into account such objectivity factors as.

Exam Probability: **Medium**

25. *Answer choices:*

(see index for correct answer)

- • a. Society of Corporate Compliance and Ethics
- • b. Fair value
- • c. Anatomy of Greed
- • d. Impact investing

Guidance: level 1

:: Generally Accepted Accounting Principles ::

In business and accounting, _____ is an entity's income minus cost of goods sold, expenses and taxes for an accounting period. It is computed as the residual of all revenues and gains over all expenses and losses for the period, and has also been defined as the net increase in shareholders' equity that results from a company's operations. In the context of the presentation of financial statements, the IFRS Foundation defines _____ as synonymous with profit and loss. The difference between revenue and the cost of making a product or providing a service, before deducting overheads, payroll, taxation, and interest payments. This is different from operating income .

26. *Answer choices:*

(see index for correct answer)

- a. Consolidation
- b. Provision
- c. Completed-contract method
- d. Net income

Guidance: level 1

:: International Financial Reporting Standards ::

_____ , usually called IFRS, are standards issued by the IFRS Foundation and the International Accounting Standards Board to provide a common global language for business affairs so that company accounts are understandable and comparable across international boundaries. They are a consequence of growing international shareholding and trade and are particularly important for companies that have dealings in several countries. They are progressively replacing the many different national accounting standards. They are the rules to be followed by accountants to maintain books of accounts which are comparable, understandable, reliable and relevant as per the users internal or external. IFRS, with the exception of IAS 29 Financial Reporting in Hyperinflationary Economies and IFRIC 7 Applying the Restatement Approach under IAS 29, are authorized in terms of the historical cost paradigm. IAS 29 and IFRIC 7 are authorized in terms of the units of constant purchasing power paradigm.IAS 2 is related to inventories in this standard we talk about the stock its production process etcIFRS began as an attempt to harmonize accounting across the European Union but the value of harmonization quickly made the concept attractive around the world. However, it has been debated whether or not de facto harmonization has occurred. Standards that were issued by IASC are still within use today and go by the name International Accounting Standards , while standards issued by IASB are called IFRS. IAS were issued between 1973 and 2001 by the Board of the International Accounting Standards Committee . On 1 April 2001, the new International Accounting Standards Board took over from the IASC the responsibility for setting International Accounting Standards. During its first meeting the new Board adopted existing IAS and Standing Interpretations Committee standards . The IASB has continued to develop standards calling the new standards " _____ ".

Exam Probability: **Low**

27. *Answer choices:*

(see index for correct answer)

- a. IAS 1
- b. IAS 39
- c. Convergence of accounting standards

- d. International Financial Reporting Standards

Guidance: level 1

:: Manufacturing ::

_____ costs are all manufacturing costs that are related to the cost object but cannot be traced to that cost object in an economically feasible way.

Exam Probability: **Medium**

28. *Answer choices:*

(see index for correct answer)

- a. Request for waiver
- b. International Manufacturing Technology Show
- c. Single-Minute Exchange of Die
- d. Manufacturing overhead

Guidance: level 1

:: Financial risk ::

The _____ on a financial investment is the expected value of its return . It is a measure of the center of the distribution of the random variable that is the return.

Exam Probability: **Medium**

29. *Answer choices:*

(see index for correct answer)

- a. Expected return
- b. Tracking error
- c. Time consistency
- d. Trading room

Guidance: level 1

:: Financial ratios ::

The _____ shows the percentage of how profitable a company's assets are in generating revenue.

Exam Probability: **Low**

30. *Answer choices:*

(see index for correct answer)

- a. Risk-adjusted return on capital
- b. Return on assets
- c. Equity ratio
- d. Expense ratio

Guidance: level 1

:: ::

An _____ is an area of the production, distribution, or trade, and consumption of goods and services by different agents. Understood in its broadest sense, 'The _____ is defined as a social domain that emphasize the practices, discourses, and material expressions associated with the production, use, and management of resources`. Economic agents can be individuals, businesses, organizations, or governments. Economic transactions occur when two parties agree to the value or price of the transacted good or service, commonly expressed in a certain currency. However, monetary transactions only account for a small part of the economic domain.

Exam Probability: **Low**

31. *Answer choices:*

(see index for correct answer)

- a. personal values
- b. imperative
- c. cultural
- d. Economy

:: Inventory ::

_____ is a system of inventory in which updates are made on a periodic basis. This differs from perpetual inventory systems, where updates are made as seen fit.

Exam Probability: **High**

32. *Answer choices:*

(see index for correct answer)

- a. GMROII
- b. Perpetual inventory
- c. Periodic inventory
- d. Ending inventory

:: Accounting terminology ::

_____ or capital expense is the money a company spends to buy, maintain, or improve its fixed assets, such as buildings, vehicles, equipment, or land. It is considered a _____ when the asset is newly purchased or when money is used towards extending the useful life of an existing asset, such as repairing the roof.

Exam Probability: **Low**

33. *Answer choices:*

(see index for correct answer)

- a. Account
- b. Fair value accounting
- c. Accrual
- d. Capital expenditure

Guidance: level 1

:: Financial ratios ::

The _____ is a financial ratio indicating the relative proportion of shareholders` equity and debt used to finance a company`s assets. Closely related to leveraging, the ratio is also known as risk, gearing or leverage. The two components are often taken from the firm`s balance sheet or statement of financial position , but the ratio may also be calculated using market values for both, if the company's debt and equity are publicly traded, or using a combination of book value for debt and market value for equity financially.

Exam Probability: **High**

34. *Answer choices:*

(see index for correct answer)

- a. Return on assets
- b. Cash conversion cycle
- c. Debt-to-equity ratio
- d. Short interest ratio

Guidance: level 1

:: Derivatives (finance) ::

A _____ or _____ row is a line of closely spaced shrubs and
sometimes trees, planted and trained to form a barrier or to mark the boundary
of an area, such as between neighbouring properties. _____ s used to
separate a road from adjoining fields or one field from another, and of
sufficient age to incorporate larger trees, are known as _____ rows. Often
they serve as windbreaks to improve conditions for the adjacent crops, as in
bocage country. When clipped and maintained, _____ s are also a simple
form of topiary.

Exam Probability: **Medium**

35. *Answer choices:*

(see index for correct answer)

- a. Bear spread
- b. Commodore option
- c. Swap ratio
- d. Bull spread

Guidance: level 1

:: Financial accounting ::

In accounting, _____ is the value of an asset according to its balance sheet account balance. For assets, the value is based on the original cost of the asset less any depreciation, amortization or impairment costs made against the asset. Traditionally, a company's _____ is its total assets minus intangible assets and liabilities. However, in practice, depending on the source of the calculation, _____ may variably include goodwill, intangible assets, or both. The value inherent in its workforce, part of the intellectual capital of a company, is always ignored. When intangible assets and goodwill are explicitly excluded, the metric is often specified to be "tangible _____".

Exam Probability: **Low**

36. *Answer choices:*

(see index for correct answer)

- a. Convenience translation
- b. Book value
- c. Carry
- d. Valuation

:: ::

_____ is the withdrawal from one's position or occupation or from one's active working life. A person may also semi-retire by reducing work hours.

Exam Probability: **High**

37. *Answer choices:*

(see index for correct answer)

- a. Retirement
- b. co-culture
- c. surface-level diversity
- d. levels of analysis

:: Inventory ::

Costs are associated with particular goods using one of the several formulas, including specific identification, first-in first-out , or average cost. Costs include all costs of purchase, costs of conversion and other costs that are incurred in bringing the inventories to their present location and condition. Costs of goods made by the businesses include material, labor, and allocated overhead. The costs of those goods which are not yet sold are deferred as costs of inventory until the inventory is sold or written down in value.

Exam Probability: **Medium**

38. *Answer choices:*

(see index for correct answer)

- a. Consignment stock
- b. Stock-taking
- c. Cost of goods sold
- d. Stock control

Guidance: level 1

:: Commerce ::

Continuation of an entity as a _____ is presumed as the basis for financial reporting unless and until the entity's liquidation becomes imminent. Preparation of financial statements under this presumption is commonly referred to as the _____ basis of accounting. If and when an entity's liquidation becomes imminent, financial statements are prepared under the liquidation basis of accounting .

39. *Answer choices:*

(see index for correct answer)

- a. Bidding
- b. Social gravity
- c. European Retail Round Table
- d. E-receipt

Guidance: level 1

:: Generally Accepted Accounting Principles ::

In accrual accounting, the revenue recognition principle states that expenses should be recorded during the period in which they are incurred, regardless of when the transfer of cash occurs. Conversely, cash basis accounting calls for the recognition of an expense when the cash is paid, regardless of when the expense was actually incurred.

Exam Probability: **High**

40. *Answer choices:*

(see index for correct answer)

- a. deferred revenue
- b. Matching principle

- c. Reserve
- d. Indian Accounting Standards

Guidance: level 1

:: Institutional investors ::

A _____ is an investment fund that pools capital from accredited investors or institutional investors and invests in a variety of assets, often with complex portfolio-construction and risk management techniques. It is administered by a professional investment management firm, and often structured as a limited partnership, limited liability company, or similar vehicle. _____ s are generally distinct from mutual funds and regarded as alternative investments, as their use of leverage is not capped by regulators, and distinct from private equity funds, as the majority of _____ s invest in relatively liquid assets. However, funds which operate similarly to _____ s but are regulated similarly to mutual funds are available and known as liquid alternative investments.

Exam Probability: **Medium**

41. *Answer choices:*

(see index for correct answer)

- a. Council of Institutional Investors
- b. Chartered Financial Analyst
- c. Gracy Title Company
- d. Davidson Kempner Capital Management

:: ::

_____ is the process whereby a business sets the price at which it will sell its products and services, and may be part of the business's marketing plan. In setting prices, the business will take into account the price at which it could acquire the goods, the manufacturing cost, the market place, competition, market condition, brand, and quality of product.

Exam Probability: **Medium**

42. *Answer choices:*

(see index for correct answer)

- a. Pricing
- b. information systems assessment
- c. corporate values
- d. similarity-attraction theory

:: Pension funds ::

_____ s typically have large amounts of money to invest and are the major investors in listed and private companies. They are especially important to the stock market where large institutional investors dominate. The largest 300 _____ s collectively hold about $6 trillion in assets. In January 2008, The Economist reported that Morgan Stanley estimates that _____ s worldwide hold over US$20 trillion in assets, the largest for any category of investor ahead of mutual funds, insurance companies, currency reserves, sovereign wealth funds, hedge funds, or private equity.

Exam Probability: **High**

43. *Answer choices:*

(see index for correct answer)

- a. Pension fund
- b. Texas Municipal Retirement System
- c. Pension led funding

Guidance: level 1

:: ::

In financial markets, a share is a unit used as mutual funds, limited partnerships, and real estate investment trusts. The owner of _____ in the corporation/company is a shareholder of the corporation. A share is an indivisible unit of capital, expressing the ownership relationship between the company and the shareholder. The denominated value of a share is its face value, and the total of the face value of issued _____ represent the capital of a company, which may not reflect the market value of those _____ .

Exam Probability: **High**

44. *Answer choices:*

(see index for correct answer)

- a. corporate values
- b. surface-level diversity
- c. Shares
- d. empathy

Guidance: level 1

:: Social security ::

_____ is "any government system that provides monetary assistance to people with an inadequate or no income." In the United States, this is usually called welfare or a social safety net, especially when talking about Canada and European countries.

45. *Answer choices:*

(see index for correct answer)

- a. Mahatma Gandhi Pravasi Suraksha Yojana
- b. Bituah Leumi
- c. Social Security Board
- d. Zak%C5%82ad Ubezpiecze%C5%84 Spo%C5%82ecznych

Guidance: level 1

:: Banking ::

A _____ is a financial account maintained by a bank for a customer. A _____ can be a deposit account, a credit card account, a current account, or any other type of account offered by a financial institution, and represents the funds that a customer has entrusted to the financial institution and from which the customer can make withdrawals. Alternatively, accounts may be loan accounts in which case the customer owes money to the financial institution.

Exam Probability: **Low**

46. *Answer choices:*

(see index for correct answer)

- a. Private money
- b. U-turn

- c. Bank account
- d. Standing order

Guidance: level 1

:: Fundamental analysis ::

_____ is the monetary value of earnings per outstanding share of common stock for a company.

Exam Probability: **Low**

47. *Answer choices:*
(see index for correct answer)

- a. Trading Advantage
- b. Goldman Sachs asset management factor model
- c. Growth stock
- d. Earnings per share

Guidance: level 1

:: Accounting terminology ::

Total _____ is a method of Accounting cost which entails the full cost of manufacturing or providing a service. TAC includes not just the costs of materials and labour, but also of all manufacturing overheads . The cost of each cost center can be direct or indirect. The direct cost can be easily identified with individual cost centers. Whereas indirect cost cannot be easily identified with the cost center. The distribution of overhead among the departments is called apportionment.

Exam Probability: **Medium**

48. *Answer choices:*

(see index for correct answer)

- a. Mark-to-market
- b. Accounting equation
- c. managerial accounting
- d. Basis of accounting

Guidance: level 1

:: Financial crises ::

A _____ is any of a broad variety of situations in which some financial assets suddenly lose a large part of their nominal value. In the 19th and early 20th centuries, many financial crises were associated with banking panics, and many recessions coincided with these panics. Other situations that are often called financial crises include stock market crashes and the bursting of other financial bubbles, currency crises, and sovereign defaults. Financial crises directly result in a loss of paper wealth but do not necessarily result in significant changes in the real economy .

Exam Probability: **High**

49. *Answer choices:*

(see index for correct answer)

- a. Financial crisis
- b. Arendal crash
- c. Panic of 1930
- d. Early 1990s recession in Finland

Guidance: level 1

:: Actuarial science ::

The _____ is the greater benefit of receiving money now rather than an identical sum later. It is founded on time preference.

Exam Probability: **Low**

50. *Answer choices:*

(see index for correct answer)

- a. Time value of money
- b. Actuarial present value
- c. Insurance cycle
- d. Reliability theory

Guidance: level 1

:: Corporate governance ::

The _____ is the officer of a company that has primary responsibility for managing the company's finances, including financial planning, management of financial risks, record-keeping, and financial reporting. In some sectors, the CFO is also responsible for analysis of data. Some CFOs have the title CFOO for chief financial and operating officer. In the United Kingdom, the typical term for a CFO is finance director . The CFO typically reports to the chief executive officer   and the board of directors and may additionally have a seat on the board.The CFO supervises the finance unit and is the chief financial spokesperson for the organization. The CFO directly assists the chief operating officer on all strategic and tactical matters relating to budget management, cost–benefit analysis, forecasting needs, and securing of new funding.

Exam Probability: **High**

51. *Answer choices:*

(see index for correct answer)

- a. Nursing management
- b. Compliance Ireland
- c. King Report on Corporate Governance
- d. Chief governance officer

Guidance: level 1

:: Loans ::

In corporate finance, a _____ is a medium- to long-term debt instrument used by large companies to borrow money, at a fixed rate of interest. The legal term "_____" originally referred to a document that either creates a debt or acknowledges it, but in some countries the term is now used interchangeably with bond, loan stock or note. A _____ is thus like a certificate of loan or a loan bond evidencing the fact that the company is liable to pay a specified amount with interest and although the money raised by the _____ s becomes a part of the company's capital structure, it does not become share capital. Senior _____ s get paid before subordinate _____ s, and there are varying rates of risk and payoff for these categories.

Exam Probability: **Medium**

52. *Answer choices:*

(see index for correct answer)

- a. Debenture
- b. SGE Loans
- c. Loan shark
- d. Loan deficiency payments

:: Notes (finance) ::

A _____ , sometimes referred to as a note payable, is a legal instrument , in which one party promises in writing to pay a determinate sum of money to the other , either at a fixed or determinable future time or on demand of the payee, under specific terms.

Exam Probability: **Low**

53. *Answer choices:*

(see index for correct answer)

- a. note payable
- b. Note issuance facility
- c. Capital note
- d. Surplus note

:: Financial economics ::

_____ , Inc. is an independent investment research and financial publishing firm based in New York City, New York, United States, founded in 1931 by Arnold Bernhard. _____ is best known for publishing The _____ Investment Survey, a stock analysis newsletter that is among the most highly regarded and widely used independent investment research resources in global investment and trading markets, tracking approximately 1,700 publicly traded stocks in over 99 industries.

Exam Probability: **Low**

54. *Answer choices:*

(see index for correct answer)

- a. Holding value
- b. International Fisher effect
- c. Value Line
- d. Value transfer system

Guidance: level 1

:: Financial accounting ::

_____ in accounting is the process of treating investments in associate companies. Equity accounting is usually applied where an investor entity holds 20–50% of the voting stock of the associate company. The investor records such investments as an asset on its balance sheet. The investor`s proportional share of the associate company`s net income increases the investment , and proportional payments of dividends decrease it. In the investor's income statement, the proportional share of the investor's net income or net loss is reported as a single-line item.

Exam Probability: **Low**

55. *Answer choices:*

(see index for correct answer)

- a. Tax amortization benefit
- b. Deferred Acquisition Costs
- c. Holding gains
- d. Financial Condition Report

Guidance: level 1

:: Financial markets ::

The _____ is the part of the capital market that deals with the issuance and sale of equity-backed securities to investors directly by the issuer. Investor buy securities that were never traded before. _____ s create long term instruments through which corporate entities raise funds from the capital market. It is also known as the New Issue Market .

56. *Answer choices:*

- a. Primary market
- b. STAMP
- c. Precautionary demand
- d. Fution

Guidance: level 1

:: Accounting ::

It is the period for which books are balanced and the financial statements are prepared. Generally, the _____ consists of 12 months. However the beginning of the _____ differs according to the jurisdiction. For example, one entity may follow the regular calendar year, i.e. January to December as the accounting year, while another entity may follow April to March as the _____ .

Exam Probability: **Medium**

57. *Answer choices:*

- a. Accounting period
- b. Cash sweep

- c. Legal cashier
- d. Engineering Accounting

Guidance: level 1

:: Financial ratios ::

The _____ is a liquidity ratio that measures whether a firm has enough resources to meet its short-term obligations. It compares a firm's current assets to its current liabilities, and is expressed as follows.

Exam Probability: **Medium**

58. *Answer choices:*

(see index for correct answer)

- a. Information ratio
- b. Cash flow return on investment
- c. Current ratio
- d. Debt-to-equity ratio

Guidance: level 1

:: Banking ::

_____ refers to a broad area of finance involving the collection, handling, and usage of cash. It involves assessing market liquidity, cash flow, and investments.

Exam Probability: **Medium**

59. *Answer choices:*

(see index for correct answer)

- a. Cash management
- b. Net stable funding ratio
- c. Christmas club
- d. Peer-to-peer lending

Guidance: level 1

Human resource management

Human resource (HR) management is the strategic approach to the effective management of organization workers so that they help the business gain a competitive advantage. It is designed to maximize employee performance in service of an employer's strategic objectives. HR is primarily concerned with the management of people within organizations, focusing on policies and on systems. HR departments are responsible for overseeing employee-benefits design, employee recruitment, training and development, performance appraisal, and rewarding (e.g., managing pay and benefit systems). HR also concerns itself with organizational change and industrial relations, that is, the balancing of organizational practices with requirements arising from collective bargaining and from governmental laws.

:: Trade unions in the United States ::

_____ is a labor union in the United States and Canada with roughly 300,000 active members. The union's members work predominantly in the hotel, food service, laundry, warehouse, and casino gaming industries. The union was formed in 2004 by the merger of Union of Needletrades, Industrial, and Textile Employees and Hotel Employees and Restaurant Employees Union .

Exam Probability: **Low**

1. *Answer choices:*

(see index for correct answer)

- a. Tennessee Nurses Association
- b. UNITE HERE
- c. American Federation of Government Employees
- d. Teaching Assistants Association

Guidance: level 1

:: ::

_____ is a form of development in which a person called a coach supports a learner or client in achieving a specific personal or professional goal by providing training and guidance. The learner is sometimes called a coachee. Occasionally, _____ may mean an informal relationship between two people, of whom one has more experience and expertise than the other and offers advice and guidance as the latter learns; but _____ differs from mentoring in focusing on specific tasks or objectives, as opposed to more general goals or overall development.

2. *Answer choices:*

(see index for correct answer)

- a. surface-level diversity
- b. empathy
- c. corporate values
- d. Coaching

Guidance: level 1

:: Employment compensation ::

The formula commonly used by compensation professionals to assess the competitiveness of an employee's pay level involves calculating a "" _____ "". _____ is the short form for Comparative ratio.

Exam Probability: **Low**

3. *Answer choices:*

(see index for correct answer)

- a. Basic Income Earth Network
- b. Compa-ratio
- c. Long service leave
- d. Pension administration in the United States

:: Workplace ::

_____ is a systematic determination of a subject's merit, worth and significance, using criteria governed by a set of standards. It can assist an organization, program, design, project or any other intervention or initiative to assess any aim, realisable concept/proposal, or any alternative, to help in decision-making; or to ascertain the degree of achievement or value in regard to the aim and objectives and results of any such action that has been completed. The primary purpose of _____ , in addition to gaining insight into prior or existing initiatives, is to enable reflection and assist in the identification of future change.

Exam Probability: **Medium**

4. *Answer choices:*

(see index for correct answer)

- a. Workplace romance
- b. Workplace spirituality
- c. Counterproductive work behavior
- d. Workplace listening

:: Recruitment ::

Recruitment refers to the overall process of attracting, shortlisting, selecting and appointing suitable candidates for jobs within an organization. Recruitment can also refer to processes involved in choosing individuals for unpaid roles. Managers, human resource generalists and recruitment specialists may be tasked with carrying out recruitment, but in some cases public-sector employment agencies, commercial recruitment agencies, or specialist search consultancies are used to undertake parts of the process. Internet-based technologies which support all aspects of recruitment have become widespread.

Exam Probability: **Medium**

5. *Answer choices:*

(see index for correct answer)

- a. The Talent Myth
- b. Purple squirrel
- c. Public employment service
- d. Employee referral

Guidance: level 1

:: ::

_____ is the withdrawal from one's position or occupation or from one's active working life. A person may also semi-retire by reducing work hours.

Exam Probability: **Low**

6. *Answer choices:*

(see index for correct answer)

- a. Retirement
- b. co-culture
- c. open system
- d. deep-level diversity

Guidance: level 1

:: Human resource management ::

_____ is athletic training in sports other than the athlete's usual sport. The goal is improving overall performance. It takes advantage of the particular effectiveness of one training method to negate the shortcomings of another.

Exam Probability: **Low**

7. *Answer choices:*

(see index for correct answer)

- a. Potential analysis
- b. Idea portal
- c. Cross-training
- d. Bradford Factor

:: Labour relations ::

_____ is a field of study that can have different meanings depending on the context in which it is used. In an international context, it is a subfield of labor history that studies the human relations with regard to work – in its broadest sense – and how this connects to questions of social inequality. It explicitly encompasses unregulated, historical, and non-Western forms of labor. Here, _____ define "for or with whom one works and under what rules. These rules determine the type of work, type and amount of remuneration, working hours, degrees of physical and psychological strain, as well as the degree of freedom and autonomy associated with the work."

Exam Probability: **Medium**

8. *Answer choices:*

(see index for correct answer)

- a. Negotiated cartelism
- b. Worker center
- c. Labor relations
- d. Open shop

:: ::

_____ is the stock of habits, knowledge, social and personality attributes embodied in the ability to perform labor so as to produce economic value.

Exam Probability: **Medium**

9. *Answer choices:*

(see index for correct answer)

- a. personal values
- b. similarity-attraction theory
- c. open system
- d. Human capital

Guidance: level 1

:: ::

_____ is a form of government characterized by strong central power and limited political freedoms. Individual freedoms are subordinate to the state and there is no constitutional accountability and rule of law under an authoritarian regime. Authoritarian regimes can be autocratic with power concentrated in one person or it can be more spread out between multiple officials and government institutions. Juan Linz's influential 1964 description of _____ characterized authoritarian political systems by four qualities.

Exam Probability: **Medium**

10. *Answer choices:*

(see index for correct answer)

- a. empathy
- b. Authoritarianism
- c. process perspective
- d. similarity-attraction theory

Guidance: level 1

:: Management ::

In the field of management, _____ involves the formulation and implementation of the major goals and initiatives taken by an organization's top management on behalf of owners, based on consideration of resources and an assessment of the internal and external environments in which the organization operates.

Exam Probability: **Medium**

11. *Answer choices:*

(see index for correct answer)

- a. Automated decision support
- b. Project management
- c. Libertarian management
- d. Strategic management

:: ::

In organizational behavior and industrial/organizational psychology, proactivity or _____ behavior by individuals refers to anticipatory, change-oriented and self-initiated behavior in situations. _____ behavior involves acting in advance of a future situation, rather than just reacting. It means taking control and making things happen rather than just adjusting to a situation or waiting for something to happen. _____ employees generally do not need to be asked to act, nor do they require detailed instructions.

Exam Probability: **Medium**

12. *Answer choices:*

(see index for correct answer)

- a. Proactive
- b. deep-level diversity
- c. personal values
- d. open system

:: ::

An _____ is a process where candidates are examined to determine their suitability for specific types of employment, especially management or military command. The candidates' personality and aptitudes are determined by techniques including interviews, group exercises, presentations, examinations and psychometric testing.

Exam Probability: **High**

13. *Answer choices:*

(see index for correct answer)

- a. information systems assessment
- b. Sarbanes-Oxley act of 2002
- c. deep-level diversity
- d. empathy

Guidance: level 1

:: Psychometrics ::

In statistics and research, _____ is typically a measure based on the correlations between different items on the same test . It measures whether several items that propose to measure the same general construct produce similar scores. For example, if a respondent expressed agreement with the statements "I like to ride bicycles" and "I've enjoyed riding bicycles in the past", and disagreement with the statement "I hate bicycles", this would be indicative of good _____ of the test.

14. *Answer choices:*

(see index for correct answer)

- a. Computerized adaptive testing
- b. Internal consistency
- c. Fuzzy concept
- d. Historiometry

Guidance: level 1

:: Human resource management ::

_____ is a process for identifying and developing new leaders who can replace old leaders when they leave, retire or die. _____ increases the availability of experienced and capable employees that are prepared to assume these roles as they become available. Taken narrowly, "replacement planning" for key roles is the heart of _____ .

Exam Probability: **Low**

15. *Answer choices:*

(see index for correct answer)

- a. The Giving of Orders
- b. Employment testing

- c. war for talent
- d. Succession planning

Guidance: level 1

:: Management ::

_____ or executive pay is composed of the financial compensation and other non-financial awards received by an executive from their firm for their service to the organization. It is typically a mixture of salary, bonuses, shares of or call options on the company stock, benefits, and perquisites, ideally configured to take into account government regulations, tax law, the desires of the organization and the executive, and rewards for performance.

Exam Probability: **Low**

16. *Answer choices:*
(see index for correct answer)

- a. Leadership Series
- b. Executive compensation
- c. Mobile sales enablement
- d. Meeting

Guidance: level 1

:: Meetings ::

A _____ is a formal meeting of the representatives of different countries, constituent states, organizations, trade unions, political parties or other groups. The term, originally denoting a parley during battle in the Late Middle Ages, is derived from the Latin _____ us.

Exam Probability: **Low**

17. *Answer choices:*

(see index for correct answer)

- a. Prayer meeting
- b. Congress
- c. Function hall
- d. Evoma

Guidance: level 1

:: Occupations ::

_____ means a restricted practice or a restriction on the use of an occupational title, requiring a license. A license created under a "practice act" requires a license before performing a certain activity, such as driving a car on public roads. A license created under a "title act" restricts the use of a given occupational title to licensees, but anyone can perform the activity itself under a less restricted title. For example, in Oregon, anyone can practice counseling, but only licensees can call themselves "Licensed Professional Counselors." Thus depending on the type of law, practicing without a license may carry civil or criminal penalties or may be perfectly legal. For some occupations and professions, licensing is often granted through a professional body or a licensing board composed of practitioners who oversee the applications for licenses. This often involves accredited training and examinations, but varies a great deal for different activities and in different countries.

Exam Probability: **Low**

18. *Answer choices:*

(see index for correct answer)

- a. Sailmaker
- b. Aeronautical operations technician
- c. Barrelman
- d. Licensure

Guidance: level 1

:: Employment compensation ::

_____ is a notional derivative of a Health Reimbursement Arrangement , a type of US employer-funded health benefit plan that reimburses employees for out-of-pocket medical expenses and, in limited cases, to pay for health insurance plan premiums.

Exam Probability: **Low**

19. *Answer choices:*

(see index for correct answer)

- a. Health Reimbursement Account
- b. Thirteenth salary
- c. Employee assistance program
- d. Take-home vehicle

Guidance: level 1

:: Unemployment ::

_____ is the support service provided by responsible organizations, keen to support individuals who are exiting the business − to help former employees transition to new jobs and help them re-orient themselves in the job market. A consultancy firm usually provides the _____ services which are paid for by the former employer and are achieved usually through practical advice, training materials and workshops. Some companies may offer psychological support.

Exam Probability: **Medium**

20. *Answer choices:*

(see index for correct answer)

- a. Employment protection legislation
- b. Outplacement
- c. Reserve army of labour
- d. Labour Force Survey

Guidance: level 1

:: ::

_____ is the process of collecting, analyzing and/or reporting information regarding the performance of an individual, group, organization, system or component. _____ is not a new concept, some of the earliest records of human activity relate to the counting or recording of activities.

Exam Probability: **Medium**

21. *Answer choices:*

(see index for correct answer)

- a. empathy
- b. surface-level diversity
- c. Performance measurement
- d. corporate values

:: Parental leave ::

_____ , or family leave, is an employee benefit available in almost all countries. The term " _____ " may include maternity, paternity, and adoption leave; or may be used distinctively from "maternity leave" and "paternity leave" to describe separate family leave available to either parent to care for small children. In some countries and jurisdictions, "family leave" also includes leave provided to care for ill family members. Often, the minimum benefits and eligibility requirements are stipulated by law.

Exam Probability: **High**

22. *Answer choices:*
(see index for correct answer)

- a. Pregnancy discrimination
- b. Equal Opportunities Commission v Secretary of State for Trade and Industry
- c. Parental leave
- d. Parental leave economics

:: Survey methodology ::

An _____ is a conversation where questions are asked and answers are given. In common parlance, the word " _____ " refers to a one-on-one conversation between an _____ er and an _____ ee. The _____ er asks questions to which the _____ ee responds, usually so information may be transferred from _____ ee to _____ er . Sometimes, information can be transferred in both directions. It is a communication, unlike a speech, which produces a one-way flow of information.

Exam Probability: **High**

23. *Answer choices:*
(see index for correct answer)

- a. Interview
- b. Political forecasting
- c. Scale analysis
- d. Sampling

Guidance: level 1

:: Ethically disputed business practices ::

An _____ in US labor law refers to certain actions taken by employers or unions that violate the National Labor Relations Act of 1935 29 U.S.C. § 151–169 and other legislation. Such acts are investigated by the National Labor Relations Board .

Exam Probability: **High**

24. *Answer choices:*

(see index for correct answer)

- a. Sugging
- b. Unfair labor practice
- c. Patent privateer
- d. Spiv

Guidance: level 1

:: ::

Refresher/ _____ is the process of learning a new or the same old skill or trade for the same group of personnel. Refresher/ _____ is required to be provided on regular basis to avoid personnel obsolescence due to technological changes & the individuals memory capacity. This short term instruction course shall serve to re-acquaint personnel with skills previously learnt or to bring one's knowledge or skills up-to-date so that skills stay sharp. This kind of training could be provided annually or more frequently as maybe required, based on the importance of consistency of the task of which the skill is involved. Examples of refreshers are cGMP, GDP, HSE trainings. _____ shall also be conducted for an employee, when the employee is rated as 'not qualified' for a skill or knowledge, as determined based on the assessment of answers in the training questionnaire of the employee.

Exam Probability: **Medium**

25. *Answer choices:*

(see index for correct answer)

- a. open system
- b. Sarbanes-Oxley act of 2002
- c. Retraining
- d. levels of analysis

Guidance: level 1

:: Labor rights ::

The _____ is the concept that people have a human _____ , or engage in productive employment, and may not be prevented from doing so. The _____ is enshrined in the Universal Declaration of Human Rights and recognized in international human rights law through its inclusion in the International Covenant on Economic, Social and Cultural Rights, where the _____ emphasizes economic, social and cultural development.

Exam Probability: **High**

26. *Answer choices:*
(see index for correct answer)

- a. Labor rights
- b. Right to work
- c. The Hyatt 100
- d. Kim Bobo

Guidance: level 1

:: ::

_____ is the process of two or more people or organizations working together to complete a task or achieve a goal. _____ is similar to cooperation. Most _____ requires leadership, although the form of leadership can be social within a decentralized and egalitarian group. Teams that work collaboratively often access greater resources, recognition and rewards when facing competition for finite resources.

Exam Probability: **High**

27. *Answer choices:*

(see index for correct answer)

- a. open system
- b. hierarchical perspective
- c. corporate values
- d. imperative

Guidance: level 1

:: Human resource management ::

_____ assesses whether a person performs a job well. _____, studied academically as part of industrial and organizational psychology, also forms a part of human resources management. Performance is an important criterion for organizational outcomes and success. John P. Campbell describes _____ as an individual-level variable, or something a single person does. This differentiates it from more encompassing constructs such as organizational performance or national performance, which are higher-level variables.

Exam Probability: **Low**

28. *Answer choices:*

(see index for correct answer)

- a. Job performance
- b. Management due diligence
- c. Multiculturalism
- d. Occupational Information Network

Guidance: level 1

:: ::

A _____ , covering letter, motivation letter, motivational letter or a letter of motivation is a letter of introduction attached to, or accompanying another document such as a résumé or curriculum vitae.

Exam Probability: **Low**

29. *Answer choices:*

(see index for correct answer)

- a. hierarchical perspective
- b. Cover letter
- c. deep-level diversity
- d. open system

Guidance: level 1

:: Organizational behavior ::

_____ is the state or fact of exclusive rights and control over property, which may be an object, land/real estate or intellectual property. _____ involves multiple rights, collectively referred to as title, which may be separated and held by different parties.

Exam Probability: **Low**

30. *Answer choices:*

(see index for correct answer)

- a. Organizational commitment
- b. Ownership
- c. Group behaviour
- d. Boreout

:: Training ::

_____ is the process of ensuring compliance with laws, regulations, rules, standards, or social norms. By enforcing laws and regulations, governments attempt to effectuate successful implementation of policies.

Exam Probability: **High**

31. *Answer choices:*

(see index for correct answer)

- a. Hot potato
- b. Enforcement
- c. ISpring Suite
- d. Strength and conditioning coach

:: ::

_____ is defined by sociologist John R. Schermerhorn as the "...degree to which the people affected by decision are treated by dignity and respect. The theory focuses on the interpersonal treatment people receive when procedures are implemented.

Exam Probability: **High**

32. *Answer choices:*
(see index for correct answer)

- a. Interactional justice
- b. levels of analysis
- c. surface-level diversity
- d. co-culture

Guidance: level 1

:: Training ::

_____ refers to practicing newly acquired skills beyond the point of initial mastery. The term is also often used to refer to the pedagogical theory that this form of practice leads to automaticity or other beneficial consequences.

Exam Probability: **Low**

33. *Answer choices:*

(see index for correct answer)

- a. National sports team
- b. Effective safety training
- c. Overlearning
- d. Leonardo da Vinci programme

Guidance: level 1

:: Hazard analysis ::

A _____ is an agent which has the potential to cause harm to a vulnerable target. The terms " _____ " and "risk" are often used interchangeably. However, in terms of risk assessment, they are two very distinct terms. A _____ is any agent that can cause harm or damage to humans, property, or the environment. Risk is defined as the probability that exposure to a _____ will lead to a negative consequence, or more simply, a _____ poses no risk if there is no exposure to that _____ .

Exam Probability: **High**

34. *Answer choices:*
(see index for correct answer)

- a. Swiss cheese model
- b. Hazardous Materials Identification System
- c. Risk assessment
- d. Hazard

:: ::

A _____ is the ability to carry out a task with determined results often within a given amount of time, energy, or both. _____ s can often be divided into domain-general and domain-specific _____ s. For example, in the domain of work, some general _____ s would include time management, teamwork and leadership, self-motivation and others, whereas domain-specific _____ s would be used only for a certain job. _____ usually requires certain environmental stimuli and situations to assess the level of _____ being shown and used.

Exam Probability: **Low**

35. *Answer choices:*

(see index for correct answer)

- a. imperative
- b. co-culture
- c. hierarchical
- d. Skill

:: Human resource management ::

_____ is the corporate management term for the act of reorganizing the legal, ownership, operational, or other structures of a company for the purpose of making it more profitable, or better organized for its present needs. Other reasons for _____ include a change of ownership or ownership structure, demerger, or a response to a crisis or major change in the business such as bankruptcy, repositioning, or buyout. _____ may also be described as corporate _____ , debt _____ and financial _____ .

Exam Probability: **Medium**

36. *Answer choices:*

(see index for correct answer)

- a. Compensation and benefits
- b. Job enlargement
- c. Recruitment process outsourcing
- d. Internal communications

Guidance: level 1

:: ::

_____ , also known as drug abuse, is a patterned use of a drug in which the user consumes the substance in amounts or with methods which are harmful to themselves or others, and is a form of substance-related disorder. Widely differing definitions of drug abuse are used in public health, medical and criminal justice contexts. In some cases criminal or anti-social behaviour occurs when the person is under the influence of a drug, and long term personality changes in individuals may occur as well. In addition to possible physical, social, and psychological harm, use of some drugs may also lead to criminal penalties, although these vary widely depending on the local jurisdiction.

Exam Probability: **Medium**

37. *Answer choices:*

(see index for correct answer)

- a. functional perspective
- b. similarity-attraction theory
- c. levels of analysis
- d. hierarchical perspective

Guidance: level 1

:: Business terms ::

Centralisation or _____ is the process by which the activities of an organization, particularly those regarding planning and decision-making, framing strategy and policies become concentrated within a particular geographical location group. This moves the important decision-making and planning powers within the center of the organisation.

Exam Probability: **Medium**

38. *Answer choices:*

(see index for correct answer)

- a. Centralization
- b. customer base
- c. organizational capital
- d. back office

Guidance: level 1

:: Self ::

_____ is a conscious or subconscious process in which people attempt to influence the perceptions of other people about a person, object or event. They do so by regulating and controlling information in social interaction. It was first conceptualized by Erving Goffman in 1959 in The Presentation of Self in Everyday Life, and then was expanded upon in 1967. An example of _____ theory in play is in sports such as soccer. At an important game, a player would want to showcase themselves in the best light possible, because there are college recruiters watching. This person would have the flashiest pair of cleats and try and perform their best to show off their skills. Their main goal may be to impress the college recruiters in a way that maximizes their chances of being chosen for a college team rather than winning the game.

Exam Probability: **High**

39. *Answer choices:*

(see index for correct answer)

- a. Impression management
- b. Self-actualization
- c. Narcissism
- d. Egocentrism

Guidance: level 1

:: Labour relations ::

_____ is the practice of hiring more workers than are needed to perform a given job, or to adopt work procedures which appear pointless, complex and time-consuming merely to employ additional workers. The term "make-work" is sometimes used as a synonym for _____ .

Exam Probability: **Low**

40. *Answer choices:*

(see index for correct answer)

- a. Picketing
- b. Big labor
- c. Featherbedding
- d. Social dialogue

Guidance: level 1

:: ::

A _____ seeks to further a particular profession, the interests of individuals engaged in that profession and the public interest. In the United States, such an association is typically a nonprofit organization for tax purposes.

Exam Probability: **Low**

41. *Answer choices:*

(see index for correct answer)

- a. corporate values
- b. empathy
- c. Sarbanes-Oxley act of 2002
- d. process perspective

Guidance: level 1

:: Problem solving ::

A _____ is a unit or formation established to work on a single defined task or activity. Originally introduced by the United States Navy, the term has now caught on for general usage and is a standard part of NATO terminology. Many non-military organizations now create " _____ s" or task groups for temporary activities that might have once been performed by ad hoc committees.

Exam Probability: **Low**

42. *Answer choices:*
(see index for correct answer)

- a. Curiosity
- b. Syntegrity
- c. Task force
- d. Troubleshooting

:: Socialism ::

In sociology, _____ is the process of internalizing the norms and ideologies of society. _____ encompasses both learning and teaching and is thus "the means by which social and cultural continuity are attained".

Exam Probability: **Medium**

43. *Answer choices:*

(see index for correct answer)

- a. State socialism
- b. Lemon socialism
- c. Sexualization
- d. Socialization

:: Unemployment benefits ::

_____ are payments made by back authorized bodies to unemployed people. In the United States, benefits are funded by a compulsory governmental insurance system, not taxes on individual citizens. Depending on the jurisdiction and the status of the person, those sums may be small, covering only basic needs, or may compensate the lost time proportionally to the previous earned salary.

Exam Probability: **High**

44. *Answer choices:*

(see index for correct answer)

- a. Unemployment benefits in Sweden
- b. Unemployment benefits
- c. National Insurance Act 1911
- d. Kela

Guidance: level 1

:: Workplace ::

A _____ is a process through which feedback from an employee's subordinates, colleagues, and supervisor, as well as a self-evaluation by the employee themselves is gathered. Such feedback can also include, when relevant, feedback from external sources who interact with the employee, such as customers and suppliers or other interested stakeholders. _____ is so named because it solicits feedback regarding an employee's behavior from a variety of points of view . It therefore may be contrasted with "downward feedback" , or "upward feedback" delivered to supervisory or management employees by subordinates only.

Exam Probability: **High**

45. *Answer choices:*
(see index for correct answer)

- a. Workplace health surveillance
- b. Feminisation of the workplace
- c. Workplace relationships
- d. Rat race

Guidance: level 1

:: Business theory ::

_____ or cultural quotient is a term used in business, education, government and academic research. _____ can be understood as the capability to relate and work effectively across cultures. Originally, the term _____ and the abbreviation "CQ" was developed by the research done by Soon Ang and Linn Van Dyne as a researched-based way of measuring and predicting intercultural performance.

Exam Probability: **Low**

46. *Answer choices:*

(see index for correct answer)

- a. Brian F. Harris
- b. Entrepreneurial leadership
- c. Cultural intelligence
- d. Complex adaptive system

Guidance: level 1

:: Labor ::

_____ s are workers whose main capital is knowledge. Examples include programmers, physicians, pharmacists, architects, engineers, scientists, design thinkers, public accountants, lawyers, and academics, and any other white-collar workers, whose line of work requires the one to "think for a living".

Exam Probability: **High**

47. *Answer choices:*

(see index for correct answer)

- a. Labor intensity
- b. Knowledge worker
- c. Means of production
- d. Man-hour

Guidance: level 1

:: ::

From an accounting perspective, _____ is crucial because _____ and _____ taxes considerably affect the net income of most companies and because they are subject to laws and regulations .

Exam Probability: **High**

48. *Answer choices:*

(see index for correct answer)

- a. similarity-attraction theory
- b. functional perspective
- c. hierarchical perspective
- d. Payroll

Guidance: level 1

:: Developmental psychology ::

_____ behavior refers to behavior that enables a person to get along in his or her environment with greatest success and least conflict with others. This is a term used in the areas of psychology and special education. _____ behavior relates to every day skills or tasks that the average person is able to complete, similar to the term life skills.

Exam Probability: **Medium**

49. *Answer choices:*

(see index for correct answer)

- a. Adult development
- b. Adaptive

Guidance: level 1

:: Project management ::

_____ is a name for various theories of human motivation built on Douglas McGregor's Theory X and Theory Y. Theories X, Y and various versions of Z have been used in human resource management, organizational behavior, organizational communication and organizational development.

Exam Probability: **High**

50. *Answer choices:*

(see index for correct answer)

- a. Lean project management
- b. Theory Z
- c. SQEP
- d. Aggregate project plan

Guidance: level 1

:: Employment compensation ::

A _____ is an agreement between a company and an employee specifying that the employee will receive certain significant benefits if employment is terminated. Most definitions specify the employment termination is as a result of a merger or takeover, also known as "Change-in-control benefits", but more recently the term has been used to describe perceived excessive CEO severance packages unrelated to change in ownership. The benefits may include severance pay, cash bonuses, stock options, or other benefits.

Exam Probability: **Low**

51. *Answer choices:*

(see index for correct answer)

- a. Family meal
- b. Severance package
- c. Golden parachute

- d. Employee stock option

Guidance: level 1

:: Employment ::

_____ is the probability that an individual will keep his/her job; a job with a high level of _____ is such that a person with the job would have a small chance of losing it.

Exam Probability: **Low**

52. *Answer choices:*
(see index for correct answer)

- a. Blacklist
- b. Workgang
- c. Service voucher
- d. Job security

Guidance: level 1

:: Leadership ::

_____ is a theory of leadership where a leader works with teams to identify needed change, creating a vision to guide the change through inspiration, and executing the change in tandem with committed members of a group; it is an integral part of the Full Range Leadership Model. _____ serves to enhance the motivation, morale, and job performance of followers through a variety of mechanisms; these include connecting the follower's sense of identity and self to a project and to the collective identity of the organization; being a role model for followers in order to inspire them and to raise their interest in the project; challenging followers to take greater ownership for their work, and understanding the strengths and weaknesses of followers, allowing the leader to align followers with tasks that enhance their performance.

Exam Probability: **Medium**

53. *Answer choices:*

(see index for correct answer)

- a. The Intangibles of Leadership
- b. Transformational leadership
- c. BTS Group
- d. Trait leadership

Guidance: level 1

:: Power (social and political) ::

_____ is a form of reverence gained by a leader who has strong interpersonal relationship skills. _____ , as an aspect of personal power, becomes particularly important as organizational leadership becomes increasingly about collaboration and influence, rather than command and control.

Exam Probability: **Medium**

54. *Answer choices:*

(see index for correct answer)

- a. Expert power
- b. Hard power
- c. need for power

Guidance: level 1

:: Management ::

In organizational studies, _____ is the efficient and effective development of an organization's resources when they are needed. Such resources may include financial resources, inventory, human skills, production resources, or information technology and natural resources.

Exam Probability: **High**

55. *Answer choices:*

(see index for correct answer)

- a. Project management simulation
- b. Financial planning
- c. Six phases of a big project
- d. Resource management

Guidance: level 1

:: ::

The _____ or labour force is the labour pool in employment. It is generally used to describe those working for a single company or industry, but can also apply to a geographic region like a city, state, or country. Within a company, its value can be labelled as its " _____ in Place". The _____ of a country includes both the employed and the unemployed. The labour force participation rate, LFPR , is the ratio between the labour force and the overall size of their cohort . The term generally excludes the employers or management, and can imply those involved in manual labour. It may also mean all those who are available for work.

Exam Probability: **Medium**

56. *Answer choices:*

(see index for correct answer)

- a. co-culture
- b. levels of analysis
- c. Workforce

- d. personal values

Guidance: level 1

:: ::

_____ is a method for employees to organize into a labor union in which a majority of employees in a bargaining unit sign authorization forms, or "cards", stating they wish to be represented by the union. Since the National Labor Relations Act became law in 1935, _____ has been an alternative to the National Labor Relations Board's election process. _____ and election are both overseen by the National Labor Relations Board. The difference is that with card sign-up, employees sign authorization cards stating they want a union, the cards are submitted to the NLRB and if more than 50% of the employees submitted cards, the NLRB requires the employer to recognize the union. The NLRA election process is an additional step with the NLRB conducting a secret ballot election after authorization cards are submitted. In both cases the employer never sees the authorization cards or any information that would disclose how individual employees voted.

Exam Probability: **Medium**

57. *Answer choices:*

(see index for correct answer)

- a. empathy
- b. deep-level diversity
- c. hierarchical perspective
- d. levels of analysis

:: Recruitment ::

A _____ or background investigation is the process of looking up and compiling criminal records, commercial records, and financial records of an individual or an organization. The frequency, purpose, and legitimacy of _____ s varies between countries, industries, and individuals. A variety of methods are used to complete such a check, from comprehensive data base search to personal references.

Exam Probability: **Medium**

58. *Answer choices:*

(see index for correct answer)

- a. Internet recruiting
- b. Vetting
- c. Probation
- d. Background check

:: Problem solving ::

In other words, _____ is a situation where a group of people meet to generate new ideas and solutions around a specific domain of interest by removing inhibitions. People are able to think more freely and they suggest as many spontaneous new ideas as possible. All the ideas are noted down and those ideas are not criticized and after _____ session the ideas are evaluated. The term was popularized by Alex Faickney Osborn in the 1953 book Applied Imagination.

Exam Probability: **Medium**

59. *Answer choices:*

(see index for correct answer)

- a. Karl Duncker
- b. Brainstorming
- c. Curiosity
- d. Circle time

Guidance: level 1

Information systems

Information systems (IS) are formal, sociotechnical, organizational systems designed to collect, process, store, and distribute information. In a sociotechnical perspective Information Systems are composed by four components: technology, process, people and organizational structure.

:: ::

A _____ is a knowledge base website on which users collaboratively modify content and structure directly from the web browser. In a typical _____ , text is written using a simplified markup language and often edited with the help of a rich-text editor.

1. *Answer choices:*

(see index for correct answer)

- a. surface-level diversity
- b. corporate values
- c. Wiki
- d. Character

Guidance: level 1

:: Network analyzers ::

A _____ , meaning "meat eater" , is an organism that derives its energy and nutrient requirements from a diet consisting mainly or exclusively of animal tissue, whether through predation or scavenging. Animals that depend solely on animal flesh for their nutrient requirements are called obligate _____ s while those that also consume non-animal food are called facultative _____ s. Omnivores also consume both animal and non-animal food, and, apart from the more general definition, there is no clearly defined ratio of plant to animal material that would distinguish a facultative _____ from an omnivore. A _____ at the top of the food chain, not preyed upon by other animals, is termed an apex predator.

Exam Probability: **Medium**

2. *Answer choices:*

(see index for correct answer)

- a. Carnivore
- b. KisMAC
- c. OpenVAS
- d. HTTP Debugger

Guidance: level 1

:: Critical thinking ::

In psychology, _____ is regarded as the cognitive process resulting in the selection of a belief or a course of action among several alternative possibilities. Every _____ process produces a final choice, which may or may not prompt action.

Exam Probability: **Low**

3. *Answer choices:*

(see index for correct answer)

- a. Emotional reasoning
- b. Decision-making
- c. Attacking Faulty Reasoning
- d. Inquiry

Guidance: level 1

:: Data management ::

Given organizations' increasing dependency on information technology to run their operations, Business continuity planning covers the entire organization, and Disaster recovery focuses on IT.

Exam Probability: **Medium**

4. *Answer choices:*

(see index for correct answer)

- a. Disaster recovery plan
- b. Very large database
- c. Workflow engine
- d. Physical schema

Guidance: level 1

:: Information systems ::

A _____ manages the creation and modification of digital content. It typically supports multiple users in a collaborative environment.

Exam Probability: **High**

5. *Answer choices:*

(see index for correct answer)

- a. Information silo
- b. Content management system
- c. Digital firm
- d. CDIS

Guidance: level 1

:: Management ::

_____ is the discipline of strategically planning for, and managing, all interactions with third party organizations that supply goods and/or services to an organization in order to maximize the value of those interactions. In practice, SRM entails creating closer, more collaborative relationships with key suppliers in order to uncover and realize new value and reduce risk of failure.

Exam Probability: **High**

6. *Answer choices:*
(see index for correct answer)

- a. Supplier relationship management
- b. Power to the edge
- c. Integrative thinking
- d. Corporate foresight

:: ::

_____ , Inc. was a company that provided human resource management systems , Financial Management Solutions , supply chain management , customer relationship management , and enterprise performance management software, as well as software for manufacturing, and student administration to large corporations, governments, and organizations. It existed as an independent corporation until its acquisition by Oracle Corporation in 2005. The _____ name and product line are now marketed by Oracle.

Exam Probability: **High**

7. *Answer choices:*

(see index for correct answer)

- a. similarity-attraction theory
- b. imperative
- c. personal values
- d. PeopleSoft

:: Credit cards ::

A _____ is a payment card issued to users to enable the cardholder to pay a merchant for goods and services based on the cardholder's promise to the card issuer to pay them for the amounts plus the other agreed charges. The card issuer creates a revolving account and grants a line of credit to the cardholder, from which the cardholder can borrow money for payment to a merchant or as a cash advance.

Exam Probability: **Medium**

8. *Answer choices:*

(see index for correct answer)

- a. Rail travel card
- b. NexG PrePaid
- c. Credit card
- d. TaiwanMoney Card

Guidance: level 1

:: Business models ::

_____ , or The Computer Utility, is a service provisioning model in which a service provider makes computing resources and infrastructure management available to the customer as needed, and charges them for specific usage rather than a flat rate. Like other types of on-demand computing , the utility model seeks to maximize the efficient use of resources and/or minimize associated costs. Utility is the packaging of system resources, such as computation, storage and services, as a metered service. This model has the advantage of a low or no initial cost to acquire computer resources; instead, resources are essentially rented.

Exam Probability: **High**

9. *Answer choices:*

(see index for correct answer)

- a. Utility computing
- b. Revenue model
- c. Entreship
- d. Sailing Ship Effect

Guidance: level 1

:: ::

A _____ is a system designed to capture, store, manipulate, analyze, manage, and present spatial or geographic data. GIS applications are tools that allow users to create interactive queries , analyze spatial information, edit data in maps, and present the results of all these operations. GIS sometimes refers to geographic information science , the science underlying geographic concepts, applications, and systems.

Exam Probability: **Low**

10. *Answer choices:*

(see index for correct answer)

- a. hierarchical
- b. surface-level diversity
- c. corporate values
- d. open system

Guidance: level 1

:: Data quality ::

_____ or data cleaning is the process of detecting and correcting corrupt or inaccurate records from a record set, table, or database and refers to identifying incomplete, incorrect, inaccurate or irrelevant parts of the data and then replacing, modifying, or deleting the dirty or coarse data. _____ may be performed interactively with data wrangling tools, or as batch processing through scripting.

11. *Answer choices:*

- a. Declarative Referential Integrity
- b. Data cleansing
- c. Data integrity
- d. Input mask

Guidance: level 1

:: Computer access control protocols ::

An _____ is a type of computer communications protocol or cryptographic protocol specifically designed for transfer of authentication data between two entities. It allows the receiving entity to authenticate the connecting entity as well as authenticate itself to the connecting entity by declaring the type of information needed for authentication as well as syntax. It is the most important layer of protection needed for secure communication within computer networks.

Exam Probability: **High**

12. *Answer choices:*

- a. Bcrypt

- b. Authentication protocol
- c. MS-CHAP
- d. POP before SMTP

Guidance: level 1

:: Identity management ::

_____ is the ability of an individual or group to seclude themselves, or information about themselves, and thereby express themselves selectively. The boundaries and content of what is considered private differ among cultures and individuals, but share common themes. When something is private to a person, it usually means that something is inherently special or sensitive to them. The domain of _____ partially overlaps with security , which can include the concepts of appropriate use, as well as protection of information. _____ may also take the form of bodily integrity.

Exam Probability: **High**

13. *Answer choices:*
(see index for correct answer)

- a. EduGAIN
- b. Identity management system
- c. Privacy
- d. Oracle Identity Management

Guidance: level 1

:: Information science ::

In discourse-based grammatical theory, _____ is any tracking of referential information by speakers. Information may be new, just introduced into the conversation; given, already active in the speakers' consciousness; or old, no longer active. The various types of activation, and how these are defined, are model-dependent.

Exam Probability: **Medium**

14. *Answer choices:*

(see index for correct answer)

- a. Digital South Asia Library
- b. Information flow
- c. Browsing
- d. Taxonomic database

Guidance: level 1

:: Ethically disputed business practices ::

_____ is the use of messaging systems to send an unsolicited message , especially advertising, as well as sending messages repeatedly on the same site. While the most widely recognized form of spam is email spam, the term is applied to similar abuses in other media: instant messaging spam, Usenet newsgroup spam, Web search engine spam, spam in blogs, wiki spam, online classified ads spam, mobile phone messaging spam, Internet forum spam, junk fax transmissions, social spam, spam mobile apps, television advertising and file sharing spam. It is named after Spam, a luncheon meat, by way of a Monty Python sketch about a restaurant that has Spam in every dish and where patrons annoyingly chant "Spam!" over and over again.

Exam Probability: **High**

15. *Answer choices:*

(see index for correct answer)

- a. Spamming
- b. Conflict of interest
- c. Market saturation
- d. Earnings management

Guidance: level 1

:: Marketing ::

_____ is a business model in which consumers create value and businesses consume that value. For example, when a consumer writes reviews or when a consumer gives a useful idea for new product development then that consumer is creating value for the business if the business adopts the input.
In the C2B model, a reverse auction or demand collection model, enables buyers to name or demand their own price, which is often binding, for a specific good or service. Inside of a consumer to business market the roles involved in the transaction must be established and the consumer must offer something of value to the business.

Exam Probability: **High**

16. *Answer choices:*

(see index for correct answer)

- a. Content creation
- b. Price war
- c. Consumer-to-business
- d. Markup

Guidance: level 1

:: Information systems ::

A _____ is an information system that supports business or organizational decision-making activities. DSSs serve the management, operations and planning levels of an organization and help people make decisions about problems that may be rapidly changing and not easily specified in advance—i.e. unstructured and semi-structured decision problems. _____ s can be either fully computerized or human-powered, or a combination of both.

Exam Probability: **Medium**

17. *Answer choices:*

(see index for correct answer)

- a. Self-service software vendors
- b. Value sensitive design
- c. Information systems
- d. Physical Internet

Guidance: level 1

:: Market research ::

_____ s are many different distantly related animals that typically have a long cylindrical tube-like body and no limbs. _____ s vary in size from microscopic to over 1 metre in length for marine polychaete _____ s , 6.7 metres for the African giant earth _____ , Microchaetus rappi, and 58 metres for the marine nemertean _____ , Lineus longissimus. Various types of _____ occupy a small variety of parasitic niches, living inside the bodies of other animals. Free-living _____ species do not live on land, but instead, live in marine or freshwater environments, or underground by burrowing.In biology, " _____ " refers to an obsolete taxon, vermes, used by Carolus Linnaeus and Jean-Baptiste Lamarck for all non-arthropod invertebrate animals, now seen to be paraphyletic. The name stems from the Old English word wyrm. Most animals called " _____ s" are invertebrates, but the term is also used for the amphibian caecilians and the slow _____ Anguis, a legless burrowing lizard. Invertebrate animals commonly called " _____ s" include annelids , nematodes , platyhelminthes , marine nemertean _____ s , marine Chaetognatha , priapulid _____ s, and insect larvae such as grubs and maggots.

Exam Probability: **Low**

18. *Answer choices:*

(see index for correct answer)

- a. Ad Tracking
- b. Preference regression
- c. DigitalMR
- d. Worm

Guidance: level 1

:: Reputation management ::

A _____ is an astronomical object consisting of a luminous spheroid of plasma held together by its own gravity. The nearest _____ to Earth is the Sun. Many other _____ s are visible to the naked eye from Earth during the night, appearing as a multitude of fixed luminous points in the sky due to their immense distance from Earth. Historically, the most prominent _____ s were grouped into constellations and asterisms, the brightest of which gained proper names. Astronomers have assembled _____ catalogues that identify the known _____ s and provide standardized stellar designations. However, most of the estimated 300 sextillion _____ s in the Universe are invisible to the naked eye from Earth, including all _____ s outside our galaxy, the Milky Way.

Exam Probability: **High**

19. *Answer choices:*
(see index for correct answer)

- a. Slashdot
- b. Raph Levien
- c. Moderation system
- d. Star

Guidance: level 1

:: Data management ::

_____ involves combining data residing in different sources and providing users with a unified view of them. This process becomes significant in a variety of situations, which include both commercial and scientific domains. _____ appears with increasing frequency as the volume and the need to share existing data explodes. It has become the focus of extensive theoretical work, and numerous open problems remain unsolved. _____ encourages collaboration between internal as well as external users

Exam Probability: **High**

20. *Answer choices:*

(see index for correct answer)

- a. Meta-data management
- b. Consistency
- c. Data set
- d. Small data

Guidance: level 1

:: Management ::

_____ is the identification of an organization's assets, followed by the development, documentation, and implementation of policies and procedures for protecting these assets.

Exam Probability: **Low**

21. *Answer choices:*

(see index for correct answer)

- a. Social business model
- b. Security management
- c. Flat organization
- d. Quality control

Guidance: level 1

:: IT risk management ::

_____ involves a set of policies, tools and procedures to enable the recovery or continuation of vital technology infrastructure and systems following a natural or human-induced disaster. _____ focuses on the IT or technology systems supporting critical business functions, as opposed to business continuity, which involves keeping all essential aspects of a business functioning despite significant disruptive events. _____ can therefore be considered as a subset of business continuity.

Exam Probability: **High**

22. *Answer choices:*

(see index for correct answer)

- a. Information assurance
- b. Business continuity
- c. Disaster recovery

:: Internet advertising ::

_____ , according to the United States federal law known as the Anti _____ Consumer Protection Act, is registering, trafficking in, or using an Internet domain name with bad faith intent to profit from the goodwill of a trademark belonging to someone else. The cybersquatter then offers to sell the domain to the person or company who owns a trademark contained within the name at an inflated price.

Exam Probability: **Medium**

23. *Answer choices:*

(see index for correct answer)

- a. LeadBolt
- b. Value Per Action
- c. Tvigle
- d. GeoEdge

:: Ubiquitous computing ::

A _____ , chip card, or integrated circuit card is a physical electronic authorization device, used to control access to a resource. It is typically a plastic credit card sized card with an embedded integrated circuit. Many _____ s include a pattern of metal contacts to electrically connect to the internal chip. Others are contactless, and some are both. _____ s can provide personal identification, authentication, data storage, and application processing. Applications include identification, financial, mobile phones , public transit, computer security, schools, and healthcare. _____ s may provide strong security authentication for single sign-on within organizations. Several nations have deployed _____ s throughout their populations.

Exam Probability: **Medium**

24. *Answer choices:*

(see index for correct answer)

- a. Ubiquitous Communicator
- b. Smart environment
- c. Martian Watches
- d. Smart card

Guidance: level 1

:: Procurement practices ::

_____ or commercially available off-the-shelf products are packaged solutions which are then adapted to satisfy the needs of the purchasing organization, rather than the commissioning of custom-made, or bespoke, solutions. A related term, Mil-COTS, refers to COTS products for use by the U.S. military.

Exam Probability: **Low**

25. *Answer choices:*

(see index for correct answer)

- a. Syndicated procurement
- b. Commercial off-the-shelf

Guidance: level 1

:: Data security ::

_____ are safeguards or countermeasures to avoid, detect, counteract, or minimize security risks to physical property, information, computer systems, or other assets.

Exam Probability: **Low**

26. *Answer choices:*

(see index for correct answer)

- a. Multi-party authorization
- b. Security controls
- c. LogLogic
- d. Security convergence

Guidance: level 1

:: Data management ::

Data aggregation is the compiling of information from databases with intent to prepare combined datasets for data processing.

Exam Probability: **Low**

27. *Answer choices:*

(see index for correct answer)

- a. Content-oriented workflow models
- b. Holistic Data Management
- c. Novell Storage Manager
- d. Data aggregator

Guidance: level 1

:: Payment systems ::

A _____ is any system used to settle financial transactions through the transfer of monetary value. This includes the institutions, instruments, people, rules, procedures, standards, and technologies that make it exchange possible. A common type of _____ is called an operational network that links bank accounts and provides for monetary exchange using bank deposits. Some _____ s also include credit mechanisms, which are essentially a different aspect of payment.

Exam Probability: **Low**

28. *Answer choices:*

(see index for correct answer)

- a. Cheque truncation system
- b. Payment system
- c. EFTPOS
- d. Currence

Guidance: level 1

:: Business models ::

_____ , a portmanteau of the words "free" and "premium", is a pricing strategy by which a product or service is provided free of charge, but money is charged for additional features, services, or virtual or physical goods. The business model has been in use by the software industry since the 1980s as a licensing scheme. A subset of this model used by the video game industry is called free-to-play.

29. *Answer choices:*

(see index for correct answer)

- a. Premium business model
- b. Cooperative
- c. Freemium
- d. Professional open source

Guidance: level 1

:: ::

Within the Internet, _____ s are formed by the rules and procedures of the _____ System . Any name registered in the DNS is a _____ . _____ s are used in various networking contexts and for application-specific naming and addressing purposes. In general, a _____ represents an Internet Protocol resource, such as a personal computer used to access the Internet, a server computer hosting a web site, or the web site itself or any other service communicated via the Internet. In 2017, 330.6 million _____ s had been registered.

Exam Probability: **High**

30. *Answer choices:*

(see index for correct answer)

- a. hierarchical
- b. interpersonal communication
- c. Domain name
- d. levels of analysis

Guidance: level 1

:: Google services ::

_____ is a web mapping service developed by Google. It offers satellite imagery, aerial photography, street maps, 360° panoramic views of streets , real-time traffic conditions, and route planning for traveling by foot, car, bicycle and air , or public transportation.

Exam Probability: **High**

31. *Answer choices:*

(see index for correct answer)

- a. App Inventor for Android
- b. Google Custom Search
- c. Google Groups
- d. Google Finance

Guidance: level 1

:: Data management ::

_____ is a set of processes and technologies that supports the collection, managing, and publishing of information in any form or medium. When stored and accessed via computers, this information may be more specifically referred to as digital content, or simply as content.

Exam Probability: **High**

32. *Answer choices:*

(see index for correct answer)

- a. Customer data management
- b. PerformancePoint
- c. Content management
- d. Content re-appropriation

Guidance: level 1

:: Virtual economies ::

_____ is an online virtual world, developed and owned by the San Francisco-based firm Linden Lab and launched on June 23, 2003. By 2013, _____ had approximately one million regular users; at the end of 2017 active user count totals "between 800,000 and 900,000". In many ways, _____ is similar to massively multiplayer online role-playing games; however, Linden Lab is emphatic that their creation is not a game: "There is no manufactured conflict, no set objective".

33. *Answer choices:*

(see index for correct answer)

- a. Megazebra
- b. EverQuest
- c. Massively multiplayer online real-time strategy game
- d. Second Life

Guidance: level 1

:: Data management ::

A _____, or metadata repository, as defined in the IBM Dictionary of Computing, is a "centralized repository of information about data such as meaning, relationships to other data, origin, usage, and format". Oracle defines it as a collection of tables with metadata. The term can have one of several closely related meanings pertaining to databases and database management systems .

Exam Probability: **Medium**

34. *Answer choices:*

(see index for correct answer)

- a. RSD
- b. World Wide Molecular Matrix

- c. Data binding
- d. Big data

Guidance: level 1

:: Data privacy ::

The _____ is an information security standard for organizations that handle branded credit cards from the major card schemes.

Exam Probability: **Medium**

35. *Answer choices:*

(see index for correct answer)

- a. Unclick
- b. Exponential mechanism
- c. Payment Card Industry Data Security Standard
- d. Article 29 Working Party

Guidance: level 1

:: ::

A _____ is a structure / access pattern specific to data warehouse environments, used to retrieve client-facing data. The _____ is a subset of the data warehouse and is usually oriented to a specific business line or team. Whereas data warehouses have an enterprise-wide depth, the information in _____ s pertains to a single department. In some deployments, each department or business unit is considered the owner of its _____ including all the hardware, software and data. This enables each department to isolate the use, manipulation and development of their data. In other deployments where conformed dimensions are used, this business unit ownership will not hold true for shared dimensions like customer, product, etc.

Exam Probability: **Medium**

36. *Answer choices:*

(see index for correct answer)

- a. deep-level diversity
- b. hierarchical perspective
- c. information systems assessment
- d. empathy

Guidance: level 1

:: Big data ::

_____ is the discovery, interpretation, and communication of meaningful patterns in data; and the process of applying those patterns towards effective decision making. In other words, _____ can be understood as the connective tissue between data and effective decision making, within an organization. Especially valuable in areas rich with recorded information, _____ relies on the simultaneous application of statistics, computer programming and operations research to quantify performance.

Exam Probability: **High**

37. *Answer choices:*

(see index for correct answer)

- a. Big Data Partnership
- b. Industrial Internet
- c. Platfora
- d. MarkLogic

Guidance: level 1

:: ::

A database is an organized collection of data, generally stored and accessed electronically from a computer system. Where databases are more complex they are often developed using formal design and modeling techniques.

Exam Probability: **Low**

38. *Answer choices:*

(see index for correct answer)

- a. empathy
- b. Database management system
- c. functional perspective
- d. deep-level diversity

Guidance: level 1

:: Computer data ::

In computer science, _____ is the ability to access an arbitrary element of a sequence in equal time or any datum from a population of addressable elements roughly as easily and efficiently as any other, no matter how many elements may be in the set. It is typically contrasted to sequential access.

Exam Probability: **High**

39. *Answer choices:*

(see index for correct answer)

- a. Text file
- b. Lilian date
- c. Random access
- d. Data in Use

:: ::

The _____ , commonly known as the Web, is an information system where documents and other web resources are identified by Uniform Resource Locators , which may be interlinked by hypertext, and are accessible over the Internet. The resources of the WWW may be accessed by users by a software application called a web browser.

Exam Probability: **Medium**

40. *Answer choices:*

(see index for correct answer)

- a. open system
- b. interpersonal communication
- c. Character
- d. cultural

:: Business ::

_____ is a sourcing model in which individuals or organizations obtain goods and services, including ideas and finances, from a large, relatively open and often rapidly-evolving group of internet users; it divides work between participants to achieve a cumulative result. The word _____ itself is a portmanteau of crowd and outsourcing, and was coined in 2005. As a mode of sourcing, _____ existed prior to the digital age .

Exam Probability: **Medium**

41. *Answer choices:*

(see index for correct answer)

- a. Accounting networks and associations
- b. CyberAlert, Inc.
- c. Ian McLeod
- d. Crowdsourcing

Guidance: level 1

:: Supply chain management ::

_____ is the removal of intermediaries in economics from a supply chain, or cutting out the middlemen in connection with a transaction or a series of transactions. Instead of going through traditional distribution channels, which had some type of intermediary , companies may now deal with customers directly, for example via the Internet. Hence, the use of factory direct and direct from the factory to mean the same thing.

42. *Answer choices:*

(see index for correct answer)

- a. ISO/PAS 28000
- b. JDA Software
- c. Gideon Hillman Consulting
- d. Disintermediation

Guidance: level 1

:: Distribution, retailing, and wholesaling ::

_____ measures the performance of a system. Certain goals are defined and the _____ gives the percentage to which those goals should be achieved. Fill rate is different from _____ .

Exam Probability: **Low**

43. *Answer choices:*

(see index for correct answer)

- a. Adjustable shelving
- b. Service level
- c. Capital City Distribution
- d. CGC Japan

:: Business planning ::

_____ is an organization's process of defining its strategy, or direction, and making decisions on allocating its resources to pursue this strategy. It may also extend to control mechanisms for guiding the implementation of the strategy. _____ became prominent in corporations during the 1960s and remains an important aspect of strategic management. It is executed by strategic planners or strategists, who involve many parties and research sources in their analysis of the organization and its relationship to the environment in which it competes.

Exam Probability: **Low**

44. *Answer choices:*

(see index for correct answer)

- a. Strategic planning
- b. Stakeholder management
- c. Community Futures
- d. Open Options Corporation

:: Information technology ::

_____ is the use of computers to store, retrieve, transmit, and manipulate data, or information, often in the context of a business or other enterprise. IT is considered to be a subset of information and communications technology . An _____ system is generally an information system, a communications system or, more specifically speaking, a computer system – including all hardware, software and peripheral equipment – operated by a limited group of users.

Exam Probability: **Medium**

45. *Answer choices:*

(see index for correct answer)

- a. Information technology
- b. ISO/IEC JTC 1/SWG 5
- c. Information and communication technologies for environmental sustainability
- d. SPAN Infotech

Guidance: level 1

:: Information systems ::

A _____ is an information system used for decision-making, and for the coordination, control, analysis, and visualization of information in an organization; especially in a company.

46. *Answer choices:*

(see index for correct answer)

- a. Internavi
- b. Management information system
- c. Digital ecosystem
- d. Local information systems

Guidance: level 1

:: Information systems ::

_____ is the process of creating, sharing, using and managing the knowledge and information of an organisation. It refers to a multidisciplinary approach to achieving organisational objectives by making the best use of knowledge.

Exam Probability: **High**

47. *Answer choices:*

(see index for correct answer)

- a. Knowledge management
- b. MIS Quarterly Executive
- c. Railway costing

- d. Earthquake Early Warning

Guidance: level 1

:: Google services ::

_____ is a discontinued image organizer and image viewer for organizing and editing digital photos, plus an integrated photo-sharing website, originally created by a company named Lifescape in 2002. In July 2004, Google acquired _____ from Lifescape and began offering it as freeware. " _____ " is a blend of the name of Spanish painter Pablo Picasso, the phrase mi casa and "pic" for pictures.

Exam Probability: **Medium**

48. *Answer choices:*
(see index for correct answer)

- a. Google Person Finder
- b. Google Friend Connect
- c. Google Sky
- d. Google Apps for Business

Guidance: level 1

:: Information science ::

_____ has been defined as "the branch of ethics that focuses on the relationship between the creation, organization, dissemination, and use of information, and the ethical standards and moral codes governing human conduct in society". It examines the morality that comes from information as a resource, a product, or as a target. It provides a critical framework for considering moral issues concerning informational privacy, moral agency , new environmental issues , problems arising from the life-cycle of information . It is very vital to understand that librarians, archivists, information professionals among others, really understand the importance of knowing how to disseminate proper information as well as being responsible with their actions when addressing information.

Exam Probability: **Medium**

49. *Answer choices:*

(see index for correct answer)

- a. Information ethics
- b. Visual Paradigm for UML
- c. Legal informatics
- d. Back-of-the-book index

Guidance: level 1

:: Management ::

A _____ describes the rationale of how an organization creates, delivers, and captures value, in economic, social, cultural or other contexts. The process of _____ construction and modification is also called _____ innovation and forms a part of business strategy.

Exam Probability: **High**

50. *Answer choices:*

(see index for correct answer)

- a. Identity formation
- b. Business model
- c. Quality, cost, delivery
- d. Project stakeholder

Guidance: level 1

:: Knowledge engineering ::

The _____ is an extension of the World Wide Web through standards by the World Wide Web Consortium . The standards promote common data formats and exchange protocols on the Web, most fundamentally the Resource Description Framework . According to the W3C, "The _____ provides a common framework that allows data to be shared and reused across application, enterprise, and community boundaries". The _____ is therefore regarded as an integrator across different content, information applications and systems.

Exam Probability: **Low**

51. *Answer choices:*

(see index for correct answer)

- a. DTRules
- b. Knowledge Collection from Volunteer Contributors
- c. Knowledge engineer
- d. Knowledge Engineering Environment

Guidance: level 1

:: Data management ::

" _____ " is a field that treats ways to analyze, systematically extract information from, or otherwise deal with data sets that are too large or complex to be dealt with by traditional data-processing application software. Data with many cases offer greater statistical power, while data with higher complexity may lead to a higher false discovery rate. _____ challenges include capturing data, data storage, data analysis, search, sharing, transfer, visualization, querying, updating, information privacy and data source. _____ was originally associated with three key concepts: volume, variety, and velocity. Other concepts later attributed with _____ are veracity and value.

Exam Probability: **Low**

52. *Answer choices:*

(see index for correct answer)

- a. Big data

- b. Clustered file system
- c. PerformancePoint
- d. Database transaction

Guidance: level 1

:: ::

_____ Holdings, Inc. is an American company operating a worldwide online payments system that supports online money transfers and serves as an electronic alternative to traditional paper methods like checks and money orders. The company operates as a payment processor for online vendors, auction sites, and many other commercial users, for which it charges a fee in exchange for benefits such as one-click transactions and password memory. _____'s payment system, also called _____ , is considered a type of payment rail.

Exam Probability: **High**

53. *Answer choices:*

(see index for correct answer)

- a. cultural
- b. Character
- c. PayPal
- d. personal values

Guidance: level 1

:: Global Positioning System ::

The _____ , originally Navstar GPS, is a satellite-based radionavigation system owned by the United States government and operated by the United States Air Force. It is a global navigation satellite system that provides geolocation and time information to a GPS receiver anywhere on or near the Earth where there is an unobstructed line of sight to four or more GPS satellites. Obstacles such as mountains and buildings block the relatively weak GPS signals.

Exam Probability: **Medium**

54. *Answer choices:*

(see index for correct answer)

- a. Receiver autonomous integrity monitoring
- b. Geo-fence
- c. Global Positioning System
- d. GpsOne

Guidance: level 1

:: Information technology management ::

_____ is a good-practice framework created by international professional association ISACA for information technology management and IT governance. _____ provides an implementable "set of controls over information technology and organizes them around a logical framework of IT-related processes and enablers."

Exam Probability: **Low**

55. *Answer choices:*

(see index for correct answer)

- a. COBIT
- b. Digital continuity
- c. Grey problem
- d. Virtual filing cabinet

Guidance: level 1

:: Networking hardware ::

A network interface controller is a computer hardware component that connects a computer to a computer network.

Exam Probability: **High**

56. *Answer choices:*

(see index for correct answer)

- a. Console server
- b. Ethernet hub
- c. bridging

Guidance: level 1

:: Enterprise modelling ::

_____ are large-scale application software packages that support business processes, information flows, reporting, and data analytics in complex organizations. While ES are generally packaged enterprise application software systems they can also be bespoke, custom developed systems created to support a specific organization's needs.

Exam Probability: **Low**

57. *Answer choices:*
(see index for correct answer)

- a. Enterprise systems
- b. SEQUAL framework
- c. GRAI method
- d. Event-driven process chain

Guidance: level 1

:: Information technology ::

_____ is the reorientation of product and service designs to focus on the end user as an individual consumer, in contrast with an earlier era of only organization-oriented offerings . Technologies whose first commercialization was at the inter-organization level thus have potential for later _____ . The emergence of the individual consumer as the primary driver of product and service design is most commonly associated with the IT industry, as large business and government organizations dominated the early decades of computer usage and development. Thus the microcomputer revolution, in which electronic computing moved from exclusively enterprise and government use to include personal computing, is a cardinal example of _____ . But many technology-based products, such as calculators and mobile phones, have also had their origins in business markets, and only over time did they become dominated by high-volume consumer usage, as these products commoditized and prices fell. An example of enterprise software that became consumer software is optical character recognition software, which originated with banks and postal systems but eventually became personal productivity software.

Exam Probability: **Low**

58. *Answer choices:*

(see index for correct answer)

- a. United States v. Ivanov
- b. Digital Researcher
- c. Enumerate
- d. Consumerization

Guidance: level 1

:: Data management ::

_____ is a data management concept concerning the capability that enables an organization to ensure that high data quality exists throughout the complete lifecycle of the data. The key focus areas of _____ include availability, usability, consistency, data integrity and data security and includes establishing processes to ensure effective data management throughout the enterprise such as accountability for the adverse effects of poor data quality and ensuring that the data which an enterprise has can be used by the entire organization.

Exam Probability: **High**

59. *Answer choices:*

(see index for correct answer)

- a. CERF
- b. Data discovery
- c. Metadirectory
- d. Data governance

Guidance: level 1

Marketing

Marketing is the study and management of exchange relationships. Marketing is the business process of creating relationships with and satisfying customers. With its focus on the customer, marketing is one of the premier components of business management.

Marketing is defined by the American Marketing Association as "the activity, set of institutions, and processes for creating, communicating, delivering, and exchanging offerings that have value for customers, clients, partners, and society at large."

:: Stock market ::

_____ is freedom from, or resilience against, potential harm caused by others. Beneficiaries of _____ may be of persons and social groups, objects and institutions, ecosystems or any other entity or phenomenon vulnerable to unwanted change by its environment.

Exam Probability: **Low**

1. *Answer choices:*

(see index for correct answer)

- a. Extended hours trading
- b. Program trading
- c. Super-majority amendment
- d. Accelerated share repurchase

Guidance: level 1

:: Brand management ::

_____ refers to the extent to which customers are able to recall or recognise a brand. _____ is a key consideration in consumer behavior, advertising management, brand management and strategy development. The consumer's ability to recognise or recall a brand is central to purchasing decision-making. Purchasing cannot proceed unless a consumer is first aware of a product category and a brand within that category. Awareness does not necessarily mean that the consumer must be able to recall a specific brand name, but he or she must be able to recall sufficient distinguishing features for purchasing to proceed. For instance, if a consumer asks her friend to buy her some gum in a "blue pack", the friend would be expected to know which gum to buy, even though neither friend can recall the precise brand name at the time.

Exam Probability: **High**

2. *Answer choices:*

(see index for correct answer)

- a. Brand-new
- b. Brand awareness
- c. Promotional apparel
- d. Principle Group

Guidance: level 1

:: ::

Advertising is a marketing communication that employs an openly sponsored, non-personal message to promote or sell a product, service or idea. Sponsors of advertising are typically businesses wishing to promote their products or services. Advertising is differentiated from public relations in that an advertiser pays for and has control over the message. It differs from personal selling in that the message is non-personal, i.e., not directed to a particular individual. Advertising is communicated through various mass media, including traditional media such as newspapers, magazines, television, radio, outdoor advertising or direct mail; and new media such as search results, blogs, social media, websites or text messages. The actual presentation of the message in a medium is referred to as an _____ , or "ad" or advert for short.

Exam Probability: **High**

3. *Answer choices:*

(see index for correct answer)

- a. open system
- b. co-culture
- c. Advertisement
- d. deep-level diversity

Guidance: level 1

:: Business terms ::

_____ occurs when a sales representative meets with a potential client for the purpose of transacting a sale. Many sales representatives rely on a sequential sales process that typically includes nine steps. Some sales representatives develop scripts for all or part of the sales process. The sales process can be used in face-to-face encounters and in telemarketing.

Exam Probability: **Low**

4. *Answer choices:*

(see index for correct answer)

- a. front office
- b. churn rate
- c. Personal selling
- d. organizational capital

Guidance: level 1

:: Management ::

_____ is the process of thinking about the activities required to achieve a desired goal. It is the first and foremost activity to achieve desired results. It involves the creation and maintenance of a plan, such as psychological aspects that require conceptual skills. There are even a couple of tests to measure someone's capability of _____ well. As such, _____ is a fundamental property of intelligent behavior. An important further meaning, often just called " _____ " is the legal context of permitted building developments.

5. *Answer choices:*

(see index for correct answer)

- a. Planning
- b. Empowerment
- c. Real property administrator
- d. Project team builder

Guidance: level 1

:: Advertising ::

A _____ is a large outdoor advertising structure , typically found in high-traffic areas such as alongside busy roads. _____ s present large advertisements to passing pedestrians and drivers. Typically showing witty slogans and distinctive visuals, _____ s are highly visible in the top designated market areas.

Exam Probability: **Medium**

6. *Answer choices:*

(see index for correct answer)

- a. Openad
- b. Advertising elasticity of demand

- c. International Standardized Commercial Identifier
- d. Van lettering

:: Retailing ::

_____ is the process of selling consumer goods or services to customers through multiple channels of distribution to earn a profit. _____ ers satisfy demand identified through a supply chain. The term " _____ er" is typically applied where a service provider fills the small orders of a large number of individuals, who are end-users, rather than large orders of a small number of wholesale, corporate or government clientele. Shopping generally refers to the act of buying products. Sometimes this is done to obtain final goods, including necessities such as food and clothing; sometimes it takes place as a recreational activity. Recreational shopping often involves window shopping and browsing: it does not always result in a purchase.

Exam Probability: **Low**

7. *Answer choices:*

(see index for correct answer)

- a. Pop-up retail
- b. Retail
- c. High-low pricing
- d. Hobby shop

:: ::

The _____ is an agreement signed by Canada, Mexico, and the United States, creating a trilateral trade bloc in North America. The agreement came into force on January 1, 1994, and superseded the 1988 Canada–United States Free Trade Agreement between the United States and Canada. The NAFTA trade bloc is one of the largest trade blocs in the world by gross domestic product.

Exam Probability: **High**

8. *Answer choices:*

(see index for correct answer)

- a. North American Free Trade Agreement
- b. empathy
- c. surface-level diversity
- d. imperative

Guidance: level 1

:: Belief ::

_____ is an umbrella term of influence. _____ can attempt to influence a person's beliefs, attitudes, intentions, motivations, or behaviors. In business, _____ is a process aimed at changing a person's attitude or behavior toward some event, idea, object, or other person, by using written, spoken words or visual tools to convey information, feelings, or reasoning, or a combination thereof. _____ is also an often used tool in the pursuit of personal gain, such as election campaigning, giving a sales pitch, or in trial advocacy. _____ can also be interpreted as using one's personal or positional resources to change people's behaviors or attitudes.Systematic _____ is the process through which attitudes or beliefs are leveraged by appeals to logic and reason. Heuristic _____ on the other hand is the process through which attitudes or beliefs are leveraged by appeals to habit or emotion.

Exam Probability: **High**

9. *Answer choices:*

(see index for correct answer)

- a. Doctrine
- b. Persuasion
- c. Real life
- d. Faith literate

Guidance: level 1

:: ::

A _____ is a research instrument consisting of a series of questions for the purpose of gathering information from respondents. The _____ was invented by the Statistical Society of London in 1838.

Exam Probability: **Medium**

10. *Answer choices:*

(see index for correct answer)

- a. Questionnaire
- b. functional perspective
- c. process perspective
- d. empathy

Guidance: level 1

:: Commodities ::

In economics, a _____ is an economic good or service that has full or substantial fungibility: that is, the market treats instances of the good as equivalent or nearly so with no regard to who produced them. Most commodities are raw materials, basic resources, agricultural, or mining products, such as iron ore, sugar, or grains like rice and wheat. Commodities can also be mass-produced unspecialized products such as chemicals and computer memory.

Exam Probability: **Low**

11. *Answer choices:*

(see index for correct answer)

- a. Commodity
- b. Sample grade
- c. IRely
- d. Commoditization

Guidance: level 1

:: Progressive Era in the United States ::

The Clayton Antitrust Act of 1914 , was a part of United States antitrust law with the goal of adding further substance to the U.S. antitrust law regime; the _____ sought to prevent anticompetitive practices in their incipiency. That regime started with the Sherman Antitrust Act of 1890, the first Federal law outlawing practices considered harmful to consumers . The _____ specified particular prohibited conduct, the three-level enforcement scheme, the exemptions, and the remedial measures.

Exam Probability: **High**

12. *Answer choices:*

(see index for correct answer)

- a. Clayton Antitrust Act
- b. Clayton Act
- c. Mann Act

:: Management ::

The term _____ refers to measures designed to increase the degree of autonomy and self-determination in people and in communities in order to enable them to represent their interests in a responsible and self-determined way, acting on their own authority. It is the process of becoming stronger and more confident, especially in controlling one`s life and claiming one`s rights. _____ as action refers both to the process of self- _____ and to professional support of people, which enables them to overcome their sense of powerlessness and lack of influence, and to recognize and use their resources. To do work with power.

Exam Probability: **Medium**

13. *Answer choices:*
(see index for correct answer)

- a. Event to knowledge
- b. Knowledge Based Decision Making
- c. Central administration
- d. Staff management

:: Direct marketing ::

_____ is a form of direct marketing using databases of customers or potential customers to generate personalized communications in order to promote a product or service for marketing purposes. The method of communication can be any addressable medium, as in direct marketing.

Exam Probability: **Medium**

14. *Answer choices:*

(see index for correct answer)

- a. Database marketing
- b. CornerWorld
- c. Time Reading Program
- d. Mailshot

Guidance: level 1

:: ::

_____ is the production of products for use or sale using labour and machines, tools, chemical and biological processing, or formulation. The term may refer to a range of human activity, from handicraft to high tech, but is most commonly applied to industrial design, in which raw materials are transformed into finished goods on a large scale. Such finished goods may be sold to other manufacturers for the production of other, more complex products, such as aircraft, household appliances, furniture, sports equipment or automobiles, or sold to wholesalers, who in turn sell them to retailers, who then sell them to end users and consumers.

15. *Answer choices:*

(see index for correct answer)

- a. Manufacturing
- b. cultural
- c. empathy
- d. personal values

Guidance: level 1

:: Budgets ::

A _____ is a financial plan for a defined period, often one year. It
may also include planned sales volumes and revenues, resource quantities, costs
and expenses, assets, liabilities and cash flows. Companies, governments,
families and other organizations use it to express strategic plans of
activities or events in measurable terms.

16. *Answer choices:*

(see index for correct answer)

- a. Budget set
- b. Operating budget

- c. Marginal budgeting for bottlenecks
- d. Budget constraint

Guidance: level 1

:: Types of marketing ::

_____ was first defined as a form of marketing developed from direct response marketing campaigns which emphasizes customer retention and satisfaction, rather than a focus on sales transactions.

Exam Probability: **Medium**

17. *Answer choices:*

(see index for correct answer)

- a. Affinity marketing
- b. Alliance marketing
- c. Relationship marketing
- d. Customer advocacy

Guidance: level 1

:: Health promotion ::

_____ is a form of advertising, it has been a large industry for some time now. Originally with newspapers and billboards, but now we have advanced to huge LCD screens and online advertisement on social medias and websites. The most common use of _____ in today's society is through social media.. It has the primary goal of achieving "social good". Traditional commercial marketing aims are primarily financial, though they can have positive social affects as well. In the context of public health, _____ would promote general health, raise awareness and induce changes in behaviour. To see _____ as only the use of standard commercial marketing practices to achieve non-commercial goals is an oversimplified view.

Exam Probability: **Low**

18. *Answer choices:*

(see index for correct answer)

- a. Rome Consensus for a Humanitarian Drug Policy
- b. Carers rights movement
- c. Social marketing
- d. Bangkok Charter

Guidance: level 1

:: ::

A brand is an overall experience of a customer that distinguishes an organization or product from its rivals in the eyes of the customer. Brands are used in business, marketing, and advertising. Name brands are sometimes distinguished from generic or store brands.

19. *Answer choices:*

(see index for correct answer)

- a. hierarchical
- b. Brand image
- c. hierarchical perspective
- d. imperative

Guidance: level 1

:: ::

_____ is a process whereby a person assumes the parenting of another, usually a child, from that person's biological or legal parent or parents. Legal _____ s permanently transfers all rights and responsibilities, along with filiation, from the biological parent or parents.

20. *Answer choices:*

(see index for correct answer)

- a. information systems assessment
- b. Adoption
- c. imperative

- d. surface-level diversity

Guidance: level 1

:: ::

A _____ service is an online platform which people use to build social networks or social relationship with other people who share similar personal or career interests, activities, backgrounds or real-life connections.

Exam Probability: **Medium**

21. *Answer choices:*

(see index for correct answer)

- a. information systems assessment
- b. Social networking
- c. co-culture
- d. similarity-attraction theory

Guidance: level 1

:: ::

In financial markets, a share is a unit used as mutual funds, limited partnerships, and real estate investment trusts. The owner of _____ in the corporation/company is a shareholder of the corporation. A share is an indivisible unit of capital, expressing the ownership relationship between the company and the shareholder. The denominated value of a share is its face value, and the total of the face value of issued _____ represent the capital of a company, which may not reflect the market value of those _____ .

Exam Probability: **Low**

22. *Answer choices:*

(see index for correct answer)

- a. Sarbanes-Oxley act of 2002
- b. co-culture
- c. similarity-attraction theory
- d. Shares

Guidance: level 1

:: Direct selling ::

_____ consists of two main business models: single-level marketing, in which a direct seller makes money by buying products from a parent organization and selling them directly to customers, and multi-level marketing , in which the direct seller may earn money from both direct sales to customers and by sponsoring new direct sellers and potentially earning a commission from their efforts.

Exam Probability: **High**

23. *Answer choices:*

(see index for correct answer)

- a. CVSL
- b. Direct Selling News
- c. Direct selling
- d. The Longaberger Company

Guidance: level 1

:: Management ::

_____ is the organizational discipline which focuses on the practical application of marketing orientation, techniques and methods inside enterprises and organizations and on the management of a firm's marketing resources and activities.

Exam Probability: **Medium**

24. *Answer choices:*

(see index for correct answer)

- a. Hierarchical organization
- b. Marketing management
- c. Reval

- d. Value migration

Guidance: level 1

:: Marketing ::

_____ is the process of using surveys to evaluate consumer acceptance of a new product idea prior to the introduction of a product to the market. It is important not to confuse _____ with advertising testing, brand testing and packaging testing; as is sometimes done. _____ focuses on the basic product idea, without the embellishments and puffery inherent in advertising.

Exam Probability: **Low**

25. *Answer choices:*

(see index for correct answer)

- a. Pricing strategies
- b. Concept testing
- c. Albuquerque Craft Beer Market
- d. NauticExpo

Guidance: level 1

:: Television commercials ::

_____ is a phenomenon whereby something new and somehow valuable is formed. The created item may be intangible or a physical object .

Exam Probability: **Low**

26. *Answer choices:*

(see index for correct answer)

- a. Trunk Monkey
- b. Creativity
- c. Godzilla vs. Charles Barkley
- d. Pretty

Guidance: level 1

:: ::

In business and engineering, new _____ covers the complete process of bringing a new product to market. A central aspect of NPD is product design, along with various business considerations. New _____ is described broadly as the transformation of a market opportunity into a product available for sale. The product can be tangible or intangible , though sometimes services and other processes are distinguished from "products." NPD requires an understanding of customer needs and wants, the competitive environment, and the nature of the market.Cost, time and quality are the main variables that drive customer needs. Aiming at these three variables, innovative companies develop continuous practices and strategies to better satisfy customer requirements and to increase their own market share by a regular development of new products. There are many uncertainties and challenges which companies must face throughout the process. The use of best practices and the elimination of barriers to communication are the main concerns for the management of the NPD .

Exam Probability: **Low**

27. *Answer choices:*

(see index for correct answer)

- a. information systems assessment
- b. levels of analysis
- c. Character
- d. Product development

Guidance: level 1

:: Workplace ::

_____ is asystematic determination of a subject's merit, worth and significance, using criteria governed by a set of standards. It can assist an organization, program, design, project or any other intervention or initiative to assess any aim, realisable concept/proposal, or any alternative, to help in decision-making; or to ascertain the degree of achievement or value in regard to the aim and objectives and results of any such action that has been completed. The primary purpose of _____ , in addition to gaining insight into prior or existing initiatives, is to enable reflection and assist in the identification of future change.

Exam Probability: **Low**

28. *Answer choices:*

(see index for correct answer)

- a. Evaluation
- b. Workplace listening
- c. Workplace strategy
- d. Toxic workplace

Guidance: level 1

:: ::

_____ , or auditory perception, is the ability to perceive sounds by detecting vibrations, changes in the pressure of the surrounding medium through time, through an organ such as the ear. The academic field concerned with _____ is auditory science.

29. *Answer choices:*

(see index for correct answer)

- a. Character
- b. cultural
- c. surface-level diversity
- d. hierarchical

Guidance: level 1

:: Monopoly (economics) ::

The _____ of 1890 was a United States antitrust law that regulates competition among enterprises, which was passed by Congress under the presidency of Benjamin Harrison.

30. *Answer choices:*

(see index for correct answer)

- a. Supracompetitive pricing
- b. Sherman Antitrust Act
- c. Trust
- d. Municipalization

Guidance: level 1

:: Product management ::

`_____` is a phrase used in the marketing industry which describes the value of having a well-known brand name, based on the idea that the owner of a well-known brand name can generate more revenue simply from brand recognition; that is from products with that brand name than from products with a less well known name, as consumers believe that a product with a well-known name is better than products with less well-known names.

Exam Probability: **Medium**

31. *Answer choices:*

(see index for correct answer)

- a. Brand extension
- b. Product information
- c. Product manager
- d. business name

Guidance: level 1

:: Marketing ::

_____ is a growth strategy that identifies and develops new market segments for current products. A _____ strategy targets non-buying customers in currently targeted segments. It also targets new customers in new segments.

Exam Probability: **High**

32. *Answer choices:*

(see index for correct answer)

- a. NauticExpo
- b. Mystery shopping
- c. Golden sample
- d. Market development

Guidance: level 1

:: Supply chain management ::

The _____ is a barcode symbology that is widely used in the United States, Canada, United Kingdom, Australia, New Zealand, in Europe and other countries for tracking trade items in stores.

Exam Probability: **Low**

33. *Answer choices:*

(see index for correct answer)

- a. Universal Product Code
- b. Transactional IT
- c. DR-DP-Matrix
- d. Astra Resources Plc

Guidance: level 1

:: ::

_____ characterises the behaviour of a system or model whose components interact in multiple ways and follow local rules, meaning there is no reasonable higher instruction to define the various possible interactions.

Exam Probability: **Low**

34. *Answer choices:*

(see index for correct answer)

- a. surface-level diversity
- b. imperative
- c. Complexity
- d. corporate values

Guidance: level 1

:: Marketing ::

_____ , in marketing, manufacturing, call centres and management, is the use of flexible computer-aided manufacturing systems to produce custom output. Such systems combine the low unit costs of mass production processes with the flexibility of individual customization.

Exam Probability: **Low**

35. *Answer choices:*

(see index for correct answer)

- a. Market share
- b. Product marketing
- c. Mass customization
- d. Competitor indexing

Guidance: level 1

:: Pricing ::

_____ is a pricing strategy in which the selling price is determined by adding a specific amount markup to a product's unit cost. An alternative pricing method is value-based pricing.

Exam Probability: **High**

36. *Answer choices:*

(see index for correct answer)

- a. Peak-load pricing
- b. Price scissors
- c. Fair trade law
- d. Net metering

Guidance: level 1

:: ::

In logic and philosophy, an _____ is a series of statements , called the premises or premisses , intended to determine the degree of truth of another statement, the conclusion. The logical form of an _____ in a natural language can be represented in a symbolic formal language, and independently of natural language formally defined " _____ s" can be made in math and computer science.

Exam Probability: **High**

37. *Answer choices:*

(see index for correct answer)

- a. Argument
- b. imperative
- c. hierarchical
- d. surface-level diversity

:: ::

_____ , also referred to as orthostasis, is a human position in which the body is held in an upright position and supported only by the feet.

Exam Probability: **High**

38. *Answer choices:*

(see index for correct answer)

- a. Standing
- b. process perspective
- c. interpersonal communication
- d. imperative

:: Television terminology ::

A _____ organization , also known as a non-business entity, not-for-profit organization, or _____ institution, is dedicated to furthering a particular social cause or advocating for a shared point of view. In economic terms, it is an organization that uses its surplus of the revenues to further achieve its ultimate objective, rather than distributing its income to the organization's shareholders, leaders, or members. _____ s are tax exempt or charitable, meaning they do not pay income tax on the money that they receive for their organization. They can operate in religious, scientific, research, or educational settings.

Exam Probability: **Low**

39. *Answer choices:*

(see index for correct answer)

- a. Satellite television
- b. Nonprofit
- c. distance learning
- d. multiplexing

Guidance: level 1

:: ::

_____ s are formal, sociotechnical, organizational systems designed to collect, process, store, and distribute information. In a sociotechnical perspective, _____ s are composed by four components: task, people, structure , and technology.

40. *Answer choices:*

(see index for correct answer)

- a. Information system
- b. deep-level diversity
- c. hierarchical
- d. imperative

Guidance: level 1

:: International trade ::

_____ or globalisation is the process of interaction and integration among people, companies, and governments worldwide. As a complex and multifaceted phenomenon, _____ is considered by some as a form of capitalist expansion which entails the integration of local and national economies into a global, unregulated market economy. _____ has grown due to advances in transportation and communication technology. With the increased global interactions comes the growth of international trade, ideas, and culture. _____ is primarily an economic process of interaction and integration that`s associated with social and cultural aspects. However, conflicts and diplomacy are also large parts of the history of _____ , and modern _____ .

Exam Probability: **Low**

41. *Answer choices:*

(see index for correct answer)

- a. Country of origin principle
- b. Globalization
- c. Kennedy Round
- d. Visible balance

Guidance: level 1

:: ::

In a supply chain, a _____ , or a seller, is an enterprise that contributes goods or services. Generally, a supply chain _____ manufactures inventory/stock items and sells them to the next link in the chain. Today, these terms refer to a supplier of any good or service.

Exam Probability: **High**

42. *Answer choices:*

(see index for correct answer)

- a. cultural
- b. functional perspective
- c. interpersonal communication
- d. Vendor

Guidance: level 1

:: Direct marketing ::

_____ is a form of advertising where organizations communicate directly to customers through a variety of media including cell phone text messaging, email, websites, online adverts, database marketing, fliers, catalog distribution, promotional letters, targeted television, newspapers, magazine advertisements, and outdoor advertising. Among practitioners, it is also known as direct response marketing.

Exam Probability: **Low**

43. *Answer choices:*

(see index for correct answer)

- a. Alticor
- b. Forced Free Trial
- c. Direct marketing
- d. Response Dynamics

Guidance: level 1

:: ::

In the broadest sense, _____ is any practice which contributes to the sale of products to a retail consumer. At a retail in-store level, _____ refers to the variety of products available for sale and the display of those products in such a way that it stimulates interest and entices customers to make a purchase.

Exam Probability: **Low**

44. *Answer choices:*

(see index for correct answer)

- a. Character
- b. similarity-attraction theory
- c. information systems assessment
- d. Merchandising

Guidance: level 1

:: Marketing ::

_____ is "commercial competition characterized by the repeated cutting of prices below those of competitors". One competitor will lower its price, then others will lower their prices to match. If one of them reduces their price again, a new round of reductions starts. In the short term, _____ s are good for buyers, who can take advantage of lower prices. Often they are not good for the companies involved because the lower prices reduce profit margins and can threaten their survival.

45. *Answer choices:*

(see index for correct answer)

- a. Mass affluent
- b. Editorial calendar
- c. Price war
- d. Marketing supply chain

Guidance: level 1

:: ::

Management is the administration of an organization, whether it is a business, a not-for-profit organization, or government body. Management includes the activities of setting the strategy of an organization and coordinating the efforts of its employees to accomplish its objectives through the application of available resources, such as financial, natural, technological, and human resources. The term "management" may also refer to those people who manage an organization.

Exam Probability: **High**

46. *Answer choices:*

(see index for correct answer)

- a. Character

- b. corporate values
- c. Manager
- d. levels of analysis

Guidance: level 1

:: ::

In _____ relations and communication science, _____ s are groups of individual people, and the _____ is the totality of such groupings. This is a different concept to the sociological concept of the Öffentlichkeit or _____ sphere. The concept of a _____ has also been defined in political science, psychology, marketing, and advertising. In _____ relations and communication science, it is one of the more ambiguous concepts in the field. Although it has definitions in the theory of the field that have been formulated from the early 20th century onwards, it has suffered in more recent years from being blurred, as a result of conflation of the idea of a _____ with the notions of audience, market segment, community, constituency, and stakeholder.

Exam Probability: **High**

47. *Answer choices:*

(see index for correct answer)

- a. Sarbanes-Oxley act of 2002
- b. cultural
- c. interpersonal communication
- d. Public

:: ::

_____ are interactive computer-mediated technologies that facilitate the creation and sharing of information, ideas, career interests and other forms of expression via virtual communities and networks. The variety of stand-alone and built-in _____ services currently available introduces challenges of definition; however, there are some common features.

Exam Probability: **Medium**

48. *Answer choices:*

(see index for correct answer)

- a. co-culture
- b. Character
- c. Social media
- d. corporate values

:: Brand management ::

_____ is defined as positive feelings towards a brand and dedication to purchase the same product or service repeatedly now and in the future from the same brand, regardless of a competitor's actions or changes in the environment. It can also be demonstrated with other behaviors such as positive word-of-mouth advocacy. _____ is where an individual buys products from the same manufacturer repeatedly rather than from other suppliers. Businesses whose financial and ethical values, for example ESG responsibilities, rest in large part on their _____ are said to use the loyalty business model.

Exam Probability: **High**

49. *Answer choices:*

(see index for correct answer)

- a. Brand-new
- b. Brand loyalty
- c. Brand Finance
- d. Saban Capital Group

Guidance: level 1

:: Marketing by medium ::

_____ or viral advertising is a business strategy that uses existing social networks to promote a product. Its name refers to how consumers spread information about a product with other people in their social networks, much in the same way that a virus spreads from one person to another. It can be delivered by word of mouth or enhanced by the network effects of the Internet and mobile networks.

50. *Answer choices:*

(see index for correct answer)

- a. Viral marketing
- b. Online advertising
- c. Social marketing intelligence
- d. New media marketing

Guidance: level 1

:: Product management ::

_____ or brand stretching is a marketing strategy in which a firm marketing a product with a well-developed image uses the same brand name in a different product category. The new product is called a spin-off. Organizations use this strategy to increase and leverage brand equity . An example of a _____ is Jello-gelatin creating Jello pudding pops. It increases awareness of the brand name and increases profitability from offerings in more than one product category.

Exam Probability: **Medium**

51. *Answer choices:*

(see index for correct answer)

- a. Product cost management

- b. Service product management
- c. Brand extension
- d. Swing tag

Guidance: level 1

:: Brand management ::

In marketing, _____ is the analysis and planning on how a brand is perceived in the market. Developing a good relationship with the target market is essential for _____ . Tangible elements of _____ include the product itself; its look, price, and packaging, etc. The intangible elements are the experiences that the consumers share with the brand, and also the relationships they have with the brand. A brand manager would oversee all aspects of the consumer's brand association as well as relationships with members of the supply chain.

Exam Probability: **Medium**

52. *Answer choices:*
(see index for correct answer)

- a. Brand management
- b. Trade symbols
- c. Superbrands
- d. Brand specialist

Guidance: level 1

:: Marketing ::

_____ is the marketing of products that are presumed to be environmentally safe. It incorporates a broad range of activities, including product modification, changes to the production process, sustainable packaging, as well as modifying advertising. Yet defining _____ is not a simple task where several meanings intersect and contradict each other; an example of this will be the existence of varying social, environmental and retail definitions attached to this term. Other similar terms used are environmental marketing and ecological marketing.

Exam Probability: **High**

53. *Answer choices:*

(see index for correct answer)

- a. Marketing automation
- b. Green marketing
- c. Field marketing
- d. Next-best-action marketing

Guidance: level 1

:: Advertising ::

_____ is the behavioral and cognitive process of selectively concentrating on a discrete aspect of information, whether deemed subjective or objective, while ignoring other perceivable information. It is a state of arousal. It is the taking possession by the mind in clear and vivid form of one out of what seem several simultaneous objects or trains of thought. Focalization, the concentration of consciousness, is of its essence. _____ has also been described as the allocation of limited cognitive processing resources.

Exam Probability: **Medium**

54. *Answer choices:*

(see index for correct answer)

- a. Family in advertising
- b. Commercial speech
- c. Attention
- d. Outsert

Guidance: level 1

:: Marketing terminology ::

_____ is used in marketing to describe the inability to assess the value gained from engaging in an activity using any tangible evidence. It is often used to describe services where there is no tangible product that the customer can purchase, that can be seen or touched.

55. *Answer choices:*

(see index for correct answer)

- a. Soft launch
- b. Product/market fit
- c. Intangibility
- d. Arrow information paradox

Guidance: level 1

:: Production and manufacturing ::

_____ consists of organization-wide efforts to "install and make permanent climate where employees continuously improve their ability to provide on demand products and services that customers will find of particular value." "Total" emphasizes that departments in addition to production are obligated to improve their operations; "management" emphasizes that executives are obligated to actively manage quality through funding, training, staffing, and goal setting. While there is no widely agreed-upon approach, TQM efforts typically draw heavily on the previously developed tools and techniques of quality control. TQM enjoyed widespread attention during the late 1980s and early 1990s before being overshadowed by ISO 9000, Lean manufacturing, and Six Sigma.

Exam Probability: **Low**

56. *Answer choices:*

(see index for correct answer)

- a. Continuous production
- b. Digital materialization
- c. Total Quality Management
- d. Common Industrial Protocol

Guidance: level 1

:: Generally Accepted Accounting Principles ::

Expenditure is an outflow of money to another person or group to pay for an item or service, or for a category of costs. For a tenant, rent is an _____ . For students or parents, tuition is an _____ . Buying food, clothing, furniture or an automobile is often referred to as an _____ . An _____ is a cost that is "paid" or "remitted", usually in exchange for something of value. Something that seems to cost a great deal is "expensive". Something that seems to cost little is "inexpensive". " _____ s of the table" are _____ s of dining, refreshments, a feast, etc.

Exam Probability: **High**

57. *Answer choices:*

(see index for correct answer)

- a. Statement of recommended practice
- b. Expense
- c. Gross sales
- d. Vendor-specific objective evidence

:: Reputation management ::

A _____ is an astronomical object consisting of a luminous spheroid of plasma held together by its own gravity. The nearest _____ to Earth is the Sun. Many other _____ s are visible to the naked eye from Earth during the night, appearing as a multitude of fixed luminous points in the sky due to their immense distance from Earth. Historically, the most prominent _____ s were grouped into constellations and asterisms, the brightest of which gained proper names. Astronomers have assembled _____ catalogues that identify the known _____ s and provide standardized stellar designations. However, most of the estimated 300 sextillion _____ s in the Universe are invisible to the naked eye from Earth, including all _____ s outside our galaxy, the Milky Way.

Exam Probability: **Low**

58. *Answer choices:*

(see index for correct answer)

- a. Star
- b. Whuffie
- c. Sybil attack
- d. Yasni

:: Human resource management ::

_____ encompasses values and behaviors that contribute to the unique social and psychological environment of a business. The _____ influences the way people interact, the context within which knowledge is created, the resistance they will have towards certain changes, and ultimately the way they share knowledge. _____ represents the collective values, beliefs and principles of organizational members and is a product of factors such as history, product, market, technology, strategy, type of employees, management style, and national culture; culture includes the organization's vision, values, norms, systems, symbols, language, assumptions, environment, location, beliefs and habits.

Exam Probability: **High**

59. *Answer choices:*

(see index for correct answer)

- a. Selection ratio
- b. Organizational culture
- c. Cross-functional team
- d. Organizational ethics

Guidance: level 1

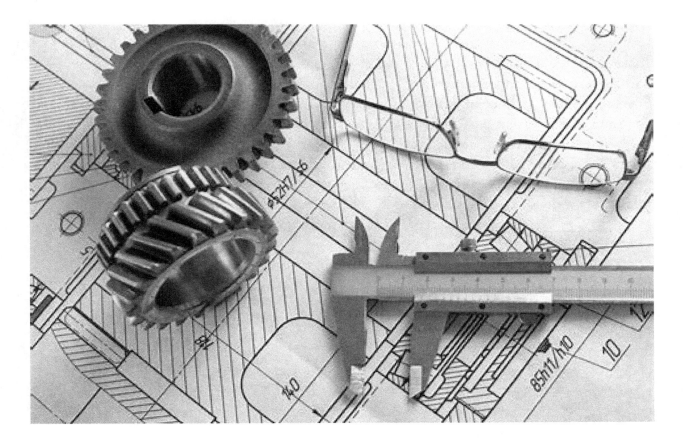

Manufacturing

Manufacturing is the production of merchandise for use or sale using labor and machines, tools, chemical and biological processing, or formulation. The term may refer to a range of human activity, from handicraft to high tech, but is most commonly applied to industrial design , in which raw materials are transformed into finished goods on a large scale. Such finished goods may be sold to other manufacturers for the production of other, more complex products, such as aircraft, household appliances, furniture, sports equipment or automobiles, or sold to wholesalers, who in turn sell them to retailers, who then sell them to end users and consumers.

:: Mereology ::

_____ , in the abstract, is what belongs to or with something, whether as an attribute or as a component of said thing. In the context of this article, it is one or more components , whether physical or incorporeal, of a person's estate; or so belonging to, as in being owned by, a person or jointly a group of people or a legal entity like a corporation or even a society. Depending on the nature of the _____ , an owner of _____ has the right to consume, alter, share, redefine, rent, mortgage, pawn, sell, exchange, transfer, give away or destroy it, or to exclude others from doing these things, as well as to perhaps abandon it; whereas regardless of the nature of the _____ , the owner thereof has the right to properly use it , or at the very least exclusively keep it.

Exam Probability: **Medium**

1. *Answer choices:*

(see index for correct answer)

- a. Property
- b. Gunk
- c. Mereological nihilism
- d. Non-wellfounded mereology

Guidance: level 1

:: ::

Some scenarios associate "this kind of planning" with learning "life skills".Schedules are necessary, or at least useful, in situations where individuals need to know what time they must be at a specific location to receive a specific service, and where people need to accomplish a set of goals within a set time period.

Exam Probability: **Medium**

2. *Answer choices:*

(see index for correct answer)

- a. functional perspective
- b. deep-level diversity
- c. interpersonal communication
- d. information systems assessment

Guidance: level 1

:: Quality awards ::

The _____ recognizes U.S. organizations in the business, health care, education, and nonprofit sectors for performance excellence. The Baldrige Award is the only formal recognition of the performance excellence of both public and private U.S. organizations given by the President of the United States. It is administered by the Baldrige Performance Excellence Program, which is based at and managed by the National Institute of Standards and Technology , an agency of the U.S. Department of Commerce.

3. *Answer choices:*

(see index for correct answer)

- a. Rajiv Gandhi National Quality Award
- b. Malcolm Baldrige National Quality Award
- c. Deming Prize
- d. Canada Awards for Excellence

Guidance: level 1

:: Auditing ::

_____ is the process of systematic examination of a quality system carried out by an internal or external _____ or or an audit team. It is an important part of an organization's quality management system and is a key element in the ISO quality system standard, ISO 9001.

Exam Probability: **Medium**

4. *Answer choices:*

(see index for correct answer)

- a. Chartered Institute of Internal Auditors
- b. Quality audit
- c. Risk-based auditing

- d. External audit

Guidance: level 1

:: Information technology management ::

_____ is the discipline of engineering concerned with the principles and practice of product and service quality assurance and control. In the software development, it is the management, development, operation and maintenance of IT systems and enterprise architectures with a high quality standard.

Exam Probability: **High**

5. *Answer choices:*

(see index for correct answer)

- a. E-Booking
- b. NetIQ
- c. Many-to-many
- d. Trustworthy Software Initiative

Guidance: level 1

:: ::

In sales, commerce and economics, a _____ is the recipient of a good, service, product or an idea - obtained from a seller, vendor, or supplier via a financial transaction or exchange for money or some other valuable consideration.

Exam Probability: **Medium**

6. *Answer choices:*

(see index for correct answer)

- a. similarity-attraction theory
- b. Sarbanes-Oxley act of 2002
- c. Customer
- d. surface-level diversity

Guidance: level 1

:: Knowledge representation ::

_____ s are causal diagrams created by Kaoru Ishikawa that show the causes of a specific event.

Exam Probability: **Medium**

7. *Answer choices:*

(see index for correct answer)

- a. Cognitive map
- b. Cutter Expansive Classification
- c. Nippon Decimal Classification
- d. Geopolitical ontology

Guidance: level 1

:: Distribution, retailing, and wholesaling ::

The _____ is a distribution channel phenomenon in which forecasts yield supply chain inefficiencies. It refers to increasing swings in inventory in response to shifts in customer demand as one moves further up the supply chain. The concept first appeared in Jay Forrester's Industrial Dynamics and thus it is also known as the Forrester effect. The _____ was named for the way the amplitude of a whip increases down its length. The further from the originating signal, the greater the distortion of the wave pattern. In a similar manner, forecast accuracy decreases as one moves upstream along the supply chain. For example, many consumer goods have fairly consistent consumption at retail but this signal becomes more chaotic and unpredictable as the focus moves away from consumer purchasing behavior.

Exam Probability: **Low**

8. *Answer choices:*

(see index for correct answer)

- a. Bridgewater House, Manchester
- b. Balance of contract
- c. 350 West Mart Center

- d. Bullwhip effect

Guidance: level 1

:: Data management ::

_____ is an object-oriented program and library developed by CERN. It was originally designed for particle physics data analysis and contains several features specific to this field, but it is also used in other applications such as astronomy and data mining. The latest release is 6.16.00, as of 2018-11-14.

Exam Probability: **Low**

9. *Answer choices:*
(see index for correct answer)

- a. Commitment ordering
- b. CommVault Systems
- c. ROOT
- d. Content repository

Guidance: level 1

:: Sensitivity analysis ::

_____ is the study of how the uncertainty in the output of a mathematical model or system can be divided and allocated to different sources of uncertainty in its inputs. A related practice is uncertainty analysis, which has a greater focus on uncertainty quantification and propagation of uncertainty; ideally, uncertainty and _____ should be run in tandem.

Exam Probability: **High**

10. *Answer choices:*

(see index for correct answer)

- a. Variance-based sensitivity analysis
- b. Fourier amplitude sensitivity testing
- c. Tornado diagram
- d. Elementary effects method

Guidance: level 1

:: Manufacturing ::

A _____ is an object used to extend the ability of an individual to modify features of the surrounding environment. Although many animals use simple _____ s, only human beings, whose use of stone _____ s dates back hundreds of millennia, use _____ s to make other _____ s. The set of _____ s needed to perform different tasks that are part of the same activity is called gear or equipment.

Exam Probability: **Low**

11. *Answer choices:*

- a. Motoman
- b. Lean manufacturing
- c. Tool
- d. Initial Reject

Guidance: level 1

:: Marketing ::

_____ or stock is the goods and materials that a business holds for the ultimate goal of resale .

Exam Probability: **Medium**

12. *Answer choices:*

- a. Prommercial
- b. Pre-order
- c. Intent scale translation
- d. Inventory

Guidance: level 1

:: Information technology management ::

_____ is a collective term for all approaches to prepare , support and help individuals, teams, and organizations in making organizational change. The most common change drivers include: technological evolution, process reviews, crisis, and consumer habit changes; pressure from new business entrants, acquisitions, mergers, and organizational restructuring. It includes methods that redirect or redefine the use of resources, business process, budget allocations, or other modes of operation that significantly change a company or organization. Organizational _____ considers the full organization and what needs to change, while _____ may be used solely to refer to how people and teams are affected by such organizational transition. It deals with many different disciplines, from behavioral and social sciences to information technology and business solutions.

Exam Probability: **Low**

13. *Answer choices:*

(see index for correct answer)

- a. Cmdbuild
- b. Change management
- c. Building lifecycle management
- d. Financial Management Standard

Guidance: level 1

:: Industrial design ::

In physics and mathematics, the _____ of a mathematical space is informally defined as the minimum number of coordinates needed to specify any point within it. Thus a line has a _____ of one because only one coordinate is needed to specify a point on it for example, the point at 5 on a number line. A surface such as a plane or the surface of a cylinder or sphere has a _____ of two because two coordinates are needed to specify a point on it for example, both a latitude and longitude are required to locate a point on the surface of a sphere. The inside of a cube, a cylinder or a sphere is three- _____ al because three coordinates are needed to locate a point within these spaces.

Exam Probability: **High**

14. *Answer choices:*

(see index for correct answer)

- a. Furniture
- b. I.D.
- c. Industrial Arts Curriculum Project
- d. Industrial design

Guidance: level 1

:: Product development ::

In business and engineering, _____ covers the complete process of bringing a new product to market. A central aspect of NPD is product design, along with various business considerations. _____ is described broadly as the transformation of a market opportunity into a product available for sale. The product can be tangible or intangible , though sometimes services and other processes are distinguished from "products." NPD requires an understanding of customer needs and wants, the competitive environment, and the nature of the market.Cost, time and quality are the main variables that drive customer needs. Aiming at these three variables, innovative companies develop continuous practices and strategies to better satisfy customer requirements and to increase their own market share by a regular development of new products. There are many uncertainties and challenges which companies must face throughout the process. The use of best practices and the elimination of barriers to communication are the main concerns for the management of the NPD .

Exam Probability: **Medium**

15. *Answer choices:*

(see index for correct answer)

- a. Product optimization
- b. Embedded intelligence
- c. New product development
- d. Specification tree

Guidance: level 1

:: Project management ::

_____ is a marketing activity that does an aggregate plan for the production process, in advance of 6 to 18 months, to give an idea to management as to what quantity of materials and other resources are to be procured and when, so that the total cost of operations of the organization is kept to the minimum over that period.

Exam Probability: **High**

16. *Answer choices:*

(see index for correct answer)

- a. Aggregate planning
- b. Alexander Laufer
- c. Design structure matrix
- d. Australian Institute of Project Management

Guidance: level 1

:: Management ::

In organizational studies, _____ is the efficient and effective development of an organization's resources when they are needed. Such resources may include financial resources, inventory, human skills, production resources, or information technology and natural resources.

Exam Probability: **Medium**

17. *Answer choices:*

(see index for correct answer)

- a. Management fad
- b. Functional management
- c. Resource management
- d. Event to knowledge

Guidance: level 1

:: Project management ::

A _____ is a professional in the field of project management. _____ s have the responsibility of the planning, procurement and execution of a project, in any undertaking that has a defined scope, defined start and a defined finish; regardless of industry. _____ s are first point of contact for any issues or discrepancies arising from within the heads of various departments in an organization before the problem escalates to higher authorities. Project management is the responsibility of a _____ . This individual seldom participates directly in the activities that produce the end result, but rather strives to maintain the progress, mutual interaction and tasks of various parties in such a way that reduces the risk of overall failure, maximizes benefits, and minimizes costs.

Exam Probability: **High**

18. *Answer choices:*

(see index for correct answer)

- a. Cone of Uncertainty
- b. Schedule
- c. Risk register
- d. Project manager

Guidance: level 1

:: Project management ::

In economics, _____ is the assignment of available resources to various uses. In the context of an entire economy, resources can be allocated by various means, such as markets or central planning.

Exam Probability: **Medium**

19. *Answer choices:*
(see index for correct answer)

- a. Resource allocation
- b. Elemental cost planning
- c. Bill of quantities
- d. Project appraisal

Guidance: level 1

:: Decision theory ::

_____ is a method developed in Japan beginning in 1966 to help transform the voice of the customer into engineering characteristics for a product. Yoji Akao, the original developer, described QFD as a "method to transform qualitative user demands into quantitative parameters, to deploy the functions forming quality, and to deploy methods for achieving the design quality into subsystems and component parts, and ultimately to specific elements of the manufacturing process." The author combined his work in quality assurance and quality control points with function deployment used in value engineering.

Exam Probability: **High**

20. *Answer choices:*

(see index for correct answer)

- a. Cognitive bias
- b. Belief structure
- c. Pignistic probability
- d. Bulk Dispatch Lapse

Guidance: level 1

:: Industrial engineering ::

_____ , in its contemporary conceptualisation, is a comparison of perceived expectations of a service with perceived performance , giving rise to the equation SQ=P-E. This conceptualistion of _____ has its origins in the expectancy-disconfirmation paradigm.

21. *Answer choices:*

(see index for correct answer)

- a. Indian Institution of Industrial Engineering
- b. Service quality
- c. Harold and Inge Marcus Department of Industrial and Manufacturing Engineering
- d. Institute of Industrial Engineers

Guidance: level 1

:: Chemical processes ::

_____ is the understanding and application of the fundamental principles and laws of nature that allow us to transform raw material and energy into products that are useful to society, at an industrial level. By taking advantage of the driving forces of nature such as pressure, temperature and concentration gradients, as well as the law of conservation of mass, process engineers can develop methods to synthesize and purify large quantities of desired chemical products. _____ focuses on the design, operation, control, optimization and intensification of chemical, physical, and biological processes. _____ encompasses a vast range of industries, such as agriculture, automotive, biotechnical, chemical, food, material development, mining, nuclear, petrochemical, pharmaceutical, and software development. The application of systematic computer-based methods to _____ is "process systems engineering".

22. *Answer choices:*

(see index for correct answer)

- a. Bioconversion
- b. Foam separation
- c. Process engineering
- d. Crystallization of polymers

Guidance: level 1

:: Materials science ::

An _____ is a polymer with viscoelasticity and very weak intermolecular forces, and generally low Young's modulus and high failure strain compared with other materials. The term, a portmanteau of elastic polymer, is often used interchangeably with rubber, although the latter is preferred when referring to vulcanisates. Each of the monomers which link to form the polymer is usually a compound of several elements among carbon, hydrogen, oxygen and silicon. _____ s are amorphous polymers maintained above their glass transition temperature, so that considerable molecular reconformation, without breaking of covalent bonds, is feasible. At ambient temperatures, such rubbers are thus relatively soft and deformable. Their primary uses are for seals, adhesives and molded flexible parts. Application areas for different types of rubber are manifold and cover segments as diverse as tires, soles for shoes, and damping and insulating elements. The importance of these rubbers can be judged from the fact that global revenues are forecast to rise to US$56 billion in 2020.

Exam Probability: **Medium**

23. *Answer choices:*

(see index for correct answer)

- a. Materials informatics
- b. Split-ring resonator
- c. Elastomer
- d. Coherent diffraction imaging

Guidance: level 1

:: Evaluation ::

_____ is a way of preventing mistakes and defects in manufactured products and avoiding problems when delivering products or services to customers; which ISO 9000 defines as "part of quality management focused on providing confidence that quality requirements will be fulfilled". This defect prevention in _____ differs subtly from defect detection and rejection in quality control and has been referred to as a shift left since it focuses on quality earlier in the process .

Exam Probability: **Low**

24. *Answer choices:*

(see index for correct answer)

- a. Australian Drug Evaluation Committee
- b. Quality assurance
- c. Princeton Application Repository for Shared-Memory Computers

- d. Common Criteria Testing Laboratory

Guidance: level 1

:: Process management ::

When used in the context of communication networks, such as Ethernet or packet radio, _____ or network _____ is the rate of successful message delivery over a communication channel. The data these messages belong to may be delivered over a physical or logical link, or it can pass through a certain network node. _____ is usually measured in bits per second , and sometimes in data packets per second or data packets per time slot.

Exam Probability: **High**

25. *Answer choices:*
(see index for correct answer)

- a. Turnaround
- b. Value grid
- c. Process modeling
- d. White Space

Guidance: level 1

:: Quality management ::

In quality management system, a _____ is a document developed by management to express the directive of the top management with respect to quality. _____ management is a strategic item.

Exam Probability: **Low**

26. *Answer choices:*

(see index for correct answer)

- a. China Quality Course
- b. Quality management
- c. Quality policy
- d. ISO 9000

Guidance: level 1

:: ::

_____ is the quantity of three-dimensional space enclosed by a closed surface, for example, the space that a substance or shape occupies or contains. _____ is often quantified numerically using the SI derived unit, the cubic metre. The _____ of a container is generally understood to be the capacity of the container; i. e., the amount of fluid that the container could hold, rather than the amount of space the container itself displaces. Three dimensional mathematical shapes are also assigned _____ s. _____ s of some simple shapes, such as regular, straight-edged, and circular shapes can be easily calculated using arithmetic formulas. _____ s of complicated shapes can be calculated with integral calculus if a formula exists for the shape's boundary. One-dimensional figures and two-dimensional shapes are assigned zero _____ in the three-dimensional space.

Exam Probability: **High**

27. *Answer choices:*

(see index for correct answer)

- a. corporate values
- b. process perspective
- c. open system
- d. Sarbanes-Oxley act of 2002

Guidance: level 1

:: Natural materials ::

_____ is a finely-grained natural rock or soil material that combines one or more _____ minerals with possible traces of quartz , metal oxides and organic matter. Geologic _____ deposits are mostly composed of phyllosilicate minerals containing variable amounts of water trapped in the mineral structure. _____ s are plastic due to particle size and geometry as well as water content, and become hard, brittle and non–plastic upon drying or firing. Depending on the soil's content in which it is found, _____ can appear in various colours from white to dull grey or brown to deep orange-red.

Exam Probability: **High**

28. *Answer choices:*

- a. Slate
- b. Cob
- c. Clay
- d. Boulder

Guidance: level 1

:: Management ::

_____ is a method of quality control which employs statistical methods to monitor and control a process. This helps to ensure that the process operates efficiently, producing more specification-conforming products with less waste . SPC can be applied to any process where the "conforming product" output can be measured. Key tools used in SPC include run charts, control charts, a focus on continuous improvement, and the design of experiments. An example of a process where SPC is applied is manufacturing lines.

Exam Probability: **Medium**

29. *Answer choices:*

(see index for correct answer)

- a. Line manager
- b. Top development
- c. Integrated master plan
- d. Real property administrator

Guidance: level 1

:: Outsourcing ::

_____ is an institutional procurement process that continuously improves and re-evaluates the purchasing activities of a company. In the services industry, _____ refers to a service solution, sometimes called a strategic partnership, which is specifically customized to meet the client's individual needs. In a production environment, it is often considered one component of supply chain management. Modern supply chain management professionals have placed emphasis on defining the distinct differences between _____ and procurement. Procurement operations support tactical day-to-day transactions such as issuing Purchase Orders to suppliers, whereas _____ represents to strategic planning, supplier development, contract negotiation, supply chain infrastructure, and outsourcing models.

Exam Probability: **High**

30. *Answer choices:*

(see index for correct answer)

- a. Harvey Nash
- b. Strategic sourcing
- c. Service level objective
- d. Government of Nova Scotia

Guidance: level 1

:: Project management ::

A _____ is a source or supply from which a benefit is produced and it has some utility. _____ s can broadly be classified upon their availability—they are classified into renewable and non-renewable _____ s.Examples of non renewable _____ s are coal ,crude oil natural gas nuclear energy etc. Examples of renewable _____ s are air,water,wind,solar energy etc. They can also be classified as actual and potential on the basis of level of development and use, on the basis of origin they can be classified as biotic and abiotic, and on the basis of their distribution, as ubiquitous and localized . An item becomes a _____ with time and developing technology. Typically, _____ s are materials, energy, services, staff, knowledge, or other assets that are transformed to produce benefit and in the process may be consumed or made unavailable. Benefits of _____ utilization may include increased wealth, proper functioning of a system, or enhanced well-being. From a human perspective a natural _____ is anything obtained from the environment to satisfy human needs and wants. From a broader biological or ecological perspective a _____ satisfies the needs of a living organism .

Exam Probability: **Medium**

31. *Answer choices:*

(see index for correct answer)

- a. Rolling Wave planning
- b. Product flow diagram
- c. Research program
- d. Resource

Guidance: level 1

:: Metal heat treatments ::

_____ is a group of industrial and metalworking processes used to alter the physical, and sometimes chemical, properties of a material. The most common application is metallurgical. Heat treatments are also used in the manufacture of many other materials, such as glass. Heat treatment involves the use of heating or chilling, normally to extreme temperatures, to achieve a desired result such as hardening or softening of a material. Heat treatment techniques include annealing, case hardening, precipitation strengthening, tempering, carburizing, normalizing and quenching. It is noteworthy that while the term heat treatment applies only to processes where the heating and cooling are done for the specific purpose of altering properties intentionally, heating and cooling often occur incidentally during other manufacturing processes such as hot forming or welding.

Exam Probability: **High**

32. *Answer choices:*

(see index for correct answer)

- a. Precipitation hardening
- b. Boriding
- c. Heat treating
- d. Tempering

Guidance: level 1

:: E-commerce ::

_____ is the activity of buying or selling of products on online services or over the Internet. Electronic commerce draws on technologies such as mobile commerce, electronic funds transfer, supply chain management, Internet marketing, online transaction processing, electronic data interchange , inventory management systems, and automated data collection systems.

Exam Probability: **High**

33. *Answer choices:*

(see index for correct answer)

- a. E-commerce
- b. The iBridge Network
- c. PayXpert
- d. Impulse economy

Guidance: level 1

:: Industrial organization ::

In economics, specifically general equilibrium theory, a perfect market is defined by several idealizing conditions, collectively called _____ . In theoretical models where conditions of _____ hold, it has been theoretically demonstrated that a market will reach an equilibrium in which the quantity supplied for every product or service, including labor, equals the quantity demanded at the current price. This equilibrium would be a Pareto optimum.

34. *Answer choices:*

- a. American system of manufacturing
- b. Perfect competition
- c. Organizational studies
- d. Switching barriers

Guidance: level 1

:: Consortia ::

A _____ is an association of two or more individuals, companies, organizations or governments with the objective of participating in a common activity or pooling their resources for achieving a common goal.

Exam Probability: **High**

35. *Answer choices:*

- a. Aero Propulsion Alliance
- b. Desertec
- c. SATURN Development Group
- d. Consortium

:: Project management ::

Rolling-wave planning is the process of project planning in waves as the project proceeds and later details become clearer; similar to the techniques used in agile software development approaches like Scrum..

Exam Probability: **Medium**

36. *Answer choices:*

(see index for correct answer)

- a. Rolling Wave planning
- b. Project manufacturing
- c. overdue
- d. Value breakdown structure

:: Unit operations ::

_____ is a discipline of thermal engineering that concerns the generation, use, conversion, and exchange of thermal energy between physical systems. _____ is classified into various mechanisms, such as thermal conduction, thermal convection, thermal radiation, and transfer of energy by phase changes. Engineers also consider the transfer of mass of differing chemical species, either cold or hot, to achieve _____ . While these mechanisms have distinct characteristics, they often occur simultaneously in the same system.

Exam Probability: **High**

37. *Answer choices:*

(see index for correct answer)

- a. Homogenization
- b. Sedimentation coefficient
- c. Heat transfer
- d. Solvent impregnated resin

Guidance: level 1

:: Materials ::

A _____ , also known as a feedstock, unprocessed material, or primary commodity, is a basic material that is used to produce goods, finished products, energy, or intermediate materials which are feedstock for future finished products. As feedstock, the term connotes these materials are bottleneck assets and are highly important with regard to producing other products. An example of this is crude oil, which is a _____ and a feedstock used in the production of industrial chemicals, fuels, plastics, and pharmaceutical goods; lumber is a _____ used to produce a variety of products including all types of furniture. The term " _____ " denotes materials in minimally processed or unprocessed in states; e.g., raw latex, crude oil, cotton, coal, raw biomass, iron ore, air, logs, or water i.e. "...any product of agriculture, forestry, fishing and any other mineral that is in its natural form or which has undergone the transformation required to prepare it for internationally marketing in substantial volumes."

Exam Probability: **Medium**

38. *Answer choices:*

(see index for correct answer)

- a. Raw material
- b. Biocompatible material
- c. Printing and writing paper
- d. Kovar

Guidance: level 1

:: Production and manufacturing ::

_____ is a concept in purchasing and project management for securing the quality and timely delivery of goods and components.

Exam Probability: **Low**

39. *Answer choices:*

(see index for correct answer)

- a. Detailed division of labor
- b. Expediting
- c. Low rate initial production
- d. Fieldbus Foundation

Guidance: level 1

:: Industrial processes ::

_____ is a technique involving the condensation of vapors and the return of this condensate to the system from which it originated. It is used in industrial and laboratory distillations. It is also used in chemistry to supply energy to reactions over a long period of time.

Exam Probability: **Medium**

40. *Answer choices:*

(see index for correct answer)

- a. Industrial wastewater treatment
- b. Process flowsheeting
- c. Curtain Coating
- d. Tumble finishing

Guidance: level 1

:: Commerce ::

A _____ is an employee within a company, business or other organization who is responsible at some level for buying or approving the acquisition of goods and services needed by the company. Responsible for buying the best quality products, goods and services for their company at the most competitive prices, _____ s work in a wide range of sectors for many different organizations. The position responsibilities may be the same as that of a buyer or purchasing agent, or may include wider supervisory or managerial responsibilities. A _____ may oversee the acquisition of materials needed for production, general supplies for offices and facilities, equipment, or construction contracts. A _____ often supervises purchasing agents and buyers, but in small companies the _____ may also be the purchasing agent or buyer. The _____ position may also carry the title "Procurement Manager" or in the public sector, "Procurement Officer". He or she can come from both an Engineering or Economics background.

Exam Probability: **Low**

41. *Answer choices:*

(see index for correct answer)

- a. Agio

- b. Barter
- c. Hong Kong Mercantile Exchange
- d. Trading post

Guidance: level 1

:: Costs ::

In process improvement efforts, _____ or cost of quality is a means to quantify the total cost of quality-related efforts and deficiencies. It was first described by Armand V. Feigenbaum in a 1956 Harvard Business Review article.

Exam Probability: **High**

42. *Answer choices:*

(see index for correct answer)

- a. Khozraschyot
- b. Road Logistics Costing in South Africa
- c. Quality costs
- d. Cost competitiveness of fuel sources

Guidance: level 1

:: Debt ::

_____ is the trust which allows one party to provide money or resources to another party wherein the second party does not reimburse the first party immediately , but promises either to repay or return those resources at a later date. In other words, _____ is a method of making reciprocity formal, legally enforceable, and extensible to a large group of unrelated people.

Exam Probability: **Medium**

43. *Answer choices:*

(see index for correct answer)

- a. Consumer debt
- b. Credit
- c. Perpetual subordinated debt
- d. Floating charge

Guidance: level 1

:: Management ::

In inventory management, _____ is the order quantity that minimizes the total holding costs and ordering costs. It is one of the oldest classical production scheduling models. The model was developed by Ford W. Harris in 1913, but R. H. Wilson, a consultant who applied it extensively, and K. Andler are given credit for their in-depth analysis.

Exam Probability: **Low**

44. *Answer choices:*

(see index for correct answer)

- a. Six phases of a big project
- b. PDCA
- c. Corporate foresight
- d. Economic order quantity

Guidance: level 1

:: Information technology management ::

_____ concerns a cycle of organizational activity: the acquisition of information from one or more sources, the custodianship and the distribution of that information to those who need it, and its ultimate disposition through archiving or deletion.

Exam Probability: **High**

45. *Answer choices:*

(see index for correct answer)

- a. Information management
- b. IT asset management
- c. Corporate Governance of ICT
- d. Change control

:: Management ::

A supply-chain network is an evolution of the basic supply chain. Due to rapid technological advancement, organisations with a basic supply chain can develop this chain into a more complex structure involving a higher level of interdependence and connectivity between more organisations, this constitutes a supply-chain network.

Exam Probability: **High**

46. *Answer choices:*

(see index for correct answer)

- a. Place management
- b. Automated decision support
- c. Concept of operations
- d. Supply chain network

:: Planning ::

_____ is a high level plan to achieve one or more goals under conditions of uncertainty. In the sense of the "art of the general," which included several subsets of skills including tactics, siegecraft, logistics etc., the term came into use in the 6th century C.E. in East Roman terminology, and was translated into Western vernacular languages only in the 18th century. From then until the 20th century, the word "_____" came to denote "a comprehensive way to try to pursue political ends, including the threat or actual use of force, in a dialectic of wills" in a military conflict, in which both adversaries interact.

Exam Probability: **Low**

47. *Answer choices:*

(see index for correct answer)

- a. Enterprise architecture planning
- b. Disruption
- c. Interactive planning
- d. Fragplan

Guidance: level 1

:: Management ::

_____ is a formal technique useful where many possible courses of action are competing for attention. In essence, the problem-solver estimates the benefit delivered by each action, then selects a number of the most effective actions that deliver a total benefit reasonably close to the maximal possible one.

48. *Answer choices:*

(see index for correct answer)

- a. Logistics support analysis
- b. Business plan
- c. Supply chain optimization
- d. Business model

Guidance: level 1

:: Information systems ::

_____ is the process of creating, sharing, using and managing the knowledge and information of an organisation. It refers to a multidisciplinary approach to achieving organisational objectives by making the best use of knowledge.

Exam Probability: **Low**

49. *Answer choices:*

(see index for correct answer)

- a. Expert system
- b. DIKW Pyramid
- c. Knowledge management

- d. Virtual information services

Guidance: level 1

:: Product management ::

_____ s, also known as Shewhart charts or process-behavior charts, are a statistical process control tool used to determine if a manufacturing or business process is in a state of control.

Exam Probability: **Medium**

50. *Answer choices:*
(see index for correct answer)

- a. Obsolescence
- b. Control chart
- c. Brand equity
- d. Brand extension

Guidance: level 1

:: Project management ::

A _____ is a type of bar chart that illustrates a project schedule, named after its inventor, Henry Gantt , who designed such a chart around the years 1910–1915. Modern _____ s also show the dependency relationships between activities and current schedule status.

Exam Probability: **High**

51. *Answer choices:*
(see index for correct answer)

- a. Confluence Project Management
- b. Master of Science in Project Management
- c. Concept note
- d. Management process

Guidance: level 1

:: Quality ::

_____ is a concept first outlined by quality expert Joseph M. Juran in publications, most notably Juran on _____ . Designing for quality and innovation is one of the three universal processes of the Juran Trilogy, in which Juran describes what is required to achieve breakthroughs in new products, services, and processes. Juran believed that quality could be planned, and that most quality crises and problems relate to the way in which quality was planned.

Exam Probability: **High**

52. *Answer choices:*

(see index for correct answer)

- a. Market Driven Quality
- b. Software Engineering Process Group
- c. Primary/secondary quality distinction
- d. Quality by Design

Guidance: level 1

:: Management ::

_____ is a process by which entities review the quality of all factors involved in production. ISO 9000 defines _____ as "A part of quality management focused on fulfilling quality requirements".

Exam Probability: **Medium**

53. *Answer choices:*

(see index for correct answer)

- a. Project team builder
- b. Quality control
- c. Sales outsourcing
- d. Operations management

Guidance: level 1

:: Industrial equipment ::

_____ s are heat exchangers typically used to provide heat to the bottom of industrial distillation columns. They boil the liquid from the bottom of a distillation column to generate vapors which are returned to the column to drive the distillation separation. The heat supplied to the column by the _____ at the bottom of the column is removed by the condenser at the top of the column.

Exam Probability: **Low**

54. *Answer choices:*
(see index for correct answer)

- a. Reboiler
- b. Derrick
- c. Multiple-effect evaporator
- d. Glass crusher

Guidance: level 1

:: Production and manufacturing ::

Automatic _____ in continuous production processes is a combination of control engineering and chemical engineering disciplines that uses industrial control systems to achieve a production level of consistency, economy and safety which could not be achieved purely by human manual control. It is implemented widely in industries such as oil refining, pulp and paper manufacturing, chemical processing and power generating plants.

Exam Probability: **Low**

55. *Answer choices:*

(see index for correct answer)

- a. Rolled throughput yield
- b. Process control
- c. Digital prototyping
- d. Highly accelerated stress audit

Guidance: level 1

:: Outsourcing ::

_____ is the practice of sourcing from the global market for goods and services across geopolitical boundaries. _____ often aims to exploit global efficiencies in the delivery of a product or service. These efficiencies include low cost skilled labor, low cost raw material and other economic factors like tax breaks and low trade tariffs. A large number of Information Technology projects and Services, including IS Applications and Mobile Apps and database services are outsourced globally to countries like Pakistan and India for more economical pricing.

56. *Answer choices:*

(see index for correct answer)

- a. Toronto-Dominion Bank
- b. Government of Nova Scotia
- c. Service-level agreement
- d. Outsourcing of animation

Guidance: level 1

:: Project management ::

_____ is the right to exercise power, which can be formalized by a state and exercised by way of judges, appointed executives of government, or the ecclesiastical or priestly appointed representatives of a God or other deities.

Exam Probability: **High**

57. *Answer choices:*

(see index for correct answer)

- a. Critical path drag
- b. Hammock activity
- c. Research program

- d. Authority

Guidance: level 1

:: Management ::

_____ is the identification, evaluation, and prioritization of risks followed by coordinated and economical application of resources to minimize, monitor, and control the probability or impact of unfortunate events or to maximize the realization of opportunities.

Exam Probability: **Low**

58. *Answer choices:*

(see index for correct answer)

- a. Adhocracy
- b. Crisis management
- c. Risk management
- d. Clean-sheet review

Guidance: level 1

:: Business process ::

A _____ or business method is a collection of related, structured activities or tasks by people or equipment which in a specific sequence produce a service or product for a particular customer or customers. _____ es occur at all organizational levels and may or may not be visible to the customers. A _____ may often be visualized as a flowchart of a sequence of activities with interleaving decision points or as a process matrix of a sequence of activities with relevance rules based on data in the process. The benefits of using _____ es include improved customer satisfaction and improved agility for reacting to rapid market change. Process-oriented organizations break down the barriers of structural departments and try to avoid functional silos.

Exam Probability: **High**

59. *Answer choices:*
(see index for correct answer)

- a. Business Process Modeling Language
- b. Business process
- c. International business development
- d. Steering committee

Guidance: level 1

Commerce

Commerce relates to "the exchange of goods and services, especially on a large scale." It includes legal, economic, political, social, cultural and technological systems that operate in any country or internationally.

:: Payment systems ::

_____ s are part of a payment system issued by financial institutions, such as a bank, to a customer that enables its owner to access the funds in the customer`s designated bank accounts, or through a credit account and make payments by electronic funds transfer and access automated teller machines . Such cards are known by a variety of names including bank cards, ATM cards, MAC , client cards, key cards or cash cards.

Exam Probability: **Low**

1. *Answer choices:*

- a. Money transmitter
- b. Uniform Customs and Practice for Documentary Credits
- c. Teller
- d. CNG Processing A/S

Guidance: level 1

:: Auctioneering ::

An _____ is a process of buying and selling goods or services by offering them up for bid, taking bids, and then selling the item to the highest bidder. The open ascending price _____ is arguably the most common form of _____ in use today. Participants bid openly against one another, with each subsequent bid required to be higher than the previous bid. An _____ eer may announce prices, bidders may call out their bids themselves , or bids may be submitted electronically with the highest current bid publicly displayed. In a Dutch _____ , the _____ eer begins with a high asking price for some quantity of like items; the price is lowered until a participant is willing to accept the _____ eer`s price for some quantity of the goods in the lot or until the seller's reserve price is met. While _____ s are most associated in the public imagination with the sale of antiques, paintings, rare collectibles and expensive wines, _____ s are also used for commodities, livestock, radio spectrum and used cars. In economic theory, an _____ may refer to any mechanism or set of trading rules for exchange.

2. *Answer choices:*

(see index for correct answer)

- a. Camden auction
- b. Virginity auction
- c. Auction
- d. How Much Wood Would a Woodchuck Chuck

Guidance: level 1

:: Cash flow ::

_____ s are narrowly interconnected with the concepts of value, interest rate and liquidity. A _____ that shall happen on a future day tN can be transformed into a _____ of the same value in t0.

3. *Answer choices:*

(see index for correct answer)

- a. Operating cash flow
- b. Cash flow forecasting
- c. Cash carrier
- d. Cash flow

:: Management ::

_____ is a process by which entities review the quality of all factors involved in production. ISO 9000 defines _____ as "A part of quality management focused on fulfilling quality requirements".

Exam Probability: **Medium**

4. *Answer choices:*

(see index for correct answer)

- a. Social business model
- b. Quality control
- c. Success-oriented management
- d. Action item

:: Supply chain management ::

A _____ is a type of auction in which the traditional roles of buyer and seller are reversed. Thus, there is one buyer and many potential sellers. In an ordinary auction , buyers compete to obtain goods or services by offering increasingly higher prices. In contrast, in a _____ , the sellers compete to obtain business from the buyer and prices will typically decrease as the sellers underbid each other.

Exam Probability: **Medium**

5. *Answer choices:*

(see index for correct answer)

- a. Reverse auction
- b. Enterprise carbon accounting
- c. DR-DP-Matrix
- d. ThoughtSpeed Corporation

Guidance: level 1

:: ::

_____ or standardisation is the process of implementing and developing technical standards based on the consensus of different parties that include firms, users, interest groups, standards organizations and governments. _____ can help maximize compatibility, interoperability, safety, repeatability, or quality. It can also facilitate commoditization of formerly custom processes. In social sciences, including economics, the idea of _____ is close to the solution for a coordination problem, a situation in which all parties can realize mutual gains, but only by making mutually consistent decisions. This view includes the case of "spontaneous _____ processes", to produce de facto standards.

Exam Probability: **Medium**

6. *Answer choices:*

(see index for correct answer)

- a. similarity-attraction theory
- b. Standardization
- c. process perspective
- d. deep-level diversity

Guidance: level 1

:: Mereology ::

_____ , in the abstract, is what belongs to or with something, whether as an attribute or as a component of said thing. In the context of this article, it is one or more components , whether physical or incorporeal, of a person's estate; or so belonging to, as in being owned by, a person or jointly a group of people or a legal entity like a corporation or even a society. Depending on the nature of the _____ , an owner of _____ has the right to consume, alter, share, redefine, rent, mortgage, pawn, sell, exchange, transfer, give away or destroy it, or to exclude others from doing these things, as well as to perhaps abandon it; whereas regardless of the nature of the _____ , the owner thereof has the right to properly use it , or at the very least exclusively keep it.

Exam Probability: **Medium**

7. *Answer choices:*

(see index for correct answer)

- a. Property
- b. Mereological essentialism
- c. Mereology
- d. Mereotopology

Guidance: level 1

:: Production economics ::

In economics and related disciplines, a _____ is a cost in making any economic trade when participating in a market.

8. *Answer choices:*

(see index for correct answer)

- a. Peer production
- b. Hicks-neutral technical change
- c. Division of work
- d. Transaction cost

Guidance: level 1

:: ::

_____ is an abstract concept of management of complex systems according to a set of rules and trends. In systems theory, these types of rules exist in various fields of biology and society, but the term has slightly different meanings according to context. For example.

Exam Probability: **Medium**

9. *Answer choices:*

(see index for correct answer)

- a. hierarchical perspective
- b. corporate values
- c. co-culture

- d. Regulation

Guidance: level 1

:: E-commerce ::

A _____ is a hosted service offering that acts as an intermediary between business partners sharing standards based or proprietary data via shared business processes. The offered service is referred to as " _____ services".

Exam Probability: **Low**

10. *Answer choices:*
(see index for correct answer)

- a. Discovery shopping
- b. The Cluetrain Manifesto
- c. Value-added network
- d. Online Shopping in Bangladesh

Guidance: level 1

:: ::

_____ is the administration of an organization, whether it is a business, a not-for-profit organization, or government body. _____ includes the activities of setting the strategy of an organization and coordinating the efforts of its employees to accomplish its objectives through the application of available resources, such as financial, natural, technological, and human resources. The term "_____" may also refer to those people who manage an organization.

Exam Probability: **Medium**

11. *Answer choices:*

(see index for correct answer)

- a. levels of analysis
- b. co-culture
- c. Sarbanes-Oxley act of 2002
- d. hierarchical perspective

Guidance: level 1

:: Workplace ::

_____ is asystematic determination of a subject's merit, worth and significance, using criteria governed by a set of standards. It can assist an organization, program, design, project or any other intervention or initiative to assess any aim, realisable concept/proposal, or any alternative, to help in decision-making; or to ascertain the degree of achievement or value in regard to the aim and objectives and results of any such action that has been completed. The primary purpose of _____ , in addition to gaining insight into prior or existing initiatives, is to enable reflection and assist in the identification of future change.

Exam Probability: **Medium**

12. *Answer choices:*

(see index for correct answer)

- a. Toxic workplace
- b. Evaluation
- c. Hostile environment sexual harassment
- d. Workplace democracy

Guidance: level 1

:: ::

_____ , in general use, is a devotion and faithfulness to a nation, cause, philosophy, country, group, or person. Philosophers disagree on what can be an object of _____ , as some argue that _____ is strictly interpersonal and only another human being can be the object of _____ . The definition of _____ in law and political science is the fidelity of an individual to a nation, either one`s nation of birth, or one`s declared home nation by oath .

Exam Probability: **Low**

13. *Answer choices:*

(see index for correct answer)

- a. surface-level diversity
- b. deep-level diversity
- c. Loyalty
- d. functional perspective

Guidance: level 1

:: Cryptography ::

In cryptography, _____ is the process of encoding a message or information in such a way that only authorized parties can access it and those who are not authorized cannot. _____ does not itself prevent interference, but denies the intelligible content to a would-be interceptor. In an _____ scheme, the intended information or message, referred to as plaintext, is encrypted using an _____ algorithm – a cipher – generating ciphertext that can be read only if decrypted. For technical reasons, an _____ scheme usually uses a pseudo-random _____ key generated by an algorithm. It is in principle possible to decrypt the message without possessing the key, but, for a well-designed _____ scheme, considerable computational resources and skills are required. An authorized recipient can easily decrypt the message with the key provided by the originator to recipients but not to unauthorized users.

Exam Probability: **Low**

14. *Answer choices:*

(see index for correct answer)

- a. plaintext
- b. Encryption
- c. cryptosystem
- d. Electronic Signature

Guidance: level 1

:: ::

In mathematics, computer science and operations research, mathematical optimization or mathematical programming is the selection of a best element from some set of available alternatives.

Exam Probability: **High**

15. *Answer choices:*

(see index for correct answer)

- a. cultural
- b. deep-level diversity
- c. Sarbanes-Oxley act of 2002
- d. Optimum

Guidance: level 1

:: E-commerce ::

_____ Inc. was an electronic money corporation founded by David Chaum in 1989. _____ transactions were unique in that they were anonymous due to a number of cryptographic protocols developed by its founder. _____ declared bankruptcy in 1998, and subsequently sold its assets to eCash Technologies, another digital currency company, which was acquired by InfoSpace on Feb. 19, 2002.

Exam Probability: **High**

16. *Answer choices:*

(see index for correct answer)

- a. DigiCash
- b. XIPWIRE
- c. Electronic trading
- d. Advance ship notice

Guidance: level 1

:: International trade ::

A _____ is a document issued by a carrier to acknowledge receipt of cargo for shipment. Although the term historically related only to carriage by sea, a _____ may today be used for any type of carriage of goods.

Exam Probability: **Low**

17. *Answer choices:*

(see index for correct answer)

- a. Hosuk Lee-Makiyama
- b. Park In-chon
- c. Silk Road
- d. Hong Kong Economic and Trade Office

Guidance: level 1

:: Industry ::

_____ , also known as flow production or continuous production, is the production of large amounts of standardized products, including and especially on assembly lines. Together with job production and batch production, it is one of the three main production methods.

Exam Probability: **High**

18. *Answer choices:*
(see index for correct answer)

- a. Exposure action value
- b. Mass production
- c. Sunset industry
- d. Takt time

Guidance: level 1

:: Business terms ::

_____ ning is an organization's process of defining its strategy, or direction, and making decisions on allocating its resources to pursue this strategy. It may also extend to control mechanisms for guiding the implementation of the strategy. _____ ning became prominent in corporations during the 1960s and remains an important aspect of strategic management. It is executed by _____ ners or strategists, who involve many parties and research sources in their analysis of the organization and its relationship to the environment in which it competes.

Exam Probability: **Medium**

19. *Answer choices:*

(see index for correct answer)

- a. Strategic plan
- b. granular
- c. Owner Controlled Insurance Program
- d. back office

Guidance: level 1

:: ::

Advertising is a marketing communication that employs an openly sponsored, non-personal message to promote or sell a product, service or idea. Sponsors of advertising are typically businesses wishing to promote their products or services. Advertising is differentiated from public relations in that an advertiser pays for and has control over the message. It differs from personal selling in that the message is non-personal, i.e., not directed to a particular individual.Advertising is communicated through various mass media, including traditional media such as newspapers, magazines, television, radio, outdoor advertising or direct mail; and new media such as search results, blogs, social media, websites or text messages. The actual presentation of the message in a medium is referred to as an _____ , or "ad" or advert for short.

Exam Probability: **High**

20. *Answer choices:*

(see index for correct answer)

- a. personal values
- b. co-culture
- c. Advertisement
- d. empathy

Guidance: level 1

:: Management ::

Logistics is generally the detailed organization and implementation of a complex operation. In a general business sense, logistics is the management of the flow of things between the point of origin and the point of consumption in order to meet requirements of customers or corporations. The resources managed in logistics may include tangible goods such as materials, equipment, and supplies, as well as food and other consumable items. The logistics of physical items usually involves the integration of information flow, materials handling, production, packaging, inventory, transportation, warehousing, and often security.

Exam Probability: **Medium**

21. *Answer choices:*

(see index for correct answer)

- a. Twelve leverage points
- b. Social risk management
- c. Allegiance
- d. Quick response manufacturing

Guidance: level 1

:: Computer access control ::

_____ is the act of confirming the truth of an attribute of a single piece of data claimed true by an entity. In contrast with identification, which refers to the act of stating or otherwise indicating a claim purportedly attesting to a person or thing's identity, _____ is the process of actually confirming that identity. It might involve confirming the identity of a person by validating their identity documents, verifying the authenticity of a website with a digital certificate, determining the age of an artifact by carbon dating, or ensuring that a product is what its packaging and labeling claim to be. In other words, _____ often involves verifying the validity of at least one form of identification.

Exam Probability: **Low**

22. *Answer choices:*

(see index for correct answer)

- a. Initiative For Open Authentication
- b. Identity provider
- c. Authentication
- d. Directory service

Guidance: level 1

:: ::

_____ is getting a diploma or academic degree or the ceremony that is sometimes associated with it, in which students become graduates. The date of _____ is often called _____ day. The _____ ceremony itself is also called commencement, convocation or invocation.

23. *Answer choices:*

(see index for correct answer)

- a. personal values
- b. Graduation
- c. similarity-attraction theory
- d. information systems assessment

Guidance: level 1

:: Stock market ::

The _____ of a corporation is all of the shares into which ownership of the corporation is divided. In American English, the shares are commonly known as " _____ s". A single share of the _____ represents fractional ownership of the corporation in proportion to the total number of shares. This typically entitles the _____ holder to that fraction of the company's earnings, proceeds from liquidation of assets , or voting power, often dividing these up in proportion to the amount of money each _____ holder has invested. Not all _____ is necessarily equal, as certain classes of _____ may be issued for example without voting rights, with enhanced voting rights, or with a certain priority to receive profits or liquidation proceeds before or after other classes of shareholders.

Exam Probability: **High**

24. *Answer choices:*

(see index for correct answer)

- a. Stock
- b. Common stock
- c. Red chip
- d. Central limit order book

Guidance: level 1

:: Income ::

In business and accounting, net income is an entity's income minus cost of goods sold, expenses and taxes for an accounting period. It is computed as the residual of all revenues and gains over all expenses and losses for the period, and has also been defined as the net increase in shareholders' equity that results from a company's operations. In the context of the presentation of financial statements, the IFRS Foundation defines net income as synonymous with profit and loss. The difference between revenue and the cost of making a product or providing a service, before deducting overheads, payroll, taxation, and interest payments. This is different from operating income .

Exam Probability: **Medium**

25. *Answer choices:*

(see index for correct answer)

- a. Bottom line
- b. Property investment calculator
- c. Income earner

- d. Private income

Guidance: level 1

:: Market research ::

_____ is an organized effort to gather information about target markets or customers. It is a very important component of business strategy. The term is commonly interchanged with marketing research; however, expert practitioners may wish to draw a distinction, in that marketing research is concerned specifically about marketing processes, while _____ is concerned specifically with markets.

Exam Probability: **Low**

26. *Answer choices:*

(see index for correct answer)

- a. Consumer neuroscience
- b. Market research and opinion polling in China
- c. Confirmit
- d. Market research

Guidance: level 1

:: Monopoly (economics) ::

A _____ exists when a specific person or enterprise is the only supplier of a particular commodity. This contrasts with a monopsony which relates to a single entity's control of a market to purchase a good or service, and with oligopoly which consists of a few sellers dominating a market. Monopolies are thus characterized by a lack of economic competition to produce the good or service, a lack of viable substitute goods, and the possibility of a high _____ price well above the seller's marginal cost that leads to a high _____ profit. The verb monopolise or monopolize refers to the process by which a company gains the ability to raise prices or exclude competitors. In economics, a _____ is a single seller. In law, a _____ is a business entity that has significant market power, that is, the power to charge overly high prices. Although monopolies may be big businesses, size is not a characteristic of a _____ . A small business may still have the power to raise prices in a small industry .

Exam Probability: **Medium**

27. *Answer choices:*

(see index for correct answer)

- a. Chamberlinian monopolistic competition
- b. Tesco Town
- c. Monopoly
- d. Regulatory economics

Guidance: level 1

:: Data interchange standards ::

_____ is the concept of businesses electronically communicating information that was traditionally communicated on paper, such as purchase orders and invoices. Technical standards for EDI exist to facilitate parties transacting such instruments without having to make special arrangements.

Exam Probability: **Medium**

28. *Answer choices:*

(see index for correct answer)

- a. Data Interchange Standards Association
- b. Electronic data interchange
- c. Uniform Communication Standard
- d. Domain Application Protocol

Guidance: level 1

:: E-commerce ::

_____ , cybersecurity or information technology security is the protection of computer systems from theft or damage to their hardware, software or electronic data, as well as from disruption or misdirection of the services they provide.

Exam Probability: **Medium**

29. *Answer choices:*

(see index for correct answer)

- a. Computer security
- b. XBRL GL
- c. Business-to-manager
- d. Discovery shopping

Guidance: level 1

:: ::

_____ is the study and management of exchange relationships. _____ is the business process of creating relationships with and satisfying customers. With its focus on the customer, _____ is one of the premier components of business management.

Exam Probability: **High**

30. *Answer choices:*

(see index for correct answer)

- a. Character
- b. Sarbanes-Oxley act of 2002
- c. hierarchical perspective
- d. interpersonal communication

Guidance: level 1

:: Information technology ::

_____ is the use of computers to store, retrieve, transmit, and manipulate data, or information, often in the context of a business or other enterprise. IT is considered to be a subset of information and communications technology . An _____ system is generally an information system, a communications system or, more specifically speaking, a computer system – including all hardware, software and peripheral equipment – operated by a limited group of users.

Exam Probability: **Medium**

31. *Answer choices:*

(see index for correct answer)

- a. Open collaboration
- b. Information and communications technology
- c. Infocommunications
- d. Information technology

Guidance: level 1

:: Regulators ::

A _____ is a public authority or government agency responsible for exercising autonomous authority over some area of human activity in a regulatory or supervisory capacity. An independent _____ is a _____ that is independent from other branches or arms of the government.

Exam Probability: **Medium**

32. *Answer choices:*

(see index for correct answer)

- a. Energy Resources Conservation Board
- b. Independent regulatory agencies in Turkey
- c. Croatian Regulatory Authority for Network Industries
- d. Alberta Energy Regulator

Guidance: level 1

:: Commerce ::

_____ , also known as duty _____ is defined by the United States Customs and Border Protection as the refund of certain duties, internal and revenue taxes and certain fees collected upon the importation of goods. Such refunds are only allowed upon the exportation or destruction of goods under U.S. Customs and Border Protection supervision. Duty _____ is an export promotions program sanctioned by the World Trade Organization and allows the refund of certain duties taxes and fees paid upon importation which was established in 1789 in order to promote U.S. innovation and manufacturing across the global market.

33. *Answer choices:*

(see index for correct answer)

- a. Kiosk
- b. Drawback
- c. Worldwide Centers of Commerce
- d. Shipping list

Guidance: level 1

:: Service industries ::

_____ are the economic services provided by the finance industry, which encompasses a broad range of businesses that manage money, including credit unions, banks, credit-card companies, insurance companies, accountancy companies, consumer-finance companies, stock brokerages, investment funds, individual managers and some government-sponsored enterprises. _____ companies are present in all economically developed geographic locations and tend to cluster in local, national, regional and international financial centers such as London, New York City, and Tokyo.

Exam Probability: **Low**

34. *Answer choices:*

(see index for correct answer)

- a. Allotment
- b. Financial services
- c. Tourism
- d. Financial services in Japan

Guidance: level 1

:: Economic globalization ::

_____ is an agreement in which one company hires another company to be responsible for a planned or existing activity that is or could be done internally,and sometimes involves transferring employees and assets from one firm to another.

Exam Probability: **High**

35. *Answer choices:*

(see index for correct answer)

- a. reshoring
- b. Outsourcing

Guidance: level 1

:: International trade ::

An _____ is a good brought into a jurisdiction, especially across a national border, from an external source. The party bringing in the good is called an _____ er. An _____ in the receiving country is an export from the sending country. _____ ation and exportation are the defining financial transactions of international trade.

Exam Probability: **Medium**

36. *Answer choices:*

(see index for correct answer)

- a. Import
- b. Extraterritorial income exclusion
- c. Trade barrier
- d. Trade in services

Guidance: level 1

:: Strategic alliances ::

A _____ is an agreement between two or more parties to pursue a set of agreed upon objectives needed while remaining independent organizations. A _____ will usually fall short of a legal partnership entity, agency, or corporate affiliate relationship. Typically, two companies form a _____ when each possesses one or more business assets or have expertise that will help the other by enhancing their businesses. _____ s can develop in outsourcing relationships where the parties desire to achieve long-term win-win benefits and innovation based on mutually desired outcomes.

37. *Answer choices:*

(see index for correct answer)

- a. Management contract
- b. Defensive termination
- c. Strategic alliance
- d. Cross-licensing

Guidance: level 1

:: ::

The _____ is a political and economic union of 28 member states that are located primarily in Europe. It has an area of 4,475,757 km2 and an estimated population of about 513 million. The EU has developed an internal single market through a standardised system of laws that apply in all member states in those matters, and only those matters, where members have agreed to act as one. EU policies aim to ensure the free movement of people, goods, services and capital within the internal market, enact legislation in justice and home affairs and maintain common policies on trade, agriculture, fisheries and regional development. For travel within the Schengen Area, passport controls have been abolished. A monetary union was established in 1999 and came into full force in 2002 and is composed of 19 EU member states which use the euro currency.

38. *Answer choices:*

(see index for correct answer)

- a. deep-level diversity
- b. levels of analysis
- c. Character
- d. co-culture

Guidance: level 1

:: Summary statistics ::

_____ is the number of occurrences of a repeating event per unit of time. It is also referred to as temporal _____ , which emphasizes the contrast to spatial _____ and angular _____ . The period is the duration of time of one cycle in a repeating event, so the period is the reciprocal of the _____ . For example: if a newborn baby's heart beats at a _____ of 120 times a minute, its period—the time interval between beats—is half a second . _____ is an important parameter used in science and engineering to specify the rate of oscillatory and vibratory phenomena, such as mechanical vibrations, audio signals , radio waves, and light.

Exam Probability: **Low**

39. *Answer choices:*

(see index for correct answer)

- a. Frequency
- b. Generalized entropy index

- c. Quartile
- d. Multiple of the median

Guidance: level 1

:: Investment ::

In finance, the benefit from an _____ is called a return. The return may consist of a gain realised from the sale of property or an _____ , unrealised capital appreciation , or _____ income such as dividends, interest, rental income etc., or a combination of capital gain and income. The return may also include currency gains or losses due to changes in foreign currency exchange rates.

Exam Probability: **High**

40. *Answer choices:*

(see index for correct answer)

- a. Tactical asset allocation
- b. Guaranteed investment contract
- c. Investment
- d. Gearing ratio

Guidance: level 1

:: Price fixing convictions ::

_____ is the flag carrier airline of the United Kingdom, headquartered at Waterside, Harmondsworth. It is the second largest airline in the United Kingdom, based on fleet size and passengers carried, behind easyJet. The airline is based in Waterside near its main hub at London Heathrow Airport. In January 2011 BA merged with Iberia, creating the International Airlines Group , a holding company registered in Madrid, Spain. IAG is the world's third-largest airline group in terms of annual revenue and the second-largest in Europe. It is listed on the London Stock Exchange and in the FTSE 100 Index. _____ is the first passenger airline to have generated more than $1 billion on a single air route in a year .

Exam Probability: **High**

41. *Answer choices:*

(see index for correct answer)

- a. Archer Daniels Midland
- b. Asahi Glass Co.
- c. Christmas tree production in Denmark
- d. British Airways

Guidance: level 1

:: ::

_____ is a means of protection from financial loss. It is a form of risk management, primarily used to hedge against the risk of a contingent or uncertain loss

42. *Answer choices:*

(see index for correct answer)

- a. Insurance
- b. hierarchical perspective
- c. imperative
- d. personal values

Guidance: level 1

:: Production economics ::

In microeconomics, _____ are the cost advantages that enterprises obtain due to their scale of operation , with cost per unit of output decreasing with increasing scale.

43. *Answer choices:*

(see index for correct answer)

- a. Foundations of Economic Analysis
- b. Marginal rate of technical substitution
- c. Split-off point
- d. Economies of scale

:: ::

> _____ is a process whereby a person assumes the parenting of another, usually a child, from that person's biological or legal parent or parents.
> Legal _____ s permanently transfers all rights and responsibilities, along with filiation, from the biological parent or parents.

Exam Probability: **High**

44. *Answer choices:*

(see index for correct answer)

- a. hierarchical perspective
- b. Adoption
- c. interpersonal communication
- d. corporate values

:: ::

A _____ manages, commands, directs, or regulates the behavior of other devices or systems using control loops. It can range from a single home heating controller using a thermostat controlling a domestic boiler to large Industrial _____ s which are used for controlling processes or machines.

Exam Probability: **Low**

45. *Answer choices:*

(see index for correct answer)

- a. functional perspective
- b. deep-level diversity
- c. Sarbanes-Oxley act of 2002
- d. imperative

Guidance: level 1

:: ::

In a supply chain, a _____ , or a seller, is an enterprise that contributes goods or services. Generally, a supply chain _____ manufactures inventory/stock items and sells them to the next link in the chain. Today, these terms refer to a supplier of any good or service.

Exam Probability: **Medium**

46. *Answer choices:*

- a. Character
- b. cultural
- c. Vendor
- d. deep-level diversity

Guidance: level 1

:: Marketing ::

_____ or stock control can be broadly defined as "the activity of checking a shop's stock." However, a more focused definition takes into account the more science-based, methodical practice of not only verifying a business' inventory but also focusing on the many related facets of inventory management "within an organisation to meet the demand placed upon that business economically." Other facets of _____ include supply chain management, production control, financial flexibility, and customer satisfaction. At the root of _____ , however, is the _____ problem, which involves determining when to order, how much to order, and the logistics of those decisions.

Exam Probability: **Medium**

47. *Answer choices:*

- a. Product bundling
- b. Franchise fee

- c. Consumer culture theory
- d. Positioning

Guidance: level 1

:: ::

_____ is an American restaurant chain and international franchise which was founded in 1958 by Dan and Frank Carney. The company is known for its Italian-American cuisine menu, including pizza and pasta, as well as side dishes and desserts. _____ has 18,431 restaurants worldwide as of December 31, 2018, making it the world`s largest pizza chain in terms of locations. It is a subsidiary of Yum! Brands, Inc., one of the world`s largest restaurant companies.

Exam Probability: **Medium**

48. *Answer choices:*

(see index for correct answer)

- a. hierarchical
- b. co-culture
- c. Sarbanes-Oxley act of 2002
- d. personal values

Guidance: level 1

:: Production economics ::

In economics long run is a theoretical concept where all markets are in equilibrium, and all prices and quantities have fully adjusted and are in equilibrium. The long run contrasts with the _____ where there are some constraints and markets are not fully in equilibrium.

Exam Probability: **Medium**

49. *Answer choices:*

(see index for correct answer)

- a. Post-Fordism
- b. Productive capacity
- c. Short run
- d. Split-off point

Guidance: level 1

:: Commercial item transport and distribution ::

Wholesaling or distributing is the sale of goods or merchandise to retailers; to industrial, commercial, institutional, or other professional business users; or to other _____ rs and related subordinated services. In general, it is the sale of goods to anyone other than a standard consumer.

Exam Probability: **Medium**

50. *Answer choices:*

(see index for correct answer)

- a. Wholesale
- b. Commodity Classification Automated Tracking System
- c. Sea protest
- d. Port centric logistics

Guidance: level 1

:: ::

_____ is the practical authority granted to a legal body to administer justice within a defined field of responsibility, e.g., Michigan tax law. In federations like the United States, areas of _____ apply to local, state, and federal levels; e.g. the court has _____ to apply federal law.

Exam Probability: **Medium**

51. *Answer choices:*

(see index for correct answer)

- a. Sarbanes-Oxley act of 2002
- b. interpersonal communication
- c. Jurisdiction
- d. empathy

:: ::

A trade fair is an exhibition organized so that companies in a specific industry can showcase and demonstrate their latest products and services, meet with industry partners and customers, study activities of rivals, and examine recent market trends and opportunities. In contrast to consumer fairs, only some trade fairs are open to the public, while others can only be attended by company representatives and members of the press, therefore _____ s are classified as either "public" or "trade only". A few fairs are hybrids of the two; one example is the Frankfurt Book Fair, which is trade only for its first three days and open to the general public on its final two days. They are held on a continuing basis in virtually all markets and normally attract companies from around the globe. For example, in the U.S., there are currently over 10,000 _____ s held every year, and several online directories have been established to help organizers, attendees, and marketers identify appropriate events.

Exam Probability: **High**

52. *Answer choices:*

(see index for correct answer)

- a. empathy
- b. cultural
- c. deep-level diversity
- d. personal values

:: Consumer theory ::

A _____ is a technical term in psychology, economics and philosophy usually used in relation to choosing between alternatives. For example, someone prefers A over B if they would rather choose A than B.

Exam Probability: **Medium**

53. *Answer choices:*

(see index for correct answer)

- a. Income elasticity of demand
- b. Preference
- c. Hicksian demand function
- d. Engel curve

Guidance: level 1

:: ::

The _____ is a U.S. business-focused, English-language international daily newspaper based in New York City. The Journal, along with its Asian and European editions, is published six days a week by Dow Jones & Company, a division of News Corp. The newspaper is published in the broadsheet format and online. The Journal has been printed continuously since its inception on July 8, 1889, by Charles Dow, Edward Jones, and Charles Bergstresser.

54. *Answer choices:*

(see index for correct answer)

- a. empathy
- b. Wall Street Journal
- c. functional perspective
- d. Character

Guidance: level 1

:: Stock market ::

_____ is freedom from, or resilience against, potential harm caused by others. Beneficiaries of _____ may be of persons and social groups, objects and institutions, ecosystems or any other entity or phenomenon vulnerable to unwanted change by its environment.

Exam Probability: **Medium**

55. *Answer choices:*

(see index for correct answer)

- a. Security
- b. Wash sale
- c. Box spread

- d. Event-driven investing

Guidance: level 1

:: Business ethics ::

_____ is a type of harassment technique that relates to a sexual nature and the unwelcome or inappropriate promise of rewards in exchange for sexual favors. _____ includes a range of actions from mild transgressions to sexual abuse or assault. Harassment can occur in many different social settings such as the workplace, the home, school, churches, etc. Harassers or victims may be of any gender.

Exam Probability: **Medium**

56. *Answer choices:*
(see index for correct answer)

- a. Sexual harassment
- b. Salad Oil Scandal
- c. Terror-free investing
- d. Anatomy of Greed

Guidance: level 1

:: ::

In international relations, _____ is – from the perspective of governments – a voluntary transfer of resources from one country to another.

Exam Probability: **Medium**

57. *Answer choices:*

(see index for correct answer)

- a. corporate values
- b. Aid
- c. co-culture
- d. Character

Guidance: level 1

:: Decision theory ::

A _____ is a deliberate system of principles to guide decisions and achieve rational outcomes. A _____ is a statement of intent, and is implemented as a procedure or protocol. Policies are generally adopted by a governance body within an organization. Policies can assist in both subjective and objective decision making. Policies to assist in subjective decision making usually assist senior management with decisions that must be based on the relative merits of a number of factors, and as a result are often hard to test objectively, e.g. work-life balance _____ . In contrast policies to assist in objective decision making are usually operational in nature and can be objectively tested, e.g. password _____ .

58. *Answer choices:*

(see index for correct answer)

- a. Utility
- b. Homothetic preferences
- c. Policy
- d. Applied information economics

Guidance: level 1

:: ::

_____ characterises the behaviour of a system or model whose components interact in multiple ways and follow local rules, meaning there is no reasonable higher instruction to define the various possible interactions.

59. *Answer choices:*

(see index for correct answer)

- a. interpersonal communication
- b. co-culture
- c. Complexity
- d. open system

Business ethics

Business ethics (also known as corporate ethics) is a form of applied ethics or professional ethics, that examines ethical principles and moral or ethical problems that can arise in a business environment. It applies to all aspects of business conduct and is relevant to the conduct of individuals and entire organizations. These ethics originate from individuals, organizational statements or from the legal system. These norms, values, ethical, and unethical practices are what is used to guide business. They help those businesses maintain a better connection with their stakeholders.

:: Television terminology ::

A _____ organization , also known as a non-business entity, not-for-profit organization, or _____ institution, is dedicated to furthering a particular social cause or advocating for a shared point of view. In economic terms, it is an organization that uses its surplus of the revenues to further achieve its ultimate objective, rather than distributing its income to the organization's shareholders, leaders, or members. _____ s are tax exempt or charitable, meaning they do not pay income tax on the money that they receive for their organization. They can operate in religious, scientific, research, or educational settings.

Exam Probability: **Low**

1. *Answer choices:*

(see index for correct answer)

- a. Nonprofit
- b. Satellite television
- c. not-for-profit
- d. distance learning

Guidance: level 1

:: ::

The Federal National Mortgage Association , commonly known as _____ , is a United States government-sponsored enterprise and, since 1968, a publicly traded company. Founded in 1938 during the Great Depression as part of the New Deal, the corporation's purpose is to expand the secondary mortgage market by securitizing mortgage loans in the form of mortgage-backed securities , allowing lenders to reinvest their assets into more lending and in effect increasing the number of lenders in the mortgage market by reducing the reliance on locally based savings and loan associations . Its brother organization is the Federal Home Loan Mortgage Corporation , better known as Freddie Mac. As of 2018, _____ is ranked #21 on the Fortune 500 rankings of the largest United States corporations by total revenue.

Exam Probability: **Low**

2. *Answer choices:*

(see index for correct answer)

- a. open system
- b. co-culture
- c. Fannie Mae
- d. Character

Guidance: level 1

:: Product certification ::

_____ is food produced by methods that comply with the standards of organic farming. Standards vary worldwide, but organic farming features practices that cycle resources, promote ecological balance, and conserve biodiversity. Organizations regulating organic products may restrict the use of certain pesticides and fertilizers in the farming methods used to produce such products. _____ s typically are not processed using irradiation, industrial solvents, or synthetic food additives.

Exam Probability: **Medium**

3. *Answer choices:*

(see index for correct answer)

- a. SGS S.A.
- b. Organic certification
- c. Hardware certification
- d. Quality Assurance International

Guidance: level 1

:: Anti-capitalism ::

_____ is a range of economic and social systems characterised by social ownership of the means of production and workers' self-management, as well as the political theories and movements associated with them. Social ownership can be public, collective or cooperative ownership, or citizen ownership of equity. There are many varieties of _____ and there is no single definition encapsulating all of them, with social ownership being the common element shared by its various forms.

4. *Answer choices:*

(see index for correct answer)

- a. Derrick Jensen
- b. Socialism
- c. Anticapitalist and Communist List
- d. Free association

Guidance: level 1

:: Confidence tricks ::

A _____ is a form of fraud that lures investors and pays profits to earlier investors with funds from more recent investors. The scheme leads victims to believe that profits are coming from product sales or other means, and they remain unaware that other investors are the source of funds. A _____ can maintain the illusion of a sustainable business as long as new investors contribute new funds, and as long as most of the investors do not demand full repayment and still believe in the non-existent assets they are purported to own.

5. *Answer choices:*

(see index for correct answer)

- a. Email fraud
- b. Badger game
- c. White van speaker scam
- d. Three-card Monte

Guidance: level 1

:: Corporate governance ::

_____ refers to the practice of members of a corporate board of directors serving on the boards of multiple corporations. A person that sits on multiple boards is known as a multiple director. Two firms have a direct interlock if a director or executive of one firm is also a director of the other, and an indirect interlock if a director of each sits on the board of a third firm. This practice, although widespread and lawful, raises questions about the quality and independence of board decisions.

Exam Probability: **High**

6. *Answer choices:*

(see index for correct answer)

- a. Australian Institute of Company Directors
- b. Control self-assessment
- c. Interlocking directorate
- d. Chief innovation officer

Guidance: level 1

:: Fraud ::

In law, _____ is intentional deception to secure unfair or unlawful gain, or to deprive a victim of a legal right. _____ can violate civil law, a criminal law, or it may cause no loss of money, property or legal right but still be an element of another civil or criminal wrong. The purpose of _____ may be monetary gain or other benefits, for example by obtaining a passport, travel document, or driver's license, or mortgage _____, where the perpetrator may attempt to qualify for a mortgage by way of false statements.

Exam Probability: **Low**

7. *Answer choices:*

(see index for correct answer)

- a. SHERIFF
- b. Voice phishing
- c. Fraud
- d. Age fabrication

Guidance: level 1

:: ::

Bernard Lawrence _____ is an American former market maker, investment advisor, financier, fraudster, and convicted felon, who is currently serving a federal prison sentence for offenses related to a massive Ponzi scheme. He is the former non-executive chairman of the NASDAQ stock market, the confessed operator of the largest Ponzi scheme in world history, and the largest financial fraud in U.S. history. Prosecutors estimated the fraud to be worth $64.8 billion based on the amounts in the accounts of _____ 's 4,800 clients as of November 30, 2008.

Exam Probability: **Low**

8. *Answer choices:*

(see index for correct answer)

- a. Madoff
- b. surface-level diversity
- c. similarity-attraction theory
- d. hierarchical perspective

Guidance: level 1

:: Anti-Revisionism ::

_____ , officially the German Democratic Republic , was a country that existed from 1949 to 1990, when the eastern portion of Germany was part of the Eastern Bloc during the Cold War. It described itself as a socialist "workers` and peasants` state", and the territory was administered and occupied by Soviet forces at the end of World War II — the Soviet Occupation Zone of the Potsdam Agreement, bounded on the east by the Oder–Neisse line. The Soviet zone surrounded West Berlin but did not include it; as a result, West Berlin remained outside the jurisdiction of the GDR.

Exam Probability: **High**

9. *Answer choices:*

(see index for correct answer)

- a. Ho Chi Minh Thought
- b. Anti-Party Group
- c. East Germany
- d. New Communist Movement

Guidance: level 1

:: Coal ::

_____ is a combustible black or brownish-black sedimentary rock, formed as rock strata called _____ seams. _____ is mostly carbon with variable amounts of other elements; chiefly hydrogen, sulfur, oxygen, and nitrogen. _____ is formed if dead plant matter decays into peat and over millions of years the heat and pressure of deep burial converts the peat into _____ . Vast deposits of _____ originates in former wetlands—called _____ forests—that covered much of the Earth's tropical land areas during the late Carboniferous and Permian times.

Exam Probability: **Low**

10. *Answer choices:*

(see index for correct answer)

- a. Coal
- b. Pulverised fuel ash
- c. Vitrinite
- d. World Coal Association

Guidance: level 1

:: Corporations law ::

A normal _____ consists of various departments that contribute to the company's overall mission and goals. Common departments include Marketing, [Finance, [[Operations managementOperations, Human Resource, and IT. These five divisions represent the major departments within a publicly traded company, though there are often smaller departments within autonomous firms. There is typically a CEO, and Board of Directors composed of the directors of each department. There are also company presidents, vice presidents, and CFOs. There is a great diversity in corporate forms as enterprises may range from single company to multi-corporate conglomerate. The four main _____ s are Functional, Divisional, Geographic, and the Matrix. Realistically, most corporations tend to have a "hybrid" structure, which is a combination of different models with one dominant strategy.

Exam Probability: **High**

11. *Answer choices:*

(see index for correct answer)

- a. Director primacy
- b. For-profit corporation
- c. Memorandum of association
- d. Constitutional documents

Guidance: level 1

:: Industrial ecology ::

_____ is a strategy for reducing the amount of waste created and released into the environment, particularly by industrial facilities, agriculture, or consumers. Many large corporations view P2 as a method of improving the efficiency and profitability of production processes by technology advancements. Legislative bodies have enacted P2 measures, such as the _____ Act of 1990 and the Clean Air Act Amendments of 1990 by the United States Congress.

Exam Probability: **Medium**

12. *Answer choices:*

(see index for correct answer)

- a. Urban metabolism
- b. Thermoeconomics
- c. Journal of Industrial Ecology
- d. Pollution Prevention

Guidance: level 1

:: Globalization-related theories ::

_____ is an economic system based on the private ownership of the means of production and their operation for profit. Characteristics central to _____ include private property, capital accumulation, wage labor, voluntary exchange, a price system, and competitive markets. In a capitalist market economy, decision-making and investment are determined by every owner of wealth, property or production ability in financial and capital markets, whereas prices and the distribution of goods and services are mainly determined by competition in goods and services markets.

Exam Probability: **High**

13. *Answer choices:*

(see index for correct answer)

- a. Capitalism
- b. Economic Development
- c. post-industrial

Guidance: level 1

:: ::

_____ is a region of India consisting of the Indian states of Bihar, Jharkhand, West Bengal, Odisha and also the union territory Andaman and Nicobar Islands. West Bengal's capital Kolkata is the largest city of this region. The Kolkata Metropolitan Area is the country's third largest.

Exam Probability: **Low**

14. *Answer choices:*

(see index for correct answer)

- a. East India
- b. cultural
- c. interpersonal communication
- d. deep-level diversity

Guidance: level 1

:: Leadership ::

_____ is a theory of leadership where a leader works with teams to identify needed change, creating a vision to guide the change through inspiration, and executing the change in tandem with committed members of a group; it is an integral part of the Full Range Leadership Model. _____ serves to enhance the motivation, morale, and job performance of followers through a variety of mechanisms; these include connecting the follower's sense of identity and self to a project and to the collective identity of the organization; being a role model for followers in order to inspire them and to raise their interest in the project; challenging followers to take greater ownership for their work, and understanding the strengths and weaknesses of followers, allowing the leader to align followers with tasks that enhance their performance.

Exam Probability: **High**

15. *Answer choices:*

(see index for correct answer)

- a. The Leadership Council
- b. Transactional leadership
- c. Transformational leadership
- d. Ethical leadership

Guidance: level 1

:: ::

_____ is a naturally occurring, yellowish-black liquid found in geological formations beneath the Earth's surface. It is commonly refined into various types of fuels. Components of _____ are separated using a technique called fractional distillation, i.e. separation of a liquid mixture into fractions differing in boiling point by means of distillation, typically using a fractionating column.

Exam Probability: **Medium**

16. *Answer choices:*

(see index for correct answer)

- a. functional perspective
- b. levels of analysis
- c. process perspective
- d. cultural

Guidance: level 1

:: ::

The _____ is an agency of the United States Department of Labor. Congress established the agency under the Occupational Safety and Health Act , which President Richard M. Nixon signed into law on December 29, 1970. OSHA's mission is to "assure safe and healthy working conditions for working men and women by setting and enforcing standards and by providing training, outreach, education and assistance". The agency is also charged with enforcing a variety of whistleblower statutes and regulations. OSHA is currently headed by Acting Assistant Secretary of Labor Loren Sweatt. OSHA's workplace safety inspections have been shown to reduce injury rates and injury costs without adverse effects to employment, sales, credit ratings, or firm survival.

Exam Probability: **High**

17. *Answer choices:*

(see index for correct answer)

- a. personal values
- b. co-culture
- c. information systems assessment
- d. hierarchical

Guidance: level 1

:: ::

A _____ is a form of business network, for example, a local organization of businesses whose goal is to further the interests of businesses. Business owners in towns and cities form these local societies to advocate on behalf of the business community. Local businesses are members, and they elect a board of directors or executive council to set policy for the chamber. The board or council then hires a President, CEO or Executive Director, plus staffing appropriate to size, to run the organization.

Exam Probability: **Low**

18. *Answer choices:*

(see index for correct answer)

- a. similarity-attraction theory
- b. interpersonal communication
- c. cultural
- d. process perspective

Guidance: level 1

:: ::

A _____ is an organization, usually a group of people or a company, authorized to act as a single entity and recognized as such in law. Early incorporated entities were established by charter . Most jurisdictions now allow the creation of new _____ s through registration.

Exam Probability: **Medium**

19. *Answer choices:*

- a. Corporation
- b. levels of analysis
- c. corporate values
- d. hierarchical

Guidance: level 1

:: ::

The _____ of 1906 was the first of a series of significant consumer protection laws which was enacted by Congress in the 20th century and led to the creation of the Food and Drug Administration. Its main purpose was to ban foreign and interstate traffic in adulterated or mislabeled food and drug products, and it directed the U.S. Bureau of Chemistry to inspect products and refer offenders to prosecutors. It required that active ingredients be placed on the label of a drug's packaging and that drugs could not fall below purity levels established by the United States Pharmacopeia or the National Formulary. The Jungle by Upton Sinclair with its graphic and revolting descriptions of unsanitary conditions and unscrupulous practices rampant in the meatpacking industry, was an inspirational piece that kept the public's attention on the important issue of unhygienic meat processing plants that later led to food inspection legislation. Sinclair quipped, "I aimed at the public's heart and by accident I hit it in the stomach," as outraged readers demanded and got the pure food law.

Exam Probability: **High**

20. *Answer choices:*

(see index for correct answer)

- a. personal values
- b. co-culture
- c. cultural
- d. surface-level diversity

Guidance: level 1

:: ::

_____ is a cognitive process that elicits emotion and rational associations based on an individual's moral philosophy or value system. _____ stands in contrast to elicited emotion or thought due to associations based on immediate sensory perceptions and reflexive responses, as in sympathetic central nervous system responses. In common terms, _____ is often described as leading to feelings of remorse when a person commits an act that conflicts with their moral values. An individual's moral values and their dissonance with familial, social, cultural and historical interpretations of moral philosophy are considered in the examination of cultural relativity in both the practice and study of psychology. The extent to which _____ informs moral judgment before an action and whether such moral judgments are or should be based on reason has occasioned debate through much of modern history between theories of modern western philosophy in juxtaposition to the theories of romanticism and other reactionary movements after the end of the Middle Ages.

Exam Probability: **High**

21. *Answer choices:*

(see index for correct answer)

- a. Sarbanes-Oxley act of 2002
- b. surface-level diversity
- c. Conscience
- d. deep-level diversity

Guidance: level 1

:: Human resource management ::

_____ encompasses values and behaviors that contribute to the unique social and psychological environment of a business. The _____ influences the way people interact, the context within which knowledge is created, the resistance they will have towards certain changes, and ultimately the way they share knowledge. _____ represents the collective values, beliefs and principles of organizational members and is a product of factors such as history, product, market, technology, strategy, type of employees, management style, and national culture; culture includes the organization's vision, values, norms, systems, symbols, language, assumptions, environment, location, beliefs and habits.

Exam Probability: **High**

22. *Answer choices:*

(see index for correct answer)

- a. E-HRM

- b. Management by observation
- c. human resource
- d. Organizational culture

Guidance: level 1

:: ::

A _____ is the ability to carry out a task with determined results often within a given amount of time, energy, or both. _____ s can often be divided into domain-general and domain-specific _____ s. For example, in the domain of work, some general _____ s would include time management, teamwork and leadership, self-motivation and others, whereas domain-specific _____ s would be used only for a certain job. _____ usually requires certain environmental stimuli and situations to assess the level of _____ being shown and used.

Exam Probability: **Low**

23. *Answer choices:*

(see index for correct answer)

- a. cultural
- b. levels of analysis
- c. Skill
- d. co-culture

Guidance: level 1

:: ::

_____ Corporation was an American energy, commodities, and services company based in Houston, Texas. It was founded in 1985 as a merger between Houston Natural Gas and InterNorth, both relatively small regional companies. Before its bankruptcy on December 3, 2001, _____ employed approximately 29,000 staff and was a major electricity, natural gas, communications and pulp and paper company, with claimed revenues of nearly $101 billion during 2000. Fortune named _____ "America's Most Innovative Company" for six consecutive years.

Exam Probability: **Low**

24. *Answer choices:*

(see index for correct answer)

- a. personal values
- b. Enron
- c. levels of analysis
- d. information systems assessment

Guidance: level 1

:: ::

_____ is a product prepared from the leaves of the _____ plant by curing them. The plant is part of the genus Nicotiana and of the Solanaceae family. While more than 70 species of _____ are known, the chief commercial crop is N. tabacum. The more potent variant N. rustica is also used around the world.

Exam Probability: **Medium**

25. *Answer choices:*

(see index for correct answer)

- a. co-culture
- b. Character
- c. Tobacco
- d. cultural

Guidance: level 1

:: Cultural appropriation ::

_____ is a social and economic order that encourages the acquisition of goods and services in ever-increasing amounts. With the industrial revolution, but particularly in the 20th century, mass production led to an economic crisis: there was overproduction—the supply of goods would grow beyond consumer demand, and so manufacturers turned to planned obsolescence and advertising to manipulate consumer spending. In 1899, a book on _____ published by Thorstein Veblen, called The Theory of the Leisure Class, examined the widespread values and economic institutions emerging along with the widespread "leisure time" in the beginning of the 20th century. In it Veblen "views the activities and spending habits of this leisure class in terms of conspicuous and vicarious consumption and waste. Both are related to the display of status and not to functionality or usefulness."

Exam Probability: **Medium**

26. *Answer choices:*

(see index for correct answer)

- a. California Indian Song
- b. Consumerism
- c. Washington Redskins
- d. Yoga piracy

Guidance: level 1

:: ::

_____ is "property consisting of land and the buildings on it, along with its natural resources such as crops, minerals or water; immovable property of this nature; an interest vested in this an item of real property, buildings or housing in general. Also: the business of _____ ; the profession of buying, selling, or renting land, buildings, or housing." It is a legal term used in jurisdictions whose legal system is derived from English common law, such as India, England, Wales, Northern Ireland, United States, Canada, Pakistan, Australia, and New Zealand.

Exam Probability: **Low**

27. *Answer choices:*

(see index for correct answer)

- a. corporate values
- b. Real estate
- c. levels of analysis
- d. Character

Guidance: level 1

:: Reputation management ::

_____ or image of a social entity is an opinion about that entity, typically as a result of social evaluation on a set of criteria.

Exam Probability: **Low**

28. *Answer choices:*

(see index for correct answer)

- a. Trust metric
- b. Whuffie
- c. The Economy of Esteem
- d. 123people

Guidance: level 1

:: Social responsibility ::

The United Nations Global Compact is a non-binding United Nations pact to encourage businesses worldwide to adopt sustainable and socially responsible policies, and to report on their implementation. The _____ is a principle-based framework for businesses, stating ten principles in the areas of human rights, labor, the environment and anti-corruption. Under the Global Compact, companies are brought together with UN agencies, labor groups and civil society. Cities can join the Global Compact through the Cities Programme.

Exam Probability: **Low**

29. *Answer choices:*

(see index for correct answer)

- a. Collective impact
- b. UN Global Compact
- c. Stanley A. Deetz

- d. United Nations Academic Impact

Guidance: level 1

:: ::

_____ or accountancy is the measurement, processing, and communication of financial information about economic entities such as businesses and corporations. The modern field was established by the Italian mathematician Luca Pacioli in 1494. _____ , which has been called the "language of business", measures the results of an organization`s economic activities and conveys this information to a variety of users, including investors, creditors, management, and regulators. Practitioners of _____ are known as accountants. The terms " _____ " and "financial reporting" are often used as synonyms.

Exam Probability: **High**

30. *Answer choices:*

(see index for correct answer)

- a. levels of analysis
- b. Accounting
- c. personal values
- d. functional perspective

Guidance: level 1

:: Business law ::

A _____ is an arrangement where parties, known as partners, agree to cooperate to advance their mutual interests. The partners in a _____ may be individuals, businesses, interest-based organizations, schools, governments or combinations. Organizations may partner to increase the likelihood of each achieving their mission and to amplify their reach. A _____ may result in issuing and holding equity or may be only governed by a contract.

Exam Probability: **Medium**

31. *Answer choices:*

(see index for correct answer)

- a. Stick licensing
- b. Unfair competition
- c. Output contract
- d. Partnership

Guidance: level 1

:: ::

A _____ is an astronomical body orbiting a star or stellar remnant that is massive enough to be rounded by its own gravity, is not massive enough to cause thermonuclear fusion, and has cleared its neighbouring region of _____ esimals.

32. *Answer choices:*

(see index for correct answer)

- a. Planet
- b. interpersonal communication
- c. deep-level diversity
- d. imperative

Guidance: level 1

:: Commercial crimes ::

_____ is an agreement between participants on the same side in a market to buy or sell a product, service, or commodity only at a fixed price, or maintain the market conditions such that the price is maintained at a given level by controlling supply and demand.

Exam Probability: **Low**

33. *Answer choices:*

(see index for correct answer)

- a. Warehouse bank
- b. Price fixing
- c. Credit card hijacking

- d. United States antitrust law

:: Majority–minority relations ::

It was established as axiomatic in anthropological research by Franz Boas in the first few decades of the 20th century and later popularized by his students. Boas first articulated the idea in 1887: "civilization is not something absolute, but ... is relative, and ... our ideas and conceptions are true only so far as our civilization goes". However, Boas did not coin the term.

Exam Probability: **Low**

34. *Answer choices:*
(see index for correct answer)

- a. positive discrimination
- b. Affirmative action
- c. Cultural relativism

:: ::

_____ was a philosopher during the Classical period in Ancient Greece, the founder of the Lyceum and the Peripatetic school of philosophy and Aristotelian tradition. Along with his teacher Plato, he is considered the "Father of Western Philosophy". His writings cover many subjects – including physics, biology, zoology, metaphysics, logic, ethics, aesthetics, poetry, theatre, music, rhetoric, psychology, linguistics, economics, politics and government. _____ provided a complex synthesis of the various philosophies existing prior to him, and it was above all from his teachings that the West inherited its intellectual lexicon, as well as problems and methods of inquiry. As a result, his philosophy has exerted a unique influence on almost every form of knowledge in the West and it continues to be a subject of contemporary philosophical discussion.

Exam Probability: **Medium**

35. *Answer choices:*

(see index for correct answer)

- a. hierarchical perspective
- b. Character
- c. Sarbanes-Oxley act of 2002
- d. Aristotle

Guidance: level 1

:: ::

_____ is an eight-block-long street running roughly northwest to southeast from Broadway to South Street, at the East River, in the Financial District of Lower Manhattan in New York City. Over time, the term has become a metonym for the financial markets of the United States as a whole, the American financial services industry , or New York–based financial interests.

Exam Probability: **Low**

36. *Answer choices:*

(see index for correct answer)

- a. information systems assessment
- b. levels of analysis
- c. personal values
- d. Wall Street

Guidance: level 1

:: Decentralization ::

_____ or sub _____ mainly refers to the unrestricted growth in many urban areas of housing, commercial development, and roads over large expanses of land, with little concern for urban planning. In addition to describing a particular form of urbanization, the term also relates to the social and environmental consequences associated with this development. In Continental Europe the term "peri-urbanisation" is often used to denote similar dynamics and phenomena, although the term _____ is currently being used by the European Environment Agency. There is widespread disagreement about what constitutes sprawl and how to quantify it. For example, some commentators measure sprawl only with the average number of residential units per acre in a given area. But others associate it with decentralization , discontinuity , segregation of uses, and so forth.

Exam Probability: **Medium**

37. *Answer choices:*

(see index for correct answer)

- a. Hacker ethic
- b. Regional autonomy
- c. Water supply and sanitation in Yemen
- d. Urban sprawl

Guidance: level 1

:: Social enterprise ::

Corporate social responsibility is a type of international private business self-regulation. While once it was possible to describe CSR as an internal organisational policy or a corporate ethic strategy, that time has passed as various international laws have been developed and various organisations have used their authority to push it beyond individual or even industry-wide initiatives. While it has been considered a form of corporate self-regulation for some time, over the last decade or so it has moved considerably from voluntary decisions at the level of individual organisations, to mandatory schemes at regional, national and even transnational levels.

Exam Probability: **High**

38. *Answer choices:*

(see index for correct answer)

- a. Corporate citizenship
- b. Social venture

Guidance: level 1

:: Financial markets ::

The _____ is a United States federal government organization, established by Title I of the Dodd–Frank Wall Street Reform and Consumer Protection Act, which was signed into law by President Barack Obama on July 21, 2010. The Office of Financial Research is intended to provide support to the council.

Exam Probability: **Medium**

39. *Answer choices:*

- a. Alternext
- b. Spot contract
- c. Financial Stability Oversight Council
- d. Limits to arbitrage

Guidance: level 1

:: Toxicology ::

_____ or lead-based paint is paint containing lead. As pigment, lead chromate , Lead oxide, , and lead carbonate are the most common forms. Lead is added to paint to accelerate drying, increase durability, maintain a fresh appearance, and resist moisture that causes corrosion. It is one of the main health and environmental hazards associated with paint. In some countries, lead continues to be added to paint intended for domestic use, whereas countries such as the U.S. and the UK have regulations prohibiting this, although _____ may still be found in older properties painted prior to the introduction of such regulations. Although lead has been banned from household paints in the United States since 1978, paint used in road markings may still contain it. Alternatives such as water-based, lead-free traffic paint are readily available, and many states and federal agencies have changed their purchasing contracts to buy these instead.

Exam Probability: **Low**

40. *Answer choices:*

- a. Lead paint
- b. The dose makes the poison
- c. Acute inhalation injury
- d. Toxicology testing

Guidance: level 1

:: Socialism ::

_____ is a label used to define the first currents of modern socialist thought as exemplified by the work of Henri de Saint-Simon, Charles Fourier, Étienne Cabet and Robert Owen.

Exam Probability: **High**

41. *Answer choices:*

(see index for correct answer)

- a. Socialism 3.0
- b. World Socialist Movement
- c. Utopian socialism
- d. Kim Se-jin

Guidance: level 1

:: Auditing ::

_____ is a general term that can reflect various types of evaluations intended to identify environmental compliance and management system implementation gaps, along with related corrective actions. In this way they perform an analogous function to financial audits. There are generally two different types of _____ s: compliance audits and management systems audits. Compliance audits tend to be the primary type in the US or within US-based multinationals.

Exam Probability: **Medium**

42. *Answer choices:*

(see index for correct answer)

- a. Sales tax audit
- b. Audit plan
- c. Control environment
- d. SOFT audit

Guidance: level 1

:: Office work ::

_____ is the process and behavior in human interactions involving power and authority. It is also a tool to assess the operational capacity and to balance diverse views of interested parties. It is also known as office politics and organizational politics.It is the use of power and social networking within an organization to achieve changes that benefit the organization or individuals within it. Influence by individuals may serve personal interests without regard to their effect on the organization itself. Some of the personal advantages may include access to tangible assets, or intangible benefits such as status or pseudo-authority that influences the behavior of others. On the other hand, organizational politics can increase efficiency, form interpersonal relationships, expedite change, and profit the organization and its members simultaneously.Both individuals and groups may engage in office politics which can be highly destructive, as people focus on personal gains at the expense of the organization. "Self-serving political actions can negatively influence our social groupings, cooperation, information sharing, and many other organizational functions." Thus, it is vital to pay attention to organizational politics and create the right political landscape. "Politics is the lubricant that oils your organization`s internal gears."
Office politics has also been described as "simply how power gets worked out on a practical, day-to-day basis."

Exam Probability: **High**

43. *Answer choices:*

(see index for correct answer)

- a. White-collar worker
- b. Workplace politics
- c. Electronic office
- d. Peter Principle

Guidance: level 1

:: Management ::

A _____ describes the rationale of how an organization creates, delivers, and captures value, in economic, social, cultural or other contexts. The process of _____ construction and modification is also called _____ innovation and forms a part of business strategy.

Exam Probability: **Low**

44. *Answer choices:*

(see index for correct answer)

- a. Business model
- b. Statistical process control
- c. Place management
- d. Business-oriented architecture

Guidance: level 1

:: Ethical banking ::

A _____ or community development finance institution - abbreviated in both cases to CDFI - is a financial institution that provides credit and financial services to underserved markets and populations, primarily in the USA but also in the UK. A CDFI may be a community development bank, a community development credit union , a community development loan fund , a community development venture capital fund , a microenterprise development loan fund, or a community development corporation.

45. *Answer choices:*

(see index for correct answer)

- a. Alfred Rexroth
- b. GLS Bank
- c. Community development financial institution
- d. Shared Interest

Guidance: level 1

:: Culture ::

_____ is a society which is characterized by individualism, which is the prioritization or emphasis, of the individual over the entire group. _____ s are oriented around the self, being independent instead of identifying with a group mentality. They see each other as only loosely linked, and value personal goals over group interests. _____ s tend to have a more diverse population and are characterized with emphasis on personal achievements, and a rational assessment of both the beneficial and detrimental aspects of relationships with others. _____ s have such unique aspects of communication as being a low power-distance culture and having a low-context communication style. The United States, Australia, Great Britain, Canada, the Netherlands, and New Zealand have been identified as highly _____ s.

Exam Probability: **High**

46. *Answer choices:*

(see index for correct answer)

- a. cultural framework
- b. Individualistic culture
- c. High-context
- d. Intracultural

Guidance: level 1

:: Law ::

_____ is a body of law which defines the role, powers, and structure of different entities within a state, namely, the executive, the parliament or legislature, and the judiciary; as well as the basic rights of citizens and, in federal countries such as the United States and Canada, the relationship between the central government and state, provincial, or territorial governments.

Exam Probability: **Medium**

47. *Answer choices:*

(see index for correct answer)

- a. Constitutional law
- b. Comparative law

Guidance: level 1

:: Business ::

_____ , or built-in obsolescence, in industrial design and economics is a policy of planning or designing a product with an artificially limited useful life, so that it becomes obsolete after a certain period of time. The rationale behind this strategy is to generate long-term sales volume by reducing the time between repeat purchases .

Exam Probability: **Low**

48. *Answer choices:*

(see index for correct answer)

- a. Planned obsolescence
- b. Business mileage reimbursement rate
- c. Free trade
- d. Business development

Guidance: level 1

:: Hazard analysis ::

Broadly speaking, a _____ is the combined effort of 1. identifying and analyzing potential events that may negatively impact individuals, assets, and/or the environment ; and 2. making judgments "on the tolerability of the risk on the basis of a risk analysis" while considering influencing factors . Put in simpler terms, a _____ analyzes what can go wrong, how likely it is to happen, what the potential consequences are, and how tolerable the identified risk is. As part of this process, the resulting determination of risk may be expressed in a quantitative or qualitative fashion. The _____ is an inherent part of an overall risk management strategy, which attempts to, after a _____ , "introduce control measures to eliminate or reduce" any potential risk-related consequences.

Exam Probability: **High**

49. *Answer choices:*

(see index for correct answer)

- a. Hazard identification
- b. Hazardous Materials Identification System
- c. Risk assessment

Guidance: level 1

:: Patent law ::

A _____ is generally any statement intended to specify or delimit the scope of rights and obligations that may be exercised and enforced by parties in a legally recognized relationship. In contrast to other terms for legally operative language, the term _____ usually implies situations that involve some level of uncertainty, waiver, or risk.

Exam Probability: **Low**

50. *Answer choices:*

(see index for correct answer)

- a. Evergreening
- b. Disclaimer
- c. Double patenting
- d. Internet as a source of prior art

Guidance: level 1

:: Market-based policy instruments ::

Cause marketing is defined as a type of corporate social responsibility, in which a company's promotional campaign has the dual purpose of increasing profitability while bettering society.

Exam Probability: **High**

51. *Answer choices:*

(see index for correct answer)

- a. Cobra effect
- b. Tax choice
- c. Cause-related marketing
- d. Public choice

Guidance: level 1

:: Social philosophy ::

The _____ describes the unintended social benefits of an individual's self-interested actions. Adam Smith first introduced the concept in The Theory of Moral Sentiments, written in 1759, invoking it in reference to income distribution. In this work, however, the idea of the market is not discussed, and the word "capitalism" is never used.

Exam Probability: **Low**

52. *Answer choices:*

(see index for correct answer)

- a. Veil of Ignorance
- b. vacancy chain
- c. Societal attitudes towards abortion
- d. Invisible hand

Guidance: level 1

:: Business ethics ::

_____ is a type of international private business self-regulation. While once it was possible to describe CSR as an internal organisational policy or a corporate ethic strategy, that time has passed as various international laws have been developed and various organisations have used their authority to push it beyond individual or even industry-wide initiatives. While it has been considered a form of corporate self-regulation for some time, over the last decade or so it has moved considerably from voluntary decisions at the level of individual organisations, to mandatory schemes at regional, national and even transnational levels.

Exam Probability: **Medium**

53. *Answer choices:*

(see index for correct answer)

- a. Terror-free investing
- b. Corporate social responsibility
- c. Financial privacy
- d. Centre for Research on Multinational Corporations

Guidance: level 1

:: ::

The _____ Group is a global financial investment management and insurance company headquartered in Des Moines, Iowa.

Exam Probability: **Medium**

54. *Answer choices:*

(see index for correct answer)

- a. hierarchical
- b. functional perspective
- c. co-culture
- d. Sarbanes-Oxley act of 2002

Guidance: level 1

:: Agricultural labor ::

The _____ of America, or more commonly just _____ , is a labor union for farmworkers in the United States. It originated from the merger of two workers' rights organizations, the Agricultural Workers Organizing Committee led by organizer Larry Itliong, and the National Farm Workers Association led by César Chávez and Dolores Huerta. They became allied and transformed from workers' rights organizations into a union as a result of a series of strikes in 1965, when the mostly Filipino farmworkers of the AWOC in Delano, California initiated a grape strike, and the NFWA went on strike in support. As a result of the commonality in goals and methods, the NFWA and the AWOC formed the _____ Organizing Committee on August 22, 1966. This organization was accepted into the AFL-CIO in 1972 and changed its name to the _____ Union.

55. *Answer choices:*

(see index for correct answer)

- a. California Agricultural Labor Relations Act
- b. United Farm Workers
- c. Agricultural gang
- d. Kibbutz

Guidance: level 1

:: ::

In regulatory jurisdictions that provide for it , _____ is a group of laws and organizations designed to ensure the rights of consumers as well as fair trade, competition and accurate information in the marketplace. The laws are designed to prevent the businesses that engage in fraud or specified unfair practices from gaining an advantage over competitors. They may also provides additional protection for those most vulnerable in society. _____ laws are a form of government regulation that aim to protect the rights of consumers. For example, a government may require businesses to disclose detailed information about products—particularly in areas where safety or public health is an issue, such as food.

56. *Answer choices:*

(see index for correct answer)

- a. co-culture
- b. surface-level diversity
- c. interpersonal communication
- d. empathy

Guidance: level 1

:: Management ::

_____ or executive pay is composed of the financial compensation and other non-financial awards received by an executive from their firm for their service to the organization. It is typically a mixture of salary, bonuses, shares of or call options on the company stock, benefits, and perquisites, ideally configured to take into account government regulations, tax law, the desires of the organization and the executive, and rewards for performance.

Exam Probability: **Medium**

57. *Answer choices:*

(see index for correct answer)

- a. Topple rate
- b. Executive compensation
- c. Operations research
- d. Project stakeholder

Guidance: level 1

:: Parental leave ::

_____ , or family leave, is an employee benefit available in almost all countries. The term "_____" may include maternity, paternity, and adoption leave; or may be used distinctively from "maternity leave" and "paternity leave" to describe separate family leave available to either parent to care for small children. In some countries and jurisdictions, "family leave" also includes leave provided to care for ill family members. Often, the minimum benefits and eligibility requirements are stipulated by law.

Exam Probability: **High**

58. *Answer choices:*

(see index for correct answer)

- a. Cleveland Board of Education v. LaFleur
- b. Sara Hlupekile Longwe
- c. Pregnancy discrimination
- d. Equal Opportunities Commission v Secretary of State for Trade and Industry

Guidance: level 1

:: Waste ::

_____ is any unwanted material in all forms that can cause harm . Many of today's household products such as televisions, computers and phones contain toxic chemicals that can pollute the air and contaminate soil and water. Disposing of such waste is a major public health issue.

Exam Probability: **Medium**

59. *Answer choices:*

(see index for correct answer)

- a. Commercial waste
- b. Toxic waste
- c. Zero waste agriculture
- d. Waste heat

Guidance: level 1

Accounting

Accounting or accountancy is the measurement, processing, and communication of financial information about economic entities such as businesses and corporations. The modern field was established by the Italian mathematician Luca Pacioli in 1494. Accounting, which has been called the "language of business", measures the results of an organization's economic activities and conveys this information to a variety of users, including investors, creditors, management, and regulators.

:: Basic financial concepts ::

_____ is a sustained increase in the general price level of goods and services in an economy over a period of time. When the general price level rises, each unit of currency buys fewer goods and services; consequently, _____ reflects a reduction in the purchasing power per unit of money a loss of real value in the medium of exchange and unit of account within the economy. The measure of _____ is the _____ rate, the annualized percentage change in a general price index, usually the consumer price index, over time. The opposite of _____ is deflation.

Exam Probability: **High**

1. *Answer choices:*

(see index for correct answer)

- a. balloon payment
- b. Base effect
- c. Maturity
- d. Present value of costs

Guidance: level 1

:: Business models ::

A _____ is a company that owns enough voting stock in another firm to control management and operation by influencing or electing its board of directors. The company is deemed a subsidiary of the _____ .

Exam Probability: **Low**

2. *Answer choices:*

(see index for correct answer)

- a. Business Model Canvas
- b. Fractional ownership
- c. Legacy carrier
- d. Parent company

Guidance: level 1

:: Generally Accepted Accounting Principles ::

Paid-in capital is capital that is contributed to a corporation by investors by purchase of stock from the corporation, the primary market, not by purchase of stock in the open market from other stockholders . It includes share capital as well as additional paid-in capital.

Exam Probability: **High**

3. *Answer choices:*

(see index for correct answer)

- a. Fixed investment
- b. Operating income
- c. Contributed capital
- d. Earnings before interest, taxes and depreciation

:: Expense ::

An _____ is the right to reimbursement of money spent by employees for work-related purposes. Some common _____ s are: administrative expense, amortization expense, bad debt expense, cost of goods sold, depreciation expense, freight-out, income tax expense, insurance expense, interest expense, loss on disposal of plant assets, maintenance and repairs expense, rent expense, salaries and wages expense, selling expense, supplies expense and utilities expense.

Exam Probability: **Low**

4. *Answer choices:*

(see index for correct answer)

- a. Operating expense
- b. Expense account
- c. Stock option expensing
- d. Interest expense

:: Real estate valuation ::

_____ or OMV is the price at which an asset would trade in a competitive auction setting. _____ is often used interchangeably with open _____ , fair value or fair _____ , although these terms have distinct definitions in different standards, and may or may not differ in some circumstances.

Exam Probability: **High**

5. *Answer choices:*

(see index for correct answer)

- a. Real estate appraisal
- b. Zillow
- c. Rate base
- d. Market value

Guidance: level 1

:: Loans ::

In corporate finance, a _____ is a medium- to long-term debt instrument used by large companies to borrow money, at a fixed rate of interest. The legal term " _____ " originally referred to a document that either creates a debt or acknowledges it, but in some countries the term is now used interchangeably with bond, loan stock or note. A _____ is thus like a certificate of loan or a loan bond evidencing the fact that the company is liable to pay a specified amount with interest and although the money raised by the _____ s becomes a part of the company's capital structure, it does not become share capital. Senior _____ s get paid before subordinate _____ s, and there are varying rates of risk and payoff for these categories.

Exam Probability: **Medium**

6. *Answer choices:*

(see index for correct answer)

- a. Debenture
- b. Student Loan Guarantor
- c. Concessionary loan
- d. Industrial loan company

Guidance: level 1

:: International accounting organizations ::

The _____ is the global organization for the accountancy profession. Founded in 1977, IFAC has more than 175 members and associates in more than 130 countries and jurisdictions, representing nearly 3 million accountants employed in public practice, industry and commerce, government, and academe. The organization supports the development, adoption and implementation of international standards for accounting education, ethics, and the public sector as well as audit and assurance. It supports four independent standard-setting boards, which establish international standards on ethics, auditing and assurance, accounting education, and public sector accounting. It also issues guidance to encourage high quality performance by professional accountants in business and small and medium accounting practices.

Exam Probability: **Low**

7. *Answer choices:*

(see index for correct answer)

- a. International Federation of Accountants
- b. Pan African Federation of Accountants
- c. World Congress of Accountants
- d. Forum of Firms

Guidance: level 1

:: Organizational theory ::

Decentralisation is the process by which the activities of an organization, particularly those regarding planning and decision making, are distributed or delegated away from a central, authoritative location or group. Concepts of _____ have been applied to group dynamics and management science in private businesses and organizations, political science, law and public administration, economics, money and technology.

Exam Probability: **Medium**

8. *Answer choices:*

(see index for correct answer)

- a. Organization theory
- b. Network-centric organization
- c. Decentralization
- d. Performance problem

Guidance: level 1

:: Taxation ::

_____ is a type of tax law that allows a person to give assets to his or her spouse with reduced or no tax imposed upon the transfer. Some _____ laws even apply to transfers made postmortem. The right to receive property conveys ownership for tax purposes. A decree of divorce transfers the right to that property by reason of the marriage and is also a transfer within a marriage. It makes no difference whether the property itself or equivalent compensation is transferred before, or after the decree dissolves the marriage. There is no U.S. estate and gift tax on transfers of any amount between spouses, whether during their lifetime or at death. There is an important exceptions for non-citizens. The U.S. federal Estate and gift tax _____ is only available if the surviving spouse is a U.S. citizen. For a surviving spouse who is not a U.S. citizen a bequest through a Qualified Domestic Trust defers estate tax until principal is distributed by the trustee, a U.S. citizen or corporation who also withholds the estate tax. Income on principal distributed to the surviving spouse is taxed as individual income. If the surviving spouse becomes a U.S. citizen, principal remaining in a Qualifying Domestic Trust may then be distributed without further tax.

Exam Probability: **High**

9. *Answer choices:*

(see index for correct answer)

- a. Fiscal burden of government
- b. Tax and spend
- c. Tax lien
- d. Marital deduction

Guidance: level 1

:: Financial ratios ::

_____ or interest coverage ratio is a measure of a company's ability to honor its debt payments. It may be calculated as either EBIT or EBITDA divided by the total interest payable.

10. *Answer choices:*

(see index for correct answer)

- a. Import ratio
- b. net margin
- c. Sustainable growth rate
- d. Theoretical ex-rights price

Guidance: level 1

:: Accounting terminology ::

_____ of something is, in finance, the adding together of interest or different investments over a period of time. It holds specific meanings in accounting, where it can refer to accounts on a balance sheet that represent liabilities and non-cash-based assets used in _____ -based accounting. These types of accounts include, among others, accounts payable, accounts receivable, goodwill, deferred tax liability and future interest expense.

11. *Answer choices:*

(see index for correct answer)

- a. Chart of accounts
- b. Basis of accounting
- c. Capital appreciation
- d. Accrual

Guidance: level 1

:: Management accounting ::

_____ is an approach to determine a product's life-cycle cost which should be sufficient to develop specified functionality and quality, while ensuring its desired profit. It involves setting a target cost by subtracting a desired profit margin from a competitive market price. A target cost is the maximum amount of cost that can be incurred on a product, however, the firm can still earn the required profit margin from that product at a particular selling price. _____ decomposes the target cost from product level to component level. Through this decomposition, _____ spreads the competitive pressure faced by the company to product's designers and suppliers. _____ consists of cost planning in the design phase of production as well as cost control throughout the resulting product life cycle. The cardinal rule of _____ is to never exceed the target cost. However, the focus of _____ is not to minimize costs, but to achieve a desired level of cost reduction determined by the _____ process.

Exam Probability: **Medium**

12. *Answer choices:*

(see index for correct answer)

- a. Certified Management Accountants of Canada
- b. Construction accounting
- c. Extended cost
- d. Target costing

Guidance: level 1

:: Business law ::

A _____ is a business entity created by two or more parties, generally characterized by shared ownership, shared returns and risks, and shared governance. Companies typically pursue _____ s for one of four reasons: to access a new market, particularly emerging markets; to gain scale efficiencies by combining assets and operations; to share risk for major investments or projects; or to access skills and capabilities.

Exam Probability: **High**

13. *Answer choices:*

(see index for correct answer)

- a. Lex mercatoria
- b. Joint venture
- c. Interest of the company
- d. Novated lease

:: ::

A _____ is a tax paid to a governing body for the sales of certain goods and services. Usually laws allow the seller to collect funds for the tax from the consumer at the point of purchase. When a tax on goods or services is paid to a governing body directly by a consumer, it is usually called a use tax. Often laws provide for the exemption of certain goods or services from sales and use tax.

Exam Probability: **Low**

14. *Answer choices:*

(see index for correct answer)

- a. Sales tax
- b. Character
- c. process perspective
- d. functional perspective

:: Taxation ::

_____ refers to instances where a taxpayer can delay paying taxes to some future period. In theory, the net taxes paid should be the same. Taxes can sometimes be deferred indefinitely, or may be taxed at a lower rate in the future, particularly for deferral of income taxes.

Exam Probability: High

15. *Answer choices:*

(see index for correct answer)

- a. Tax basis
- b. Taxable income
- c. Energy tax
- d. Voluntary taxation

Guidance: level 1

:: Capital gains taxes ::

A _____ refers to profit that results from a sale of a capital asset, such as stock, bond or real estate, where the sale price exceeds the purchase price. The gain is the difference between a higher selling price and a lower purchase price. Conversely, a capital loss arises if the proceeds from the sale of a capital asset are less than the purchase price.

Exam Probability: Low

16. *Answer choices:*

(see index for correct answer)

- a. Capital gain
- b. Capital gains tax
- c. Capital cost tax factor

Guidance: level 1

:: Accounting terminology ::

_____ is an independent, objective assurance and consulting activity designed to add value to and improve an organization's operations. It helps an organization accomplish its objectives by bringing a systematic, disciplined approach to evaluate and improve the effectiveness of risk management, control and governance processes. _____ achieves this by providing insight and recommendations based on analyses and assessments of data and business processes. With commitment to integrity and accountability, _____ provides value to governing bodies and senior management as an objective source of independent advice. Professionals called internal auditors are employed by organizations to perform the _____ activity.

Exam Probability: **High**

17. *Answer choices:*

(see index for correct answer)

- a. Chart of accounts
- b. Impairment cost

- c. Accounts receivable
- d. Internal auditing

Guidance: level 1

:: Management accounting ::

In business, a _____ is a division that gains revenue from product sales or service provided. The manager in _____ is accountable for revenue only.

Exam Probability: **High**

18. *Answer choices:*
(see index for correct answer)

- a. Direct material usage variance
- b. Profit center
- c. Revenue center
- d. Institute of Certified Management Accountants

Guidance: level 1

:: Supply chain management terms ::

In business and finance, _____ is a system of organizations, people, activities, information, and resources involved in moving a product or service from supplier to customer. _____ activities involve the transformation of natural resources, raw materials, and components into a finished product that is delivered to the end customer. In sophisticated _____ systems, used products may re-enter the _____ at any point where residual value is recyclable. _____ s link value chains.

Exam Probability: **High**

19. *Answer choices:*

(see index for correct answer)

- a. Capital spare
- b. Consumables
- c. Supply chain
- d. Final assembly schedule

Guidance: level 1

:: Production and manufacturing ::

_____ consists of organization-wide efforts to "install and make permanent climate where employees continuously improve their ability to provide on demand products and services that customers will find of particular value." "Total" emphasizes that departments in addition to production are obligated to improve their operations; "management" emphasizes that executives are obligated to actively manage quality through funding, training, staffing, and goal setting. While there is no widely agreed-upon approach, TQM efforts typically draw heavily on the previously developed tools and techniques of quality control. TQM enjoyed widespread attention during the late 1980s and early 1990s before being overshadowed by ISO 9000, Lean manufacturing, and Six Sigma.

Exam Probability: **High**

20. *Answer choices:*

(see index for correct answer)

- a. Total quality management
- b. Nuffield Tools and Gauges
- c. STEP-NC
- d. Product layout

Guidance: level 1

:: Project management ::

_____ is the widespread practice of collecting information and attempting to spot a pattern. In some fields of study, the term "_____" has more formally defined meanings.

Exam Probability: **Low**

21. *Answer choices:*

(see index for correct answer)

- a. Bid manager
- b. Trend analysis
- c. Transport Initiatives Edinburgh
- d. Resource allocation

Guidance: level 1

:: Management accounting ::

_____ is a professional certification credential in the management accounting and financial management fields. The certification signifies that the person possesses knowledge in the areas of financial planning, analysis, control, decision support, and professional ethics. The CMA is a U.S.-based, globally recognized certification offered by the Institute of Management Accountants.

Exam Probability: **Low**

22. *Answer choices:*

(see index for correct answer)

- a. Certified Management Accountants of Canada
- b. Target income sales

- c. Hedge accounting
- d. Variable Costing

Guidance: level 1

:: Management accounting ::

_____ is a professional business study of Accounts and management in which we learn importance of accounts in our management system.

Exam Probability: **Low**

23. *Answer choices:*

(see index for correct answer)

- a. Fixed assets management
- b. Accounting management
- c. Target costing
- d. Certified Management Accountant

Guidance: level 1

:: Taxation ::

A _____ is a person or organization subject to pay a tax. _____ s have an Identification Number, a reference number issued by a government to its citizens.

Exam Probability: **Low**

24. *Answer choices:*

(see index for correct answer)

- a. Tax refund
- b. Tax basis
- c. Tax cap
- d. Taxpayer

Guidance: level 1

:: ::

The _____ is a private, non-profit organization standard-setting body whose primary purpose is to establish and improve Generally Accepted Accounting Principles within the United States in the public's interest. The Securities and Exchange Commission designated the FASB as the organization responsible for setting accounting standards for public companies in the US. The FASB replaced the American Institute of Certified Public Accountants' Accounting Principles Board on July 1, 1973.

Exam Probability: **High**

25. *Answer choices:*

(see index for correct answer)

- a. Financial Accounting Standards Board
- b. Character
- c. empathy
- d. functional perspective

Guidance: level 1

:: ::

The _____ of 1938 29 U.S.C. § 203 is a United States labor law that creates the right to a minimum wage, and "time-and-a-half" overtime pay when people work over forty hours a week. It also prohibits most employment of minors in "oppressive child labor". It applies to employees engaged in interstate commerce or employed by an enterprise engaged in commerce or in the production of goods for commerce, unless the employer can claim an exemption from coverage.

Exam Probability: **Low**

26. *Answer choices:*

(see index for correct answer)

- a. imperative
- b. personal values
- c. Fair Labor Standards Act

- d. co-culture

Guidance: level 1

:: ::

_____ is a process whereby a person assumes the parenting of another, usually a child, from that person's biological or legal parent or parents.
Legal _____ s permanently transfers all rights and responsibilities, along with filiation, from the biological parent or parents.

Exam Probability: **High**

27. *Answer choices:*

(see index for correct answer)

- a. Character
- b. Adoption
- c. information systems assessment
- d. cultural

Guidance: level 1

:: Financial statements ::

_____ s - are the "Financial statements of a group in which the assets, liabilities, equity, income, expenses and cash flows of the parent company and its subsidiaries are presented as those of a single economic entity", according to International Accounting Standard 27 "Consolidated and separate financial statements", and International Financial Reporting Standard 10 " _____ s".

28. *Answer choices:*

(see index for correct answer)

- a. Financial report
- b. Statement on Auditing Standards No. 70: Service Organizations
- c. Quarterly finance report
- d. Balance sheet

Guidance: level 1

:: Organizational structure ::

An _____ defines how activities such as task allocation, coordination, and supervision are directed toward the achievement of organizational aims.

29. *Answer choices:*

(see index for correct answer)

- a. Unorganisation
- b. Organizational structure
- c. Blessed Unrest
- d. Followership

Guidance: level 1

:: Asset ::

In financial accounting, an _____ is any resource owned by the business. Anything tangible or intangible that can be owned or controlled to produce value and that is held by a company to produce positive economic value is an _____ . Simply stated, _____ s represent value of ownership that can be converted into cash . The balance sheet of a firm records the monetary value of the _____ s owned by that firm. It covers money and other valuables belonging to an individual or to a business.

Exam Probability: **Low**

30. *Answer choices:*
(see index for correct answer)

- a. Current asset
- b. Asset

Guidance: level 1

:: Generally Accepted Accounting Principles ::

_____ is a measure of a fixed or current asset's worth when held in inventory, in the field of accounting. NRV is part of the Generally Accepted Accounting Principles and International Financial Reporting Standards that apply to valuing inventory, so as to not overstate or understate the value of inventory goods. _____ is generally equal to the selling price of the inventory goods less the selling costs . Therefore, it is expected sales price less selling costs . NRV prevents overstating or understating of an assets value. NRV is the price cap when using the Lower of Cost or Market Rule.

Exam Probability: **Medium**

31. *Answer choices:*

(see index for correct answer)

- a. Earnings before interest, taxes and depreciation
- b. Net realizable value
- c. Normal balance
- d. Matching principle

Guidance: level 1

:: Foreign exchange market ::

A currency , in the most specific sense is money in any form when in use or circulation as a medium of exchange, especially circulating banknotes and coins. A more general definition is that a currency is a system of money in common use, especially for people in a nation. Under this definition, US dollars , pounds sterling , Australian dollars , European euros , Russian rubles and Indian Rupees are examples of currencies. These various currencies are recognized as stores of value and are traded between nations in foreign exchange markets, which determine the relative values of the different currencies. Currencies in this sense are defined by governments, and each type has limited boundaries of acceptance.

Exam Probability: **Low**

32. *Answer choices:*

(see index for correct answer)

- a. Billion Dollar Day
- b. VND Index
- c. Exorbitant privilege
- d. Monetary unit

Guidance: level 1

:: Stock market ::

_____ is a form of corporate equity ownership, a type of security. The terms voting share and ordinary share are also used frequently in other parts of the world; " _____ " being primarily used in the United States. They are known as Equity shares or Ordinary shares in the UK and other Commonwealth realms. This type of share gives the stockholder the right to share in the profits of the company, and to vote on matters of corporate policy and the composition of the members of the board of directors.

Exam Probability: **Low**

33. *Answer choices:*

(see index for correct answer)

- a. Common stock
- b. Security
- c. Central limit order book
- d. Shadow stock

Guidance: level 1

:: ::

The U.S. _____ is an independent agency of the United States federal government. The SEC holds primary responsibility for enforcing the federal securities laws, proposing securities rules, and regulating the securities industry, the nation's stock and options exchanges, and other activities and organizations, including the electronic securities markets in the United States.

34. *Answer choices:*

(see index for correct answer)

- a. interpersonal communication
- b. empathy
- c. Securities and Exchange Commission
- d. information systems assessment

Guidance: level 1

:: Accounting in the United States ::

The _____ is a private-sector, nonprofit corporation created by the Sarbanes–Oxley Act of 2002 to oversee the audits of public companies and other issuers in order to protect the interests of investors and further the public interest in the preparation of informative, accurate and independent audit reports. The PCAOB also oversees the audits of broker-dealers, including compliance reports filed pursuant to federal securities laws, to promote investor protection. All PCAOB rules and standards must be approved by the U.S. Securities and Exchange Commission .

Exam Probability: **High**

35. *Answer choices:*

(see index for correct answer)

- a. Association of Certified Fraud Examiners
- b. Public Company Accounting Oversight Board
- c. National Association of State Boards of Accountancy
- d. Certified Public Accountant

Guidance: level 1

:: Accounting source documents ::

_____ is a letter sent by a customer to a supplier to inform the supplier that their invoice has been paid. If the customer is paying by cheque, the _____ often accompanies the cheque. The advice may consist of a literal letter or of a voucher attached to the side or top of the cheque.

Exam Probability: **Medium**

36. *Answer choices:*

(see index for correct answer)

- a. Credit memo
- b. Remittance advice
- c. Purchase order
- d. Parcel audit

Guidance: level 1

:: Financial ratios ::

A _____ or accounting ratio is a relative magnitude of two selected numerical values taken from an enterprise's financial statements. Often used in accounting, there are many standard ratios used to try to evaluate the overall financial condition of a corporation or other organization. _____ s may be used by managers within a firm, by current and potential shareholders of a firm, and by a firm's creditors. Financial analysts use _____ s to compare the strengths and weaknesses in various companies. If shares in a company are traded in a financial market, the market price of the shares is used in certain _____ s.

Exam Probability: **Medium**

37. *Answer choices:*

(see index for correct answer)

- a. Financial ratio
- b. Capital recovery factor
- c. Return on net assets
- d. Debt service ratio

Guidance: level 1

:: ::

A _____ is a fund into which a sum of money is added during an employee's employment years, and from which payments are drawn to support the person's retirement from work in the form of periodic payments. A _____ may be a "defined benefit plan" where a fixed sum is paid regularly to a person, or a "defined contribution plan" under which a fixed sum is invested and then becomes available at retirement age. _____ s should not be confused with severance pay; the former is usually paid in regular installments for life after retirement, while the latter is typically paid as a fixed amount after involuntary termination of employment prior to retirement.

Exam Probability: **Medium**

38. *Answer choices:*

(see index for correct answer)

- a. levels of analysis
- b. imperative
- c. empathy
- d. Pension

Guidance: level 1

:: ::

In the field of analysis of algorithms in computer science, the _____ is a method of amortized analysis based on accounting. The _____ often gives a more intuitive account of the amortized cost of an operation than either aggregate analysis or the potential method. Note, however, that this does not guarantee such analysis will be immediately obvious; often, choosing the correct parameters for the _____ requires as much knowledge of the problem and the complexity bounds one is attempting to prove as the other two methods.

Exam Probability: **High**

39. *Answer choices:*

(see index for correct answer)

- a. levels of analysis
- b. similarity-attraction theory
- c. Character
- d. hierarchical perspective

Guidance: level 1

:: Land value taxation ::

_____ , sometimes referred to as dry _____ , is the solid surface of Earth that is not permanently covered by water. The vast majority of human activity throughout history has occurred in _____ areas that support agriculture, habitat, and various natural resources. Some life forms have developed from predecessor species that lived in bodies of water.

40. *Answer choices:*

(see index for correct answer)

- a. Prosper Australia
- b. Harry Gunnison Brown
- c. Land value tax
- d. Land

Guidance: level 1

:: International trade ::

In finance, an _____ is the rate at which one currency will be exchanged for another. It is also regarded as the value of one country's currency in relation to another currency. For example, an interbank _____ of 114 Japanese yen to the United States dollar means that ¥114 will be exchanged for each US$1 or that US$1 will be exchanged for each ¥114. In this case it is said that the price of a dollar in relation to yen is ¥114, or equivalently that the price of a yen in relation to dollars is $1/114.

Exam Probability: **High**

41. *Answer choices:*

(see index for correct answer)

- a. Exchange rate

- b. Kennedy Round
- c. Denied trade screening
- d. Trade and Investment Framework Agreement

Guidance: level 1

:: United States Generally Accepted Accounting Principles ::

A _____ is a set of U.S. government financial statements comprising the financial report of a state, municipal or other governmental entity that complies with the accounting requirements promulgated by the Governmental Accounting Standards Board . GASB provides standards for the content of a CAFR in its annually updated publication Codification of Governmental Accounting and Financial Reporting Standards. The U.S. Federal Government adheres to standards determined by the Federal Accounting Standards Advisory Board .

Exam Probability: **Low**

42. *Answer choices:*

(see index for correct answer)

- a. Cost segregation study
- b. Single Audit
- c. Asset retirement obligation
- d. Accounting for leases in the United States

Guidance: level 1

:: E-commerce ::

A _____ is a plastic payment card that can be used instead of cash when making purchases. It is similar to a credit card, but unlike a credit card, the money is immediately transferred directly from the cardholder's bank account when performing a transaction.

Exam Probability: **Low**

43. *Answer choices:*

(see index for correct answer)

- a. Dragonpay
- b. Mobile banking
- c. Debit card
- d. Point of sale

Guidance: level 1

:: Financial ratios ::

The _____ is a liquidity ratio that measures whether a firm has enough resources to meet its short-term obligations. It compares a firm's current assets to its current liabilities, and is expressed as follows.

Exam Probability: **Low**

44. *Answer choices:*

(see index for correct answer)

- a. Return on event
- b. Like for like
- c. Current ratio
- d. Total revenue share

Guidance: level 1

:: Password authentication ::

A _____ , or sometimes redundantly a PIN number, is a numeric or alpha-numeric password used in the process of authenticating a user accessing a system.

Exam Probability: **Medium**

45. *Answer choices:*

(see index for correct answer)

- a. Password length parameter
- b. Passwd
- c. Personal identification number
- d. Passphrase

Guidance: level 1

_____ or accountancy is the measurement, processing, and communication of financial information about economic entities such as businesses and corporations. The modern field was established by the Italian mathematician Luca Pacioli in 1494. _____ , which has been called the "language of business", measures the results of an organization's economic activities and conveys this information to a variety of users, including investors, creditors, management, and regulators. Practitioners of _____ are known as accountants. The terms " _____ " and "financial reporting" are often used as synonyms.

Exam Probability: **Low**

46. *Answer choices:*

(see index for correct answer)

- a. co-culture
- b. Accounting
- c. empathy
- d. hierarchical perspective

Guidance: level 1

:: Notes (finance) ::

A _____ , sometimes referred to as a note payable, is a legal instrument , in which one party promises in writing to pay a determinate sum of money to the other , either at a fixed or determinable future time or on demand of the payee, under specific terms.

Exam Probability: **Low**

47. *Answer choices:*

(see index for correct answer)

- a. note payable
- b. Note issuance facility
- c. Promissory note
- d. Treasury Note

Guidance: level 1

:: Investment ::

In economics, _____ is spending which increases the availability of fixed capital goods or means of production and goods inventories. It is the total spending on newly produced physical capital and on inventories —that is, gross investment—minus replacement investment, which simply replaces depreciated capital goods. It is productive capital formation plus net additions to the stock of housing and the stock of inventories.

Exam Probability: **Medium**

48. *Answer choices:*

(see index for correct answer)

- a. Net investment
- b. Multi-manager investment
- c. Dispersion
- d. Asset Liquidation Marketing Integration Within Asset Management Framework

Guidance: level 1

:: Organizational behavior ::

_____ is the state or fact of exclusive rights and control over property, which may be an object, land/real estate or intellectual property. _____ involves multiple rights, collectively referred to as title, which may be separated and held by different parties.

Exam Probability: **Medium**

49. *Answer choices:*

(see index for correct answer)

- a. Nut Island effect
- b. Ownership
- c. Behavioral systems analysis
- d. Organizational commitment

:: Financial ratios ::

_____ or asset turns is a financial ratio that measures the efficiency of a company's use of its assets in generating sales revenue or sales income to the company.

Exam Probability: **Medium**

50. *Answer choices:*

(see index for correct answer)

- a. Implied multiple
- b. Debt-to-equity ratio
- c. Debt service coverage ratio
- d. Asset turnover

:: ::

An _____ is a systematic and independent examination of books, accounts, statutory records, documents and vouchers of an organization to ascertain how far the financial statements as well as non-financial disclosures present a true and fair view of the concern. It also attempts to ensure that the books of accounts are properly maintained by the concern as required by law. _____ ing has become such a ubiquitous phenomenon in the corporate and the public sector that academics started identifying an " _____ Society". The _____ or perceives and recognises the propositions before them for examination, obtains evidence, evaluates the same and formulates an opinion on the basis of his judgement which is communicated through their _____ ing report.

Exam Probability: **Low**

51. *Answer choices:*

(see index for correct answer)

- a. functional perspective
- b. similarity-attraction theory
- c. deep-level diversity
- d. Audit

Guidance: level 1

:: Options (finance) ::

A _____ bond is a type of bond that allows the issuer of the bond to retain the privilege of redeeming the bond at some point before the bond reaches its date of maturity. In other words, on the call date, the issuer has the right, but not the obligation, to buy back the bonds from the bond holders at a defined call price. Technically speaking, the bonds are not really bought and held by the issuer but are instead cancelled immediately.

Exam Probability: **High**

52. *Answer choices:*

(see index for correct answer)

- a. Interest rate guarantee
- b. Chooser option
- c. Swaption
- d. Compound option

Guidance: level 1

:: Generally Accepted Accounting Principles ::

In accounting, _____ is the income that a business have from its normal business activities, usually from the sale of goods and services to customers. _____ is also referred to as sales or turnover. Some companies receive _____ from interest, royalties, or other fees. _____ may refer to business income in general, or it may refer to the amount, in a monetary unit, earned during a period of time, as in "Last year, Company X had _____ of $42 million". Profits or net income generally imply total _____ minus total expenses in a given period. In accounting, in the balance statement it is a subsection of the Equity section and _____ increases equity, it is often referred to as the "top line" due to its position on the income statement at the very top. This is to be contrasted with the "bottom line" which denotes net income .

Exam Probability: **Low**

53. *Answer choices:*
(see index for correct answer)

- a. Revenue
- b. Indian Accounting Standards
- c. Statement of recommended practice
- d. Engagement letter

Guidance: level 1

:: Accounting systems ::

In bookkeeping, a _____ statement is a process that explains the difference on a specified date between the bank balance shown in an organization's bank statement, as supplied by the bank and the corresponding amount shown in the organization's own accounting records.

Exam Probability: **High**

54. *Answer choices:*

(see index for correct answer)

- a. Counting house
- b. Standard accounting practice
- c. Inflation accounting
- d. Bank reconciliation

Guidance: level 1

:: Management accounting ::

A _____ is a part of a business which is expected to make an identifiable contribution to the organization's profits.

Exam Probability: **Low**

55. *Answer choices:*

(see index for correct answer)

- a. Notional profit
- b. Holding cost
- c. Profit center
- d. Direct material usage variance

Guidance: level 1

:: ::

An inheritance or _____ is a tax paid by a person who inherits money or property or a levy on the estate of a person who has died.

Exam Probability: **Low**

56. *Answer choices:*

(see index for correct answer)

- a. Estate tax
- b. open system
- c. Character
- d. surface-level diversity

Guidance: level 1

:: Costs ::

The _____ is computed by dividing the total cost of goods available for sale by the total units available for sale. This gives a weighted-average unit cost that is applied to the units in the ending inventory.

Exam Probability: **Medium**

57. *Answer choices:*

(see index for correct answer)

- a. Average cost
- b. Cost curve
- c. Psychic cost
- d. Explicit cost

Guidance: level 1

:: Finance ::

_____ , in finance and accounting, means stated value or face value. From this come the expressions at par , over par and under par .

Exam Probability: **Medium**

58. *Answer choices:*

(see index for correct answer)

- a. Sponging-house
- b. Debt-snowball method
- c. Par value
- d. trading volume

Guidance: level 1

:: Generally Accepted Accounting Principles ::

An _____ or profit and loss account is one of the financial statements of a company and shows the company's revenues and expenses during a particular period.

Exam Probability: **Medium**

59. *Answer choices:*

(see index for correct answer)

- a. Operating income before depreciation and amortization
- b. Income statement
- c. Normal balance
- d. Construction in progress

Guidance: level 1

INDEX: Correct Answers

Foundations of Business

1. d: Partnership

2. a: Preferred stock

3. b: Firm

4. b: Specification

5. d: E-commerce

6. : Internal Revenue Service

7. : Employment

8. a: Negotiation

9. b: Training

10. c: Industrial Revolution

11. a: Technology

12. : Investment

13. a: Integrity

14. d: Review

15. c: Bribery

16. d: Target market

17. b: Cash flow

18. b: Stock exchange

19. : Competitive advantage

20. c: Gross domestic product

21. d: Foreign direct investment

22. a: Purchasing

23. a: Working capital

24. d: Good

25. c: Capitalism

26. : Economy

27. : Small business

28. d: Free trade

29. a: Demand

30. a: Financial services

31. d: Scheduling

32. c: Credit card

33. : Meeting

34. : Customs

35. c: Exercise

36. a: Bankruptcy

37. : Loan

38. b: Trade agreement

39. : Analysis

40. d: Present value

41. d: Raw material

42. c: Economic growth

43. c: Comparative advantage

44. d: Federal Trade Commission

45. b: Solution

46. a: Opportunity cost

47. d: Dividend

48. d: Authority

49. b: Industry

50. a: Asset

51. a: Law

52. b: Size

53. c: Alliance

54. a: Ownership

55. b: Competitor

56. a: Business plan

57. c: Preference

58. d: Franchising

59. a: Revenue

Management

1. a: Cross-functional team

2. c: Best practice

3. d: Resource management

4. d: Reinforcement

5. d: Supply chain management

6. c: Strategic management

7. a: Decentralization

8. a: Interdependence

9. c: Skill

10. d: Myers-Briggs type

11. a: Individualism

12. d: Creativity

13. c: Control chart

14. b: Patent

15. a: Ratio

16. c: Organizational structure

17. c: Sales

18. d: Checklist

19. d: Specification

20. : Continuous improvement

21. c: Organizational commitment

22. c: Criticism

23. : Standard deviation

24. c: Decision tree

25. d: Ambiguity

26. : Information

27. b: Economies of scale

28. c: Job design

29. b: SWOT analysis

30. d: Organizational culture

31. a: Training

32. : Mission statement

33. a: Inventory control

34. d: Leadership development

35. b: Collaboration

36. a: Delegation

37. c: Distance

38. c: Justice

39. : Resource

40. c: Span of control

41. b: Motivation

42. : Human capital

43. : Labor relations

44. d: Process control

45. d: Code

46. b: Threat

47. a: Goal setting

48. a: Expert power

49. a: Cooperative

50. b: Subsidiary

51. b: Export

52. b: Proactive

53. b: Office

54. : Training and development

55. b: Quality control

56. a: Job description

57. a: Linear programming

58. a: Human resources

59. a: Enron

Business law

1. a: Delegation

2. : Disparagement

3. c: Market value

4. d: Complaint

5. : Estoppel

6. d: Insolvency

7. b: Indictment

8. d: Aid

9. a: Shares

10. : Bankruptcy

11. c: Broker

12. d: Jury

13. c: Sherman Act

14. d: Employment law

15. c: False imprisonment

16. c: Proximate cause

17. b: Punitive

18. : Technology

19. a: Foreclosure

20. c: Joint venture

21. c: Argument

22. c: Amendment

23. a: Fiduciary

24. : Federal government

25. : Rehabilitation Act

26. : Personnel

27. a: Implied authority

28. c: Charter

29. d: Sherman Antitrust

30. : Lien

31. b: Risk

32. b: Criminal procedure

33. c: Surety

34. c: Industry

35. a: Accord and satisfaction

36. d: Economic Espionage Act

37. b: Utility

38. a: Summary judgment

39. c: Creditor

40. a: Employment discrimination

41. : Negotiation

42. c: Mediation

43. : Warehouse receipt

44. c: Promissory note

45. a: Bailee

46. d: Manufacturing

47. c: Collective bargaining

48. d: Injunction

49. d: Cyberspace

50. : Verdict

51. a: Copyright

52. : Arbitration clause

53. : Tangible

54. b: Antitrust

55. : Perfection

56. c: Exclusionary rule

57. a: Perfect tender

58. : Firm

59. b: Parol evidence

Finance

1. : Stock price

2. b: Subsidiary ledger

3. b: Financial ratio

4. b: Capital market

5. b: Working capital

6. d: Presentation

7. : Deferral

8. b: Normal balance

9. : Preference

10. : Copyright

11. a: Dividend

12. b: Activity-based costing

13. c: Saving

14. c: Liquidity

15. c: Ending inventory

16. : Securities and Exchange Commission

17. a: Fraud

18. a: Money market

19. d: Consideration

20. d: Debt ratio

21. d: Investment

22. b: Sinking fund

23. : Accrual

24. c: Asset

25. b: Fair value

26. d: Net income

27. d: International Financial Reporting Standards

28. d: Manufacturing overhead

29. a: Expected return

30. b: Return on assets

31. d: Economy

32. c: Periodic inventory

33. d: Capital expenditure

34. c: Debt-to-equity ratio

35. : Hedge

36. b: Book value

37. a: Retirement

38. c: Cost of goods sold

39. : Going concern

40. b: Matching principle

41. : Hedge fund

42. a: Pricing

43. a: Pension fund

44. c: Shares

45. : Social security

46. c: Bank account

47. d: Earnings per share

48. : Absorption costing

49. a: Financial crisis

50. a: Time value of money

51. : Chief financial officer

52. a: Debenture

53. : Promissory note

54. c: Value Line

55. : Equity method

56. a: Primary market

57. a: Accounting period

58. c: Current ratio

59. a: Cash management

Human resource management

1. b: UNITE HERE

2. d: Coaching

3. b: Compa-ratio

4. : Evaluation

5. d: Employee referral

6. a: Retirement

7. c: Cross-training

8. c: Labor relations

9. d: Human capital

10. b: Authoritarianism

11. d: Strategic management

12. a: Proactive

13. : Assessment center

14. b: Internal consistency

15. d: Succession planning

16. b: Executive compensation

17. b: Congress

18. d: Licensure

19. a: Health Reimbursement Account

20. b: Outplacement

21. c: Performance measurement

22. c: Parental leave

23. a: Interview

24. b: Unfair labor practice

25. c: Retraining

26. b: Right to work

27. : Collaboration

28. a: Job performance

29. b: Cover letter

30. b: Ownership

31. b: Enforcement

32. a: Interactional justice

33. c: Overlearning

34. d: Hazard

35. d: Skill

36. : Restructuring

37. : Substance abuse

38. a: Centralization

39. a: Impression management

40. c: Featherbedding

41. : Professional association

42. c: Task force

43. d: Socialization

44. b: Unemployment benefits

45. : 360-degree feedback

46. c: Cultural intelligence

47. b: Knowledge worker

48. d: Payroll

49. b: Adaptive

50. b: Theory Z

51. c: Golden parachute

52. d: Job security

53. b: Transformational leadership

54. d: Referent power

55. d: Resource management

56. c: Workforce

57. : Card check

58. d: Background check

59. b: Brainstorming

Information systems

1. c: Wiki

2. a: Carnivore

3. b: Decision-making

4. a: Disaster recovery plan

5. b: Content management system

6. a: Supplier relationship management

7. d: PeopleSoft

8. c: Credit card

9. a: Utility computing

10. : Geographic information system

11. b: Data cleansing

12. b: Authentication protocol

13. c: Privacy

14. b: Information flow

15. a: Spamming

16. c: Consumer-to-business

17. : Decision support system

18. d: Worm

19. d: Star

20. : Data integration

21. b: Security management

22. c: Disaster recovery

23. : Cybersquatting

24. d: Smart card

25. b: Commercial off-the-shelf

26. b: Security controls

27. d: Data aggregator

28. b: Payment system

29. c: Freemium

30. c: Domain name

31. : Google Maps

32. c: Content management

33. d: Second Life

34. : Data dictionary

35. c: Payment Card Industry Data Security Standard

36. : Data mart

37. : Analytics

38. b: Database management system

39. c: Random access

40. : World Wide Web

41. d: Crowdsourcing

42. d: Disintermediation

43. b: Service level

44. a: Strategic planning

45. a: Information technology

46. b: Management information system

47. a: Knowledge management

48. : Picasa

49. a: Information ethics

50. b: Business model

51. : Semantic Web

52. a: Big data

53. c: PayPal

54. c: Global Positioning System

55. a: COBIT

56. d: Network interface card

57. a: Enterprise systems

58. d: Consumerization

59. d: Data governance

Marketing

1. : Security

2. b: Brand awareness

3. c: Advertisement

4. c: Personal selling

5. a: Planning

6. : Billboard

7. b: Retail

8. a: North American Free Trade Agreement

9. b: Persuasion

10. a: Questionnaire

11. a: Commodity

12. b: Clayton Act

13. : Empowerment

14. a: Database marketing

15. a: Manufacturing

16. : Budget

17. c: Relationship marketing

18. c: Social marketing

19. b: Brand image

20. b: Adoption

21. b: Social networking

22. d: Shares

23. c: Direct selling

24. b: Marketing management

25. b: Concept testing

26. b: Creativity

27. d: Product development

28. a: Evaluation

29. : Hearing

30. b: Sherman Antitrust Act

31. : Brand equity

32. d: Market development

33. a: Universal Product Code

34. c: Complexity

35. c: Mass customization

36. : Cost-plus pricing

37. a: Argument

38. a: Standing

39. b: Nonprofit

40. a: Information system

41. b: Globalization

42. d: Vendor

43. c: Direct marketing

44. d: Merchandising

45. c: Price war

46. c: Manager

47. d: Public

48. c: Social media

49. b: Brand loyalty

50. a: Viral marketing

51. c: Brand extension

52. a: Brand management

53. b: Green marketing

54. c: Attention

55. c: Intangibility

56. c: Total Quality Management

57. b: Expense

58. a: Star

59. b: Organizational culture

Manufacturing

1. a: Property

2. : Scheduling

3. b: Malcolm Baldrige National Quality Award

4. b: Quality audit

5. : Quality Engineering

6. c: Customer

7. : Ishikawa diagram

8. d: Bullwhip effect

9. c: ROOT

10. : Sensitivity analysis

11. c: Tool

12. d: Inventory

13. b: Change management

14. : Dimension

15. c: New product development

16. a: Aggregate planning

17. c: Resource management

18. d: Project manager

19. a: Resource allocation

20. : Quality function deployment

21. b: Service quality

22. c: Process engineering

23. c: Elastomer

24. b: Quality assurance

25. : Throughput

26. c: Quality policy

27. : Volume

28. c: Clay

29. : Statistical process control

30. b: Strategic sourcing

31. d: Resource

32. c: Heat treating

33. a: E-commerce

34. b: Perfect competition

35. d: Consortium

36. a: Rolling Wave planning

37. c: Heat transfer

38. a: Raw material

39. b: Expediting

40. : Reflux

41. : Purchasing manager

42. c: Quality costs

43. b: Credit

44. d: Economic order quantity

45. a: Information management

46. d: Supply chain network

47. : Strategy

48. : Pareto analysis

49. c: Knowledge management

50. b: Control chart

51. : Gantt chart

52. d: Quality by Design

53. b: Quality control

54. a: Reboiler

55. b: Process control

56. : Global sourcing

57. d: Authority

58. c: Risk management

59. b: Business process

Commerce

1. : Payment card

2. c: Auction

3. d: Cash flow

4. b: Quality control

5. a: Reverse auction

6. b: Standardization

7. a: Property

8. d: Transaction cost

9. d: Regulation

10. c: Value-added network

11. : Management

12. b: Evaluation

13. c: Loyalty

14. b: Encryption

15. d: Optimum

16. a: DigiCash

17. : Bill of lading

18. b: Mass production

19. a: Strategic plan

20. c: Advertisement

21. : Logistics Management

22. c: Authentication

23. b: Graduation

24. a: Stock

25. a: Bottom line

26. d: Market research

27. c: Monopoly

28. b: Electronic data interchange

29. a: Computer security

30. : Marketing

31. d: Information technology

32. : Regulatory agency

33. b: Drawback

34. b: Financial services

35. b: Outsourcing

36. a: Import

37. c: Strategic alliance

38. : European Union

39. a: Frequency

40. c: Investment

41. d: British Airways

42. a: Insurance

43. d: Economies of scale

44. b: Adoption

45. : Control system

46. c: Vendor

47. : Inventory control

48. : Pizza Hut

49. c: Short run

50. a: Wholesale

51. c: Jurisdiction

52. : Trade show

53. b: Preference

54. b: Wall Street Journal

55. a: Security

56. a: Sexual harassment

57. b: Aid

58. c: Policy

59. c: Complexity

Business ethics

1. a: Nonprofit

2. c: Fannie Mae

3. : Organic food

4. b: Socialism

5. : Ponzi scheme

6. c: Interlocking directorate

7. c: Fraud

8. a: Madoff

9. c: East Germany

10. a: Coal

11. : Corporate structure

12. d: Pollution Prevention

13. a: Capitalism

14. a: East India

15. c: Transformational leadership

16. : Petroleum

17. : Occupational Safety and Health Administration

18. : Chamber of Commerce

19. a: Corporation

20. : Pure Food and Drug Act

21. c: Conscience

22. d: Organizational culture

23. c: Skill

24. b: Enron

25. c: Tobacco

26. b: Consumerism

27. b: Real estate

28. : Reputation

29. b: UN Global Compact

30. b: Accounting

31. d: Partnership

32. a: Planet

33. b: Price fixing

34. c: Cultural relativism

35. d: Aristotle

36. d: Wall Street

37. d: Urban sprawl

38. a: Corporate citizenship

39. c: Financial Stability Oversight Council

40. a: Lead paint

41. c: Utopian socialism

42. : Environmental audit

43. b: Workplace politics

44. a: Business model

45. c: Community development financial institution

46. b: Individualistic culture

47. a: Constitutional law

48. a: Planned obsolescence

49. c: Risk assessment

50. b: Disclaimer

51. c: Cause-related marketing

52. d: Invisible hand

53. b: Corporate social responsibility

54. : Principal Financial

55. b: United Farm Workers

56. : Consumer Protection

57. b: Executive compensation

58. : Parental leave

59. b: Toxic waste

Accounting

1. : Inflation

2. d: Parent company

3. c: Contributed capital

4. b: Expense account

5. d: Market value

6. a: Debenture

7. a: International Federation of Accountants

8. c: Decentralization

9. d: Marital deduction

10. : Times interest earned

11. d: Accrual

12. d: Target costing

13. b: Joint venture

14. a: Sales tax

15. : Tax deferral

16. a: Capital gain

17. d: Internal auditing

18. c: Revenue center

19. c: Supply chain

20. a: Total quality management

21. b: Trend analysis

22. : Certified Management Accountant

23. b: Accounting management

24. d: Taxpayer

25. a: Financial Accounting Standards Board

26. c: Fair Labor Standards Act

27. b: Adoption

28. : Consolidated financial statement

29. b: Organizational structure

30. b: Asset

31. b: Net realizable value

32. d: Monetary unit

33. a: Common stock

34. c: Securities and Exchange Commission

35. b: Public Company Accounting Oversight Board

36. b: Remittance advice

37. a: Financial ratio

38. d: Pension

39. : Accounting method

40. d: Land

41. a: Exchange rate

42. : Comprehensive annual financial report

43. c: Debit card

44. c: Current ratio

45. c: Personal identification number

46. b: Accounting

47. c: Promissory note

48. a: Net investment

49. b: Ownership

50. d: Asset turnover

51. d: Audit

52. : Callable

53. a: Revenue

54. d: Bank reconciliation

55. c: Profit center

56. a: Estate tax

57. a: Average cost

58. c: Par value

59. b: Income statement

CPSIA information can be obtained
at www.ICGtesting.com
Printed in the USA
LVHW060133011119
635715LV00014B/359/P